TRAVEL GUIDE

NEW YORK CITY

ACKNOWLEDGMENTS

We gratefully acknowledge the help of our representatives for their efficient and perceptive inspections of the lodgings listed. ForbesTravel Guide is also grateful to the talented writers who contributed to this book.

Front and Back Cover images: ©IStock
ISBN: 978-1-936010-04-2
Manufactured in the USA
10 9 8 7 6 5 4 3 2 1

CONTENTS

NEW YORK CITY

FIVE STAR HOTELS

Four Seasons Hotel New York *(page 104)*

Mandarin Oriental, New York *(page 118)*

The Peninsula New York *(page 109)*

The Ritz-Carlton New York, Central Park *(page109)*

The St. Regis, New York *(page 110)*

Trump International Hotel & Tower *(page 119)*

FIVE STAR RESTAURANTS

Jean Georges *(page 90)*
Le Bernardin *(page 75)*
Masa *(page 90)*
Per Se *(page 90)*

FIVE STAR SPAS

The Peninsula Spa by ESPA *(page 121)*
The Spa at Mandarin Oriental, New York *(page 121)*

FOUR STAR HOTELS

The Carlyle, A Rosewood Hotel, *(page 115)*
The Lowell, New York *(page 116)*
The New York Palace *(page 108)*

The Ritz-Carlton New York, Battery Park *(page 98)*

FOUR STAR RESTAURANTS

Adour Alain Ducasse *(page 69)*
Asiate *(page 88)*
Aureole *(page 70)*
Bouley *(page 79)*
Country *(page 83)*
Daniel *(page 86)*
Del Posto *(page 56)*
Eleven Madison Park *(page 84)*
Gilt *(page 73)*
Gordon Ramsay at the London, New York *(page 74)*
Gotham Bar and Grill *(page 65)*
Gramercy Tavern *(page 84)*
Kai *(page 87)*
L'Atelier de Joel Robuchon *(page 74)*
La Grenouille *(page 75)*
Le Cirque *(page 76)*
The Modern *(page 76)*
Picholine *(page 91)*
Sugiyama *(page 79)*

FOUR STAR SPA

The Spa at Four Seasons Hotel New York *(page 121)*

STAR ATTRACTIONS

If you've been a reader of Mobil Travel Guide, you will have heard that this historic brand partnered with another storied media name, Forbes, in 2009 to create a new entity, Forbes Travel Guide. For more than 50 years, Mobil Travel Guide assisted travelers in making smart decisions about where to stay and dine when traveling. With this new partnership, our mission has not changed: We're committed to the same rigorous inspections of hotels, restaurants and spas—the most comprehensive in the industry with more than 500 standards tested at each property we visit—to help you cut through the clutter and make easy and informed decisions on where to spend your time and travel budget. Our team of anonymous inspectors are constantly on the road, sleeping in hotels, eating in restaurants and making spa appointments, evaluating those exacting standards to determine a property's rating.

What kinds of standards are we looking for when we visit a property? We're looking for more than just high-thread count sheets, pristine spa treatment rooms and white linen-topped tables. We look for service that's attentive, individualized and unforgettable. We note how long it takes to be greeted when you sit down at your table, or to be served when you order room service, or whether the hotel staff can confidently help you when you've forgotten that one essential item that will make or break your trip. Unlike any other travel ratings entity, we visit each and every place we rate, testing hundreds of attributes to compile our ratings, and our ratings cannot be bought or influenced. The Forbes Five Star rating is the most prestigious achievement in hospitality—while we rate more than 8,000 properties in the U.S., Canada, Hong Kong, Macau and Beijing, for 2010, we have awarded Five Star designations to only 53 hotels, 21 restaurants and 18 spas. When you travel with Forbes, you can travel with confidence, knowing that you'll get the very best experience, no matter who you are.

With our new City Guide series, you can also count on a local perspective, in the form of a fresh, witty, insider voice. We employ local writers and inspectors who are well-connected in their respective cities to give you the very latest information on what's going on around town. As you are reading these pages, we hope you get a real flavor of the city and that you feel even more inspired to visit and take it all in. All of our books in the City Guide series include vibrant photos and easy-to-use maps to help you find your way to the city's best attractions. We understand the importance of making the most of your time. That's why the most trusted name in travel is now Forbes Travel Guide.

STAR RATED HOTELS

Whether you're looking for the ultimate in luxury or the best value for your travel budget, we have a hotel recommendation for you. To help you pinpoint properties that meet your needs, Forbes Travel Guide classifies each lodging by type according to the following characteristics:

★★★★★These exceptional properties provide a memorable experience through virtually flawless service and the finest of amenities. Staff are intuitive, engaging and passionate, and eagerly deliver service above and beyond the guests' expectations. The hotel was designed with the guest's comfort in mind, with particular attention paid to craftsmanship and quality of product. A Five-Star property is a destination unto itself.

★★★★These properties provide a distinctive setting, and a guest will find many interesting and inviting elements to enjoy throughout the property. Attention to detail is prominent throughout the property, from design concept to quality of products provided. Staff are accommodating and take pride in catering to the guest's specific needs throughout their stay.

★★★These well-appointed establishments have enhanced amenities that provide travelers with a strong sense of location, whether for style or function. They may have a distinguishing style and ambience in both the public spaces and guest rooms; or they may be more focused on functionality, providing guests with easy access to local events, meetings or tourism highlights.

★★The Two Star hotel is considered a clean, comfortable and reliable establishment that has expanded amenities, such as a full-service restaurant.

★The One Star lodging is a limited-service hotel or inn that is considered a clean, comfortable and reliable establishment.

For every property, we also provide pricing information. All prices quoted are accurate at the time of publication; however, prices cannot be guaranteed.

STAR RATED RESTAURANTS

Every restaurant in this book has been visited by Forbes Travel Guide's team of experts and comes highly recommended as an outstanding dining experience.

★★★★★Forbes Five-Star restaurants deliver a truly unique and distinctive dining experience. A Five-Star restaurant consistently provides exceptional food, superlative service and elegant décor. An emphasis is placed on originality and personalized, attentive and discreet service. Every detail that surrounds the experience is attended to by a warm and gracious dining room team.

★★★★These are exciting restaurants with often well-known chefs that feature creative and complex foods and emphasize various culinary techniques and a focus on seasonality. A highly-trained dining room staff provides refined personal service and attention.

★★★Three Star restaurants offer skillfully-prepared food with a focus on a specific style or cuisine. The dining room staff provides warm and professional service in a comfortable atmosphere. The décor is well-coordinated with quality fixtures and decorative items, and promotes a comfortable ambience.

★★The Two Star restaurant serves fresh food in a clean setting with efficient service. Value is considered in this category, as is family friendliness.

★The One Star restaurant provides a distinctive experience through culinary specialty, local flair or individual atmosphere.

Because menu prices can fluctuate, we list a pricing range rather than specific prices. The pricing ranges are per diner, and assume that you order an appetizer or dessert, an entrée and one drink.

STAR RATED SPAS

Forbes Travel Guide's spa ratings are based on objective evaluations of more than 450 attributes. About half of these criteria assess basic expectations, such as staff courtesy, the technical proficiency and skill of the employees and whether the facility is clean and maintained properly. Several standards address issues that impact a guest's physical comfort and convenience, as well as the staff's ability to impart a sense of personalized service. Additional criteria measure the spa's ability to create a completely calming ambience.

★★★★★Stepping foot in a Five Star Spa will result in an exceptional experience with no detail overlooked. These properties wow their guests with extraordinary design and facilities, and uncompromising service. Expert staff cater to your every whim and pamper you with the most advanced treatments and skin care lines available. These spas often offer exclusive treatments and may emphasize local elements.

★★★★Four Star spas provide a wonderful experience in an inviting and serene environment. A sense of personalized service is evident from the moment you check in and receive your robe and slippers. The guest's comfort is always of utmost concern to the well-trained staff.

★★★These spas offer well-appointed facilities with a full complement of staff to ensure that guests' needs are met. The spa facilities include clean and appealing treatment rooms, changing areas and a welcoming reception desk.

★ BEST BETS

EMPIRE STATE BUILDING

BIG APPLE BESTS

How do you navigate one of largest cities in the world? You start by choosing the right hotel, eating at some of its top restaurants (and sampling its iconic foods in between) and visiting a few of its beloved sights. Whether you've got 24 hours or a long weekend, you can customize your visit to New York to include some of the city's newest attractions, as well as old favorites. Here's how to do exactly that.

WHAT ARE NEW YORK'S TOP HOTELS?

For the utmost in luxury, make a reservation at the **Mandarin Oriental, New York** (page 118). Rooms start on the 38th floor of the Time Warner Center, overlooking Columbus Circle, midtown Manhattan, the Hudson River and Central Park. The hotel itself is beautiful and offers every amenity, including a heavenly spa (page 121), but you'll also find plenty to do right in the building, since the Time Warner Center is full of shops and restaurants.

You can never go wrong at the **Four Seasons Hotel New York** (page 104), where many of the rooms are larger than most New York apartments—and you get the signature top-notch service.

The **Ritz-Carlton New York, Central Park** (page 109) is an Uptown classic that epitomizes New York glamour and sophistication at every turn, and is probably one of the best properties in the hotel chain. Rooms are plush and luxurious, and guests barely lift a finger from the time they arrive. You also can't beat the location, right across the street from the park (visitors in park-view rooms even get telescopes).

Many consider the **Royalton Hotel** (page 110) to be the original boutique hotel: It's the one that set the standard for hipness with its famously intense Philippe Starck design. A recent renovation upped the sophistication level in a quiet, clubby way.

If downtown chic is more your style, opt for **The Bowery Hotel** (page 97). One of New York's newer high-end hot spots, the boutique property has swank guest suites with marble baths, iPod stereo systems and—lest you forget you're in a downtown neighborhood long-known for its gritty character—floor-to-ceiling windows that overlook some remaining tenement housing.

For a downtown vibe with more classic accommodations, try **The Ritz-Carlton, Battery Park** (page 98). Top-notch views of the Statue of Liberty, Ellis Island, New York Harbor and the downtown skyline make the Ritz's quieter downtown waterfront location on the southwestern tip of Manhattan a great excuse to avoid the chaotic Midtown hotel scene.

WHAT ARE NEW YORK'S BEST FOOD EXPERIENCES?

Eating is a quintessential part of any visit to New York; critics often label this the best restaurant city in the world, and you'd be hard-pressed to find a global cuisine not represented. It's easy to drop hundreds here on meals created by some of the most recognizable names in the culinary stratosphere. The Food Network superstar chef Mario Batali has—count them—nine restaurants in New York, including the cozy, classic Italian spot **Babbo** (page 61) and the 24,000-square-foot, super-fancy **Del Posto** (page 56). You can try the cuisines of other celebrity chefs at **Jean Georges** (page 90), **Per Se** (page 90) and **Masa** (page 90). Then there are all the great, classic New York restaurants, from **Le Bernardin** (page 75) to **Gramercy Tavern** (page 84) to the **Four Seasons** (page 73), a Mid-Century Modern masterpiece where power deals are still made over long lunches.

THE METROPOLITAN MUSEUM OF ART

You can also get a good taste of the Big Apple without breaking the bank, and you can do it around the clock. Dozens of divey-and-delicious Chinatown eateries are open until the wee hours of the morning, and the hunger pang-inducing smell of $1.25 grilled hot dogs at **Gray's Papaya** *(page 58)* wafts through the Upper West Side luring in both the over-served and light-of-wallet 24 hours a day. Just a few blocks away, you can get hot bagels straight from the oven at the no-frills **H&H Bagels** *(page 58)*. **Ess-a-Bagel** *(page 58)* is a more full-service bagel bakery, serving up lox and other smoked fish. Grabbing a coffee to go along with it? Forget the overwrought Starbucks-style terminology: In New York, a "regular" coffee is one with plain old milk and sugar added.

Even though it's not in its original East Village location (or even on Second Avenue), make a pilgrimage to **Second Avenue Deli** *(page 58)* for a hot pastrami on rye or a soothing bowl of matzah ball soup. Just looking for a nosh? Stop at a sidewalk cart for a hot pretzel or warm bag of roasted chestnuts. Sweet tooths have to try big-as-your-head, spongy black-and-white (half chocolate/half vanilla) cookies, sold at delis and bakeries throughout the city, or line up with the masses craving sinfully good cupcakes at **Magnolia Bakery** *(401 Bleecker St., 212-462-2572; www.magnoliacupcakes.com)*. Remember to choose carefully—the bakery limits the number you can buy when demand outreaches supply.

WHAT ARE NEW YORK'S BEST CULTURAL EXPERIENCES?

Culture fans should check out the latest exhibition at the Met (the **Metropolitan Museum of Art**) or MoMA (the **Museum of Modern Art**) *(page 36)*. Or plan a trip to see the next big names in contemporary art at the always buzzed-about Whitney Biennial at the **Whitney Museum of American Art** *(page 43)*.

See a household name or two put their acting chops on the line at a broadway show, or try some edgier theater off- (or off- off-) Broadway (line up at the TKTS booth in Times Square—at Broadway and 47th Street—for

WHAT'S THE BEST OF NEW YORK SHOPPING?

Grab a coffee at Dean and Deluca *(560 Broadway, at Prince Street, 212-226-6800; www.deandeluca.com)* and spend the afternoon in Soho—New York's cobble-stoned answer to an outdoor shopping mall, packed with one-off boutiques. Or stop in at one of the city's infamous department stores—Macy's Herald Square *(page 24)*, Saks Fifth Avenue *(page 136)* and Bloomingdale's *(page 136)* attract all manner of shoppers, while a design-conscious set shops Barneys New York *(page 136)*, Henri Bendel *(page 136)* and Bergdorf Goodman *(page 136)*. The favorite of label-loving bargain hunters, meanwhile, is Century 21 *(page 133)*, the well-known and loved discount department store. Those really in the know shop the bevy of "private" sample sales that offer everything from housewares to handbags held in warehouses and office spaces around the city *(page 142)*.

same-day show discounts). Come summer, fans of the Bard start queuing up early in the morning for free tickets (distributed only on the day of the performance) to the **Public Theater's Shakespeare in the Park** productions at Central Park's outdoor **Delacorte Theater** *(212-539-8500; www.publictheater.org)*. You don't need a ticket, though, to take in free summertime performances of the **New York Philharmonic** and the **Metropolitan Opera** *(page 162)*, or the colorful characters hanging out on the park's Great Lawn. More free entertainment can be had sitting in the audience of the many TV shows taped here, though you'll need to reserve well in advance to attend *Late Show with David Letterman, The View, Saturday Night Live* and other popular picks. Spring and Fall are marked by the trendsetters who come to see the newest styles during **New York Fashion Week**. (Beginning September 2010, shows will move from Bryant Park to Lincoln Center.)

WHAT'S THE BEST NIGHTLIFE?

Dive bars? Check. Classic Cocktails? Check. The Next Big Thing or a world-class mezzo soprano live on stage? New York's got that, too. For a step back in time, go to Midtown's sophisticated, old-school **King Cole Bar Lounge** *(page 150)*, which claims to be the birthplace of the Bloody Mary (though here it's called a Red Snapper, and you'd better ask for it that way). And yes, that's Maxfield Parrish's famous mural of the nursery rhyme icon behind the bar. Share a pint with academic-types from NYU and a boho West Village crowd at **Kettle of Fish** *(page 148)*, where the vintage Ms. Pac-Man Machine is always busy. If you want panorama and a flute of bubbly, try **Rare View** *(page 155)* in the Shelburne Murray Hill Hotel for a look at the Empire State and Chrysler buildings that will take your breath away. **Arlene's Grocery** *(page 160)* had a former life as a bodega, but these days it's better known as one of the city's best live music venues. You can catch up-and-comers who sing everything from rock to reggae for less than the price of one cocktail elsewhere in town. Or buy tickets in advance and bring along your best jewels to get decked out for a night at **The Metropolitan Opera** *(page 162)*, where renowned singers Beverly Sills and Leontyne Price have graced the stage.

WHAT ARE THE CAN'T-MISS SIGHTS?

Hands down, the best deal in the city for day-tripping tourists is the free round-trip ride on the **Staten Island Ferry** *(page 28)*, which crosses New York Harbor and gives commuters and visitors up-close views of the **Statue of Liberty** *(page 30)* and **Ellis Island** *(page 27)*.

The skyline is the star of the show atop New York's tallest structure, the 1,454-foot **Empire State Building** *(page 35)*. You can take in the view from sky decks on the 86th and 102nd floors; when you're looking at it from a distance, check out the changing colors of the tower lights to mark everything from holidays to events like the New York City Marathon.

Visitors can't get past the lobby of the city's second tallest building, the stunning, 1,047-foot **Chrysler Building** *(page 34)*, but that in itself is a marble- and granite-filled Art Deco masterpiece worth a visit. The 70th-floor **Top of the Rock Observation Deck** *(page 38)* reopened in 2005 after a 25-year hiatus and $75 million expansion to offer 360-degree views of Midtown.

Roughly 30 million people pass through **Times Square** *(Broadway at 42nd Street)* every year to see the flashing lights and billboards, shop the flagship chain stores and eat at theme restaurants. Locals may begrudge the spectacle, but no one misses its former incarnation when it was awash in peep shows and condemned buildings. You can get maps, discount theater tickets and use public restrooms at the **Times Square Information Center** *(Seventh Avenue between 46th and 47th streets, 212-768-1560; www.timesquarenyc.org)*

It's mostly a construction zone right now, but the site of the **World Trade Center** until the 9/11 terrorist attacks still draws crowds who come to pay their respects to victims of the tragic day. One World Trade Center (previously called the Freedom Tower), and a memorial and museum are still under construction

You could easily spend an entire weekend exploring New York City's playground, **Central Park** *(page 42)*. Stop at the visitor's center, called the Dairy—mid-park at 65th Street—for a map and a calendar of events. Jog around the reservoir or rent ice skates at Wollman Rink or Lasker Rink, which becomes a swimming pool in the summer. Rent a rowboat at Loeb Boathouse or a kite from Big City Kites at Lexington and 82nd Street and walk over to the park to catch the breeze on the Great Lawn. If you have kids, visit one of the 19 themed playgrounds, the zoo and petting zoo, the Carousel, the storytelling hour at the Hans Christian Andersen statue and the Model Boat Pond, where serious modelers race their tiny remote-controlled boats on weekends.

For an awesome view of Lower Manhattan, Brooklyn and New York Harbor, take a 40-minute stroll across downtown's historic **Brooklyn Bridge**, the first bridge to cross the East River to Brooklyn. The circa 1883 bridge was and still is a monument to American engineering and creativity. Two massive stone pylons, each pierced with two soaring Gothic arches, rise 272 feet to support an intricate web of cables. At the Brooklyn end of the bridge is a half-mile promenade with equally grand views.

Though the recent recession stirs passionate viewpoints about its influence, for much of the nation's history, **Wall Street** *(page 30)* has been the symbol of American capitalism, renowned around the world. The street begins at Broadway, where you'll find Trinity Church (built in 1846 and a symbol of the city's strength when it survived the nearby 9/11 terrorist attacks), and stretches east of the East River. If you walk the street's six or so blocks, you'll pass the **Federal Hall National Monument**, the site where George Washington took the Oath of Office and became the first President of the United States in 1789. Step inside the building to view the impressive rotunda and check out an exhibit on the Constitution. Just half a block south of Wall Street, on Broad Street, is the **New York Stock Exchange**, where fortunes are made and lost with every clang of the opening bell.

★HISTORY

HOW WAS NEW YORK FOUNDED?

Explorer Giovanni da Verrazano could not have possibly dreamed of what lay ahead for the land he saw when he sailed into New York Harbor in 1524, or the millions of people who would come to inhabit it. New York City has taken on many faces during its history. It's a constantly evolving place where the one thing that never changes is its importance as one of the great metropolises of the world.

Verrazano, commissioned by the French to find a shortcut to the Orient, didn't find what he was looking for upon discovery of New York. In fact, he never even set foot on dry land before leaving again. It wasn't until 85 years later that Henry Hudson came through and saw that it was a place worth sticking around due to its potential to be a strategic location as a thoroughfare for commerce. By 1624, the first Dutch settlers arrived, giving Manhattan Island the name New Amsterdam. Legend has it that Peter Minuit soon "purchased" for 60 guilders all 14,000 acres of the island from the Native Americans who were living there. The amount is estimated now as somewhere between $24 and $500—a rip-off on either end of that spectrum, and perhaps the city's very first real estate scam.

Forty years into Dutch rule, English warships arrived to take over the prospering colony. The Dutch quickly surrendered, and New Amsterdam became New York, named for the brother of King Charles, the Duke of York. In 1733, a German immigrant named John Peter Zenger founded the *New-York Weekly Journal*, one of the city's first newspapers, in which he criticized local government. He was imprisoned and then later acquitted of libel, paving the way for a free press in New York City and, later, the country-to-be as a whole.

By 1740, New York was a thriving port and an important link in the slave trade, but many residents were growing tired of British rule, especially its ever-increasing taxation on the American colonies. Anti-British sentiment grew here as well as in the other colonies under the leadership of politically vociferous New Yorkers like Alexander Hamilton and John Jay. By 1776, 400 British ships, including 73 warships, had arrived in New York Harbor with 32,000 troops to quell the impending revolution. Nonetheless, the Declaration of Independence was adopted on July Fourth of that year, and New Yorkers pulled down a statue of King George III in Bowling Green, the oldest public park in New York City (and now the home of Charging Bull, a statue originally installed on Wall Street as a publicity stunt by artist Arturo DiModica). The battle for New York officially began soon after, and the British wound up occupying the city until 1783, when the Treaty of Paris finally ended the American Revolution.

HOW DID NEW YORK BECOME A MAJOR METROPOLIS?

New York City became the first capital of the United States of America in 1789, and George Washington took the oath of office to become the nation's first president in the city's Federal Hall. The following year, the capital moved to Philadelphia, but New York soon established itself as a global center of financial importance. Thanks in large part to the business savvy of Hamilton, 1792 saw the founding of what would come to be known as the New York Stock Exchange. (Hamilton also founded the *New York Evening Post* newspaper, still in circulation today as the *New York Post*. After contributing so much to a young New York, he famously died in a duel across the Hudson in New Jersey with vice president and political rival Aaron Burr.)

Despite widespread outbreaks of both cholera and yellow fever, New York's population exploded in the early 1800s. Immigrants kept arriving, with Germans,

WHAT WAS NEW YORK LIKE IN THE '70s and '80s?

By the 1970s, New York, like many other American cities, was a crime-ridden, gritty version of its former self. Times Square was a seedy mecca of X-rated movie theaters; the subways were dirty, graffitti-ridden and often dangerous to ride; and residents started fleeing to the suburbs. In 1975, the city government narrowly avoided bankruptcy with the help of a federal loan and debt assistance. But that was after then-President Gerald Ford initially said he'd veto any federal bailout, prompting the infamous 1975 *New York Daily News* headline "Ford to City: Drop Dead." (Ford never actually said those exact words, and the paper still endorsed him for President the following year.) From 1976 to 1977, the city was terrorized by the random shootings committed by serial killer David Berkowitz, nicknamed the Son of Sam, who murdered six people and injured seven others before being caught in August 1977, when he claimed he had been possessed by his neighbor's dog. Earlier that summer, a blackout turned the electricity off across the city for two steamy July days, prompting widespread looting, rioting and arson that destroyed entire blocks. Those events helped Mayor Ed Koch win the election, with promises to bring the city back to its former glory.

And the city did rebound with the mammoth success of Wall Street in the 1980s. The period was considered an era of relentless greed everywhere, but more noticeably here, as evidenced in pop culture portrayals of the New York investment bankers who considered themselves "masters of the universe" in Tom Wolfe's book *The Bonfire of the Vanities*, as well as Michael Douglas' Oscar-winning portrayal of corporate raider Gordon Gekko in the movie *Wall Street*. It was evident that New York had clearly returned to its powerhouse role on the worldwide financial scene. Still, racial tensions increased by the end of the decade, prompted by several high-profile crimes against African-Americans, including the shooting death of 16-year-old Yusuf Hawkins in Brooklyn. The 1989 election of David Dinkins, the city's first African-American mayor, was thought at least to be in part a result of voters wanting to ease those tensions.

Irish and Scandinavians helping the population reach almost 125,000. When the Erie Canal opened in 1825, the city began handling more trade than all other U.S. ports combined. In 1831, the city's first public transportation system began operation, with horse-drawn buses pulling passengers. Tension among immigrants of varying backgrounds and financial woes that affected the national banking, real estate and commerce sectors marked the middle of that century in New York, resulting in plenty of violence and civil unrest. By 1863, with the Civil War in full swing, the Draft Riots—prompted by opposition of the rich hiring less-fortunate substitutes to go to war for them—left more than 1,000 people dead and many more injured.

New York City suffered little damage in the war, and after its end, the city's population swelled to two million, aided by an influx of many Southern migrants. This led to the development of new technologies for the city, including electricity for public consumption, the first telephone exchange and elevated railways to move the throngs about town. Names like Carnegie, Rockefeller and Morgan made New York the headquarters for their businesses—Standard Oil and U.S. Steel among them—and reaped fortunes while solidifying New York's importance on the global business scene. Meanwhile, in 1886, the Statue of Liberty—a beacon to those less fortunate seeking a piece of the riches—was delivered as a gift from the French and posited in New York Harbor. It served as a symbol of freedom and opportunity to thousands of foreigners who could see Lady Liberty as they made their way by boat to neighboring Ellis Island, the main entry point for immigrants entering the United States until 1954.

By the end of the century, with the population continuing to surge, people lived in and around all of Manhattan, and there were fragmented governments ruling bits and pieces of the city, causing plenty of confusion. In 1898, the boroughs of Manhattan, Brooklyn, Queens, the Bronx and Staten Island merged to form New York City—becoming the country's largest city, which it remains today. Meanwhile, NYC continued to grow, boasting roughly 70 skyscrapers in its already land-strapped confines by 1913, most notable among them the 700-foot-tall Metropolitan Life Tower in Madison Square and the Woolworth Building, a 792-footer on Broadway. A $35 million underground transit system was completed in 1904; today, it remains one of the most extensive and busiest in the world, covering 842 miles, and is open 24 hours a day, 365 days a year.

Local women suffragists put plenty of pressure on the state government to earn women the right to vote, staging some of the largest rallies in the country. A referendum was originally defeated in 1914, but a state law was eventually passed in 1917, and New York led the way for the ratification of the 19th Amendment to the U.S. Constitution in 1920, allowing women across the country the freedom to vote.

While business and politics kept New Yorkers on their toes, the city, with its mix of cultures and allure of excitement, became a breeding ground for a thriving cultural scene. A well-known group of writers, critics and actors met for lunch almost daily from 1919 to 1927 in the Algonquin Hotel at what became known as the Algonquin Round Table. People such as Dorothy Parker, Harpo Marx and Tallulah Bankhead were a part of the group, who were famous for their wit and the practical jokes they played upon one another. (Part of this group founded *The New Yorker* magazine in 1925.) The Roaring Twenties also saw the birth of the Harlem Renaissance, when African-American writers, including Langston Hughes and Zora Neale Hurston, made a name for themselves. It was the heyday of the Cotton Club—where the likes of Cab Calloway, Ella Fitzgerald, Count Basie and Duke Ellington entertained—but black patrons, ironically, were usually denied admission. Broadway thrived, too, thanks to the genius of composers including Irving Berlin, George and Ira Gershwin, and Richard Rodgers and Oscar Hammerstein II. Jerome Kern's *Show Boat*, considered the first modern musical, opened to raves in 1927.

The good times came to an end in New York City, as they did elsewhere in the country, on October 29, 1929, when the stock market crashed and the nation plunged into a deep depression. The city's population by that time had skyrocketed to 5.6 million, and roughly one million of its citizens were out of work. Shanty towns dotted city parks, and thousands waited in bread lines. The election of popular Mayor Fiorello LaGuardia ushered in brighter times, as he cracked down on crime, brought the World's Fair to town and helped the city's factories and ports become an important part of the war effort during World War II. At the same time, urban planner Robert Moses beautified the city's landscape with parks, beaches and playgrounds and restored a run-down Central Park back to its former glory after many years of neglect. But he was a controversial figure, criticized for ignoring ethnic neighborhoods and hurting places like Coney Island and the South Bronx with the building of expressways and tunnels.

The United Nations made its home in New York City following the war, and throngs of new immigrants, mainly from Puerto Rico and Asia, arrived. A new generation of artists, including Beat Generation writers Allen Ginsberg, Jack Kerouac and William S. Burroughs, and painter Jackson Pollock, became well known as non-conformists during the 1950s. When the 1960s and the Age of Aquarius dawned, Bob Dylan and Andy Warhol burst onto the scene. The modern gay-rights movement saw its birth in New York City in 1969 with the Stonewall Riots, which involved several days of violent conflicts between police and activists that centered around a gay club called the Stonewall Inn.

HOW HAS THE CITY CHANGED IN THE NEW MILLENNIUM?

In the 1990s, crime rates dropped, the city cleaned itself up and once again became a place where people from near and far wanted to live, work and play. New York reaped disproportionate benefits during the dot-com boom late in the decade, when then-Mayor Rudolph Giuliani was simultaneously taking a tough stance on crime (some thought too tough) and turning down-and-out areas like Times Square into places that more resembled Disneyland, to the delight of tourists.

New York City was forever changed by the events of September 11, 2001. Terrorists hijacked four U.S. planes, crashing two of them into the twin towers of the World Trade Center, resulting in the collapse of both buildings and the death of almost 3,000 people, including many firemen, policemen and rescue workers. Yet, true to its nature, the city—which now boasts a population of more than eight million people who speak nearly 170 languages—banned together to regain its stamina. While there have been many difficulties, including heavy debate about the future of the World Trade Center site, New York City remains as strong as ever, and Ground Zero will become a multi-use area to include parks, a cultural center and memorial, plus five office towers, including a new 1,776-foot skyscraper to be called One World Trade Center (previously named the Freedom Tower), expected to be completed by 2013. Already opened on the World Trade Center site is the 52-story 7 World Trade Center *(www.wtc. com)*, which is New York's first certified "green" office building complete with a public park, a Jeff Koons sculpture in the public space and a Jenny Holzer installation, which is the largest in America, in the lobby.

The global recession of the last two years has hit the city hard, with thousands of bankers down and out on Wall Street, shops and restaurants closing and a crumbling real estate market. The upside of the financial malaise that still grips the city at press time is that rents and real estate have come down in price, allowing New Yorkers some breathing room in maintaining a more realistic standard of living. And for many in the nation's top city, it's a return to simpler things, from dining at home with friends (or at the home of a chef at one of the city's newest supper clubs, *page 63*) to spending the day in Central Park, an experience that comes with no price tag but plenty of pay-off.

STATUE OF LIBERTY

BRIGHT LIGHTS, BIG CITY

Exhilarating, intriguing, overwhelming—New York City can be all of those things. More than 8.2 million people live here, and another 40 million visit each year. The Big Apple offers a kaleidoscope of world-class cultural attractions, restaurants, shops, ethnic neighborhoods and, yes, even spots for outdoor sports and recreation within the concrete jungle. Truth is, the most populous city in America can be all at once the most welcoming, crowded, expensive, budget-friendly, gritty, elegant place you'll ever visit—your perceptions can shift as quickly as the bustling sidewalk before you. Even the messy bits (getting lost, getting snubbed, getting overwhelmed) can be part of the fun.

JUST HOW DIVERSE IS NEW YORK CITY?

The common term "melting pot" has long been used to describe the dense, immigrant-heavy neighborhoods on Manhattan's Lower East Side. Today, that influx continues throughout New York City—more than a third of the population is foreign-born, and roughly 170 languages are spoken here. This packed-to-the-gills city is made up of scores of individual neighborhoods, all with personalities that are markedly distinct. Within just a five-mile radius in Manhattan, you can buy frogs and paper fans at a street market in Chinatown, feast on cannoli in Little Italy, stroll cobblestoned, tree-lined streets and browse the city's largest collection of rare books in Greenwich Village, rollerblade along the Hudson River in Lower Manhattan, gallery hop and hobnob with artistic types and then dance the night away at clubs in Chelsea. The Upper West Side is a bagel-and-lox lover's paradise full of stroller-pushing moms, while the Upper East Side is a tony neighborhood big on high-end shops and old-school manners. In between, Midtown is a combo of tourist mecca and bustling business.

WHAT'S THE BEST WAY TO BLEND IN LIKE A LOCAL?

Learn some lingo to boost your street cred. Houston ("Hew-ston") is a city in Texas; Houston ("How-ston") is the street that divides Greenwich Village and Soho. Subway lines are referred to by number or letter (1, 2, 3, A, C, E), not color.

HOW EXPENSIVE IS MANHATTAN?

The global recession may have drowned out the real estate market for the moment, but if there's one thing New Yorkers love gossiping about, it's real estate. Nowhere in America is housing pricier than in Manhattan, and nowhere is the rental market more competitive. It's renters—not landlords—who can expect to fork over as much as $10,000 in broker's fees and deposits, plus prove that they make 40 times the rent before pocketing the keys to a pint-sized apartment (where it's not uncommon to find the fridge a step or two from the bathtub). Rents vary widely by neighborhood, but a not-so-special one-bedroom in Greenwich Village likely goes for about $3,100 a month. While owning may be smarter in the long-run, it'll definitely cost you: The median price of a 734-square-foot, one-bedroom apartment in Manhattan is a whopping $778,961, according to Miller Samuel, a real estate appraisal and consulting firm. For all but the most affluent, living in Manhattan means scaling down and getting creative (the farther you head into the outer boroughs, the more room you'll have and the less you'll pay). Don't be surprised to hear stories of two friends splitting a tiny studio and illegal sublets in subpar but rent-controlled apartment, where price ceilings are legally set until a tenant moves out. Those stories you've heard about New Yorkers perusing newspaper obituary pages for apartment finds aren't the stuff of urban legend. It's every man for himself when it comes to finding a place to live in New York City.

HOW INFLUENTIAL IS NEW YORK CITY?

When New Yorkers describe their town as the center of the universe, they're not (just) being egomaniacs—more media is pumped out of here than in any other city in the world. New York is home to newspapers with an international influence (think *The New York Times* and *The Wall Street Journal*) and magazine publishers (Hearst, Condé Nast, Time Inc.), plus some of the biggest book publishing houses (Random House, HarperCollins, Simon & Schuster) and record companies (Sony, Warner Music Group) in the world. All four major American broadcast networks are headquartered in the city; and CNN and other cable outlets and masters of the Web such as Google and AOL have offices here. In short, if it's read, watched, surfed or listened to, there's a good chance it was produced in New York City.

New York City is also one of the largest regional economies in the world—you can almost feel the money pulsing through Manhattan. Wall Street, an unassuming strip of asphalt that's home to a gobsmacking financial history, is the location of the New York Stock Exchange, which is by far the largest exchange in the world. Nearby, the Federal Reserve Bank of New York helps implement national monetary policy, and houses a vault 80 feet underground that holds more gold than any other depository in the world—even Fort Knox. More *Fortune* 500 companies are headquartered in the Big Apple than anywhere else, from household names like AOL, Verizon and American Express to financial behemoths like JPMorgan Chase and Citigroup.

HOW GOOD IS THEATER IN NEW YORK?

If you can make it here, you'll make it anywhere: Theater thrives in New York like in no other city, which is why actors from the world over flock here hoping to get their big break. For most visitors, a Broadway show tops

ARE NEW YORKERS ACTUALLY RUDE?

Former Mayor Rudy Giuliani famously turned many of the most sleazy, crime-ridden pockets of the city (including peep show-laden Times Square) into family-friendly (some argue theme park-like) destinations during the 1990s, and the attacks on 9/11 united New Yorkers and gave them a sense of solidarity with their neighbors. Still, New York has a reputation for being a bit rude. In reality, New Yorkers just don't like their fast-paced lives slowed down. So when you're playing pedestrian, observe some unspoken rules of the road: Don't stop in the middle of the sidewalk to take pictures or look at your map. Instead, move to the side and let foot traffic flow. While strolling with friends and family is a great way to spend a day, walking four abreast while you all look skyward will earn you more than one scowl, and maybe even a shove. But there are friendly faces on the crowded sidewalks, too. Most people don't mind giving directions, and you may even get an added smile—or better yet, a tip about something you wouldn't have thought of yourself. (We've got one if you're brave enough to drive: Unlike almost anywhere else in the country, it's illegal to make a right turn on a red light here.)

CENTRAL PARK

their must-see list. More than 12 million theater tickets are sold in the city each year for shows ranging from lavish, outsized musical productions that have been going strong for years to tiny, shoestring-budget shows that pop up for one night only. Broadway puts on everything from classics like *The Phantom of the Opera* (the longest-running musical ever, with more than 8,500 performances under its belt) to poppy-and-pink *Legally Blonde* (a musical based on the movie), and far more serious fare, like Chekhov's *The Seagull*. So no matter what your taste, something is sure to stir you on Broadway. (On the off chance that nothing floats your boat, try more eclectic Off-Broadway and Off-Off-Broadway productions. You just might catch the next big thing before everyone else does.)

WHERE IS NEW YORK'S GREATEST ARCHITECTURE?

New York City is constantly reinventing itself, and nowhere is that more apparent than in the city's architecture. It's experiencing one of its largest building booms in decades, drawing world-class architects to add their touches to a skyline that already boasts nearly every structural style. Notable recent additions include British architect Sir Norman Foster's Hearst Tower, Spanish architect Santiago Calatrava's World Trade Center tranportation hub (still under construction at Ground Zero), Italian architect Renzo Piano's Morgan Library & Museum, plus the IAC/InterActiveCorp building by American Frank Gehry. To get the inside scoop on some of the city's most famous buildings (as well as its hidden gems), your best bet is an architectural tour, which generally costs $15 to $40. Opt for either a neighborhood-specific walking tour—**Municipal Art Society of New York** *(212-935-3960; www.mas.org)* or **Big Onion Walking Tours** *(212-439-1090; www.bigonion.com)* or a building-focused bus ride on a double-decker *(Gray Line, 800-669-0051; www.coachusa.com)*. Or gawk at the big picture with a skyline cruise *(NY Waterway Tours, 800-533-3779; www.nywaterway.com)*.

WHAT TO SEE

SOLOMON R. GUGGENHEIM MUSEUM

ONLY IN NEW YORK

It's a refrain you'll often hear echoed throughout the city's streets and corridors. The city that never sleeps is home to some of the most exceptional attractions anywhere, many of them highly prized for their cultural and historical significance. Besides the world-class museums, shopping and entertainment venues New York offers, there's another attraction that can't be replicated elsewhere: the colorful cast of characters who give the city its soul. After you've spent a day touring the city's top sights, take a seat in Central Park or at a café in Union Square and participate in the city's best free attraction: people watching. Without the intangible energy of New York's residents, the Statue of Liberty becomes just another heap of scrap metal and the lights of Times Square go dark. It's more than just iconic landmarks that make this city one of a kind. New York has a pulsing electricity all its own—something that has to be experienced to be understood.

CHELSEA/HELL'S KITCHEN/GARMENT DISTRICT

There's something for everyone in Chelsea, which lies to the north of Greenwich Village on Manhattan's west side. Long known as a home to both art galleries and gay culture, the neighborhood is also loved by foodies who frequent the gourmet stalls and restaurants at Chelsea Market, and fitness-minded types who come to Chelsea Piers, a riverfront sports complex containing batting cages, volleyball courts and an ice rink. To the north, hugging the Hudson River, Hell's Kitchen once had a reputation as a crime-ridden, decaying part of the city. Gentrification means that these days, strollers line the sidewalks and brunch at one of the many bistros lining Ninth Avenue is the most common sight. Unfortunately, you won't find ateliers and couture shops in the Garment District, which sits in Midtown between the Javits Convention Center and the Empire State Building—just the warehouses used by garment manufacturers and offices of big and small names in the world of fashion.

CHELSEA MARKET
75 Ninth Ave., Chelsea, 212-243-6005; www.chelseamarket.com
This sprawling urban marketplace has the stuff to make foodies take notice and picky eaters cry uncle. Once home to the Oreo cookie factory (they also made Fig Newtons and Saltines), Chelsea Market encompasses an entire city block and houses gourmet-goods shops, drool-worthy restaurants and even a few TV studios (Food Network and Oxygen most notably). You better come hungry if you're going to scratch the surface of this gastronomical playland. Calm a nagging sweet tooth with luscious brownies at Fat Witch bakery *(212-419-4824; www.fatwitch.com)* or load up on carbs at Amy's Bread *(212-462-4338; www.amysbread.com)*. Fill your pantry with olive oil and pastas at Buon Italia *(212-633-9090; www.buonitalia.com)* or dine on tuna pizza or rack of lamb at *Iron Chef* Masaharu Morimoto's eponymous restaurant *(212-989-8883; www.morimotonyc.com)*. Once you're full, burn off some calories by shopping for housewares at Bowery Kitchen Supply *(212-376-4982; www.bowerykitchens.com)* or Moroccan sconces at Imports from Marrakesh *(212-675-9700; www.importsfrommarrakesh.com)*. *Monday-Saturday 7 a.m.-10 p.m., Sunday 8 a.m.-8 p.m.*

NEW YORK PUBLIC LIBRARY

CHELSEA PIERS
Between 17th and 23rd streets at the Hudson River, Chelsea, 212-336-6666; www.chelseapiers.com
Long a mooring point for luxury liners (the *Titanic* was bound for Chelsea Piers when it struck that iceberg in April 1912), the Hudson River docks fell into a slow but steady decline as the jet-setting lifestyle sank nautical travel. Thanks to a $100 million renovation in the 1990s, Piers 59 through 62 were transformed into a 28-acre sports and entertainment complex boasting a 40-lane bowling alley, golf club (where swingers can tee off on 51-simulated championship courses), ice skating rinks, rock climbing wall, swimming pool, restaurants and a spa *(page 127)*.
Hours vary by business.

MACY'S HERALD SQUARE
151 West 34th St., Garment District, 212-695-4400; www.macys.com
They don't call Macy's flagship the "World's Largest Store" without reason. With more than one million square feet of retail space, the shopping mecca might better be described as a small (and sometimes chaotic) city. Nine floors hold an expansive inventory of designer perfumes, handbags, clothing and housewares, plus eateries like Au Bon Pain and Starbucks for refueling. The behemoth also sponsors several holiday extravaganzas every year, most famously the Macy's Thanksgiving Day Parade, when crowds cram the streets to catch glimpses of celebrity-studded floats and balloons

WHAT IS THE NEWEST ATTRACTION IN NYC?
The High Line *(page 40)* Built upon an elevated railroad track which had been out of commission for nearly 20 years, this park offers New Yorkers an unexpected green space that runs from the Meatpacking District to Chelsea, and stretches one-and-a-half miles up the island's West Side, with another stretch scheduled to be completed in 2010.

WHICH PARKS, BESIDES CENTRAL, ARE THE BEST TO VISIT?
Bryant Park *(page 33)* Locals love the Reading Room, an open-air library where you can sit and read books and magazines, as well as viewing free movies in the green space come summer.

Riverside Park *(page 47)* Yet another Frederick Law Olmsted-designed recreational area, the park has basketball courts, baseball and soccer fields, playgrounds, dog runs, a skate park and even a public marina.

Union Square Park *(page 41)* This European-style piazza brims with all sorts of activity and people, including students, home cooks who come to browse the market, dog walkers and protesters.

Washington Square Park *(page 33)* The quirky park is known for its famous landmark, the Washington Arch, an Arc de Triomphe replica. The space was also a gathering spot for hippies and artists in the 1960s.

as they glide down Broadway and end up in front of the store.
Monday-Saturday 10 a.m.-9:30 p.m., Sunday 11 a.m.-8:30 p.m.

CHINATOWN/LITTLE ITALY/NOLITA

Your senses will be on high alert when you head downtown and hit Chinatown. The visual and aural assault of crowds haggling for deals on knock-off designer handbags and tchotchkes in crammed retail stalls on Canal Street is only overshadowed by the aromas wafting from the fresh seafood shops. It's your taste buds that reap the real reward, thanks to what seems like an endless array of dim sum and noodle restaurants. If you prefer prosciutto to Peking duck, Little Italy is literally just steps away. It may be more tourist-trap than true Italian nowadays, except during the Feast of San Gennaro festival each September *(www.sangennaro.org)*, when it's worth a squeeze through the crowds for a paper bag full of warm zeppoles (fried dough balls with powdered sugar). Nolita (just north of Little Italy, like its name suggests) mixes independent (and often tiny) bars and restaurants with one-of-a-kind boutiques.

CHINATOWN/LITTLE ITALY
Chinatown: Essex, Worth, Grand and East Broadway streets; www.explorechinatown.com. Little Italy: Houston to Canal streets and Lafayette Street to the Bowery; www.littleitalynyc.com
One moment you're picking through rare fruits and examining fresh seafood and the next, you're spooning gelato and sampling chicken parmesan. It's hard not to notice the curious juxtaposition of Chinatown and Little Italy—two neighborhoods that couldn't be more different and that have somehow morphed into one. It's tempting to make food the focus of your excursion to these ethnic enclaves (for good reason), but there is so much more to these diverse neighborhoods. In Chinatown, stop at Chatham Square to pose by the Kim Lau Memorial Arch traditional Chinatown gate or head for Great World Inc. *(32 E. Broadway, 212-925-6606)*, a video store that stocks thousands of martial arts titles. In Little Italy, get a pie at the city's oldest pizza joint (it's been around since 1905) at Lombardi's *(32 Spring St., 212-941-7994: www.lombardisoriginalpizza.com)* and be sure to pay a visit to St. Patrick's Old Cathedral *(263 Mulberry St., 212-226-8075; www.oldcathedral.org)*, the original St. Pat's.

EAST VILLAGE/LOWER EAST SIDE

Long associated with the immigrants and working class who occupied the tenements here (especially Eastern European Jews), the Lower East Side's landscape changed in the 1990s to one with more art galleries, alt-rock venues, and hipster-haunt restaurants and bars than cheap apartments and kosher delis. The East Village was once considered a part of this low-income neighborhood, but the area east of the Bowery from Houston to 14th streets eventually developed a counter-culture vibe where artists and activists like Andy Warhol, Keith Haring, Abbie Hoffman and The Velvet Underground made names for themselves. Gentrification—most notably by ever-expanding New York University—has led to a shift in the arts scene to the Williamsburg section of Brooklyn and other parts of the city.

LOWER EAST SIDE TENEMENT MUSEUM
108 Orchard St., Lower East Side, 212-982-8420; www.tenement.org

Looking to profit from the rising number of immigrants flooding New York in the mid-1800s, Lukas Glockner opened a cheap tenement at 97 Orchard Street to house them. Between 1863 and 1935, more than 7,000 tenants—primarily the poor and working class—occupied his sparse Lower East Side apartment building. It later fell into disrepair but was refurbished and opened as a museum in 1988—the first of its kind. Visitors take guided tours to learn about the immigrant experience and the traditions they brought with them from all over the world.

Admission: adults $20, students and seniors $15. Daily 10 a.m.-6 p.m.

FINANCIAL DISTRICT/BATTERY PARK CITY

There's more to the downtown Financial District than the New York Stock Exchange and a bunch of stiff suits. Even if it's a bear market, Wall Street's power inspires optimism, and if things are looking up, you can drop a pretty penny at South Street Seaport's touristy shops and restaurants. The area is also a somber stop for visitors who want a look at Ground Zero—and surrounding street vendors are at the ready, hawking everything from commemorative snow globes to t-shirts. A good place to escape them is adjacent Battery Park City, a planned community on the southern tip of Manhattan where you'll find sweeping views of New York Harbor and the Statue of Liberty.

BOWLING GREEN
Broadway and Whitehall Street, Battery Park

This small, wedge-shaped plaza has at least two claims to historical fame. In 1626, it was the spot where Dutch governor Peter Minuit allegedly purchased Manhattan for $24 worth of goods, leading some to call this grassy parcel the birthplace of New York. It also happens to be New York City's first official park. Today, most visitors know it as the home of the 7,000 pound bronze sculpture Charging Bull. The bull represents financial optimism when stock prices are rising (contrasted with a bear market, when prices are falling). But according to its sculptor, Arturo Di Modica, it also represents "the strength, power and hope of the American people for the future." He first installed the piece illegally next to the New York Stock Exchange as guerrilla art, and it was impounded by police. After a public outcry, it was placed—legally this time—at its current location.

WHAT ARE NEW YORK'S CAN'T-MISS FIRST VISIT SIGHTS?

Central Park *(pages 29, 42)* The most frequently visited urban park in the United States, Central Park is a tranquil oasis in the heart of Manhattan.

Empire State Building *(page 35)* As New York's tallest—and most famous— skyscraper, it's no wonder many a movie moment has transpired atop this majestic marvel.

Rockefeller Center *(page 38)* Many well-known tenants are housed in the center of this 19-building complex, including Radio City Music Hall, NBC studios and the famous Rockefeller Center Christmas tree.

Times Square *(page 39)* Once a crime-riddled area, today's Times Square is a 24-hour tourist's haven, overflowing with shopping, dining and cultural activities.

CASTLE CLINTON NATIONAL MONUMENT

Battery Park at New York Harbor, 212-344-7220; www.nps.gov/cacl

This is where you hop the ferry to Ellis Island and the Statue of Liberty. Arguably one of New York's most storied sights, this monument, completed in 1811, began as a fort for protecting the island from British invasion during the War of 1812. The large circular structure was then converted into a theater where concerts and scientific demonstrations frequently got top billing. After 30 years as an entertainment venue, the building once again changed purposes, becoming an immigrant-landing depot until Ellis Island opened in the 1890s. A stint as an aquarium followed before the site was converted into a national monument where you can eat a picnic lunch, take a guided tour and get the ferry to Ellis Island and the Statue of Liberty. *Daily 8:30 a.m.-5 p.m.*

ELLIS ISLAND

212-561-4588; www.ellisisland.org

More than 40 percent of Americans can trace their ancestors' first steps on U.S. soil to the country's first federal immigration station, which opened in the shadow of the Statue of Liberty in 1892. Roughly 12 million immigrants seeking the American dream passed through here before the station closed in 1954. Now it's open to visitors as an interactive museum, where you can take a self-guided tour of the grounds and check out photographs, artifacts and search records to locate family members.

Daily 9:30 a.m.-5:15 p.m. Check Web site for seasonal changes in hours.

GROUND ZERO

Lower Manhattan, bound by the West Side Highway and Vesey, Liberty and Church streets, Financial District

Nine years after the attacks of September 11, 2001, the old World Trade Center site is alive with the sound of jackhammers and bulldozers as new buildings begin to take shape against lower Manhattan's skyline. The first completed building, the office complex at 7 World Trade Center, opened its doors in May 2006. But for the most part, the site is still shrouded by chain link fences and barricades. The National September 11 Memorial and Museum is scheduled for a 2011 opening, but in the meantime, there are a variety of ways to pay tribute and recognize the events of September 11th. Pedestrian bridges across West Street, located on both Liberty and

ELLIS ISLAND

Vesey streets, provide a view of the site, as does the PATH train station and the World Financial Center in nearby Battery Park. The Tribute WTC Visitor Center *(120 Liberty St., 866-737-1184; www.tributewtc.org)* houses numerous artifacts and highlights the stories of those lost during the tragedy.

SOUTH STREET SEAPORT
Fulton and South streets, Pier 17, Financial District, 212-732-7678;
www.southstreetseaport.com
Part mall, part historic landmark, Lower Manhattan's South Street Seaport has a little something for everyone. In the shopping center you'll find all the usual suspects (Abercrombie & Fitch, Bath and Body Works, Gap, Victoria's Secret) plus a TKTS discount ticket booth *(page 167),* in addition to restaurants like the Pan-Asian Pacific Grill and food-court fare including Subway sandwiches and pizza. It's the South Street Seaport Museum, however, that really captures the spirit of the former commercial and transportation hub. The museum boasts an extensive collection of luxury liner memorabilia; visitors can see a scale model of the *Titanic* and a vast collection of cigarette cards, china, medals and tea sets from other cruise ships of yore. The site also features a recreated working paper press that makes cards and stationery to order, printed on 19th century treadle-powered equipment.
Monday-Saturday 10 a.m.-9 p.m., Sunday 11 a.m.-8 p.m. Restaurants and bars have extended hours.

STATEN ISLAND FERRY
1 Whitehall St., Battery Park, 718-815-2628; www.nyc.gov
Commutes aren't supposed to be romantic, but that's the best way to describe the 5.2-mile run between St. George Terminal in Staten Island and the Whitehall Terminal in lower Manhattan. Sure, pragmatists would point out that the ferries provide Staten Islanders with free (that's right, free!) transportation to their Manhattan day jobs. But those with a little imagination

WHAT'S THE BEST WAY TO SEE CENTRAL PARK IN ONE DAY?

It would be tough to see everything this expansive 843-acre park has to offer in just one day (or even two). But with a little planning, you can take in many of the must-see sites in the country's most well-known park. Here's how:

10 A.M.

Start with a bike ride along the park's six-mile loop of paved pathway. The Loeb Central Park Boathouse *(Park Drive North between East 74th and East 75th streets, 212-517-2233; www.thecentralparkboathouse.com)* offers an array of cycle rentals, including tandems and cruisers. If a run is more your style, there's a popular one-and-a-half mile running track surrounding the Jacqueline Kennedy Onassis Reservoir. Or saddle up for a horseback ride along the park's six-mile bridle path; rides start at the North Meadow Recreation Center *(midpark; enter at West 96th Street, 212-348-4867)*. You can simply ride the painted wooden version on the park's carousel *(www.centralparkcarousel.com)* at 64th Street—a mere two bucks gets you a three-and-a-half-minute ride.

NOON

Sure, you could make do with a hot dog or braided pretzel from one of the park's many concession stands, but you can do better than that. After dropping off your bike, enjoy a serene lunch by the lake at the boathouse's restaurant *(midpark; around 72nd Street, 212-517-2233)*, where you can watch rowboats, ducks and even an occasional gondola float by. Options run from quick-and-easy sandwiches at the Express Café to the decadent entrées at the Lakeside Dining area.

1:30 P.M.

The park may be a testament to Mother Nature's handiwork, but many of the awe-inspiring man-made wonders here are worth a look, too. Head southwest to take in the "heart" of Central Park—Bethesda Terrace, which overlooks the lake and Bethesda Fountain. The site is a popular filming location. Next, walk northeast to see one of the park's oldest landmarks—Cleopatra's Needle. A 69-foot-tall obelisk nestled behind the south side of the Metropolitan Museum of Art, the sculpture came from Egypt in 1881 and dates back to about 1500 B.C.

3 P.M.

Grab a cab just outside the park's bounds heading south along Fifth Avenue for a quick trip to Central Park Zoo *(www.centralparkzoo.com)* at 64th Street. The zoo—open 365 days a year—is organized by climate zones, so you can chill out with the polar bears, check out parrots in the rain forest exhibit, and visit rare red pandas in their jungle habitat, all in one trip. Or spend some quiet time in Strawberry Fields, the stretch of park from 71st to 74th streets dedicated to John Lennon. In the center is the famous "Imagine" mosaic that was donated by the city of Naples, Italy.

5 P.M.

Have a cocktail at Tavern on the Green's 40-foot Garden Bar *(Central Park at West 67th Street, 212-873-3200; www.tavernonthegreen.com)*, which was crafted from trees harvested from the city's parks. For dinner, the Time Warner Center located just outside the park is home to some of the city's top restaurants.

8 P.M.

During the summer, the New York Public Theater *(425 Lafayette St., 212-539-8500; www.publictheater.org)* hosts Shakespeare in the Park, performing the Bard's greatest hits like *Hamlet* and more recent productions like *Hair*—often with a Hollywood star or two. The Great Lawn also puts on concerts by the New York Philharmonic *(www.nyphil.org)* and The Metropolitan Opera *(www.metoperafamily.com)*.

know the 25-minute ride is a tourist treasure, too, far more a sightseeing pleasure cruise than weary work trip. From the decks, passengers can take in picturesque views of the Statue of Liberty, Ellis Island and Manhattan's scraper-filled skyline.
Check Web site for schedule.

STATUE OF LIBERTY
Liberty Island, 212-363-3200; www.nps.gov/stli
Perhaps the most enduring symbol of America's promise of freedom and democracy, the Liberty Enlightening the World statue (its formal name) has served as a beacon welcoming immigrants and visitors for more than 120 years. A gift of friendship from the French, the monument was dedicated on October 28, 1886, and stands more than 305 feet from the ground to the top of the torch. Designer Frederic-Auguste Bartholdi placed several symbolic touches throughout the monument: The seven rays of Lady Liberty's crown represent the seven seas and continents of the world, and the tablet she holds in her left hand reads in Roman numerals "July 4, 1776." The lady was restored for her centennial on July 2, 1986. Visitors are allowed onto the Statue's observation deck and can also get an inside view through a glass ceiling with a new lighting and video system.
Admission: adults $12, seniors $10, children 4-12 $5, children 3 and under free. Daily 8:30 a.m.-6 p.m. (hours are adjusted seasonally). Ferries run daily from 8:30 a.m.-4:30 p.m. from Castle Clinton in Battery Park. Visit www.statuecruises.com for more information.

WALL STREET
Between Broadway and South Street near the East River, Financial District
A flurry of crisp business suits and Blackberrys, Wall Street is a stretch of pavement that has become synonymous with the U.S. financial industry. The street begins at Broadway, where you'll find Trinity Church, and stretches east to the East River.

Named for the blockade constructed by Dutch colonists to protect themselves from British attacks, today Wall Street is known far better as the home of financially and historically relevant sights, including the New York Stock Exchange and Federal Hall. The NYSE, also known as the "Big Board," is the largest exchange in the world based on the value of its securities. As the nation's first capitol, Federal Hall was the sight of George Washington's inauguration, the first congressional meeting and the signing of the Bill of Rights. Since 9/11, the Exchange is no longer open to the public. You can, however, tour the Federal Reserve Bank *(33 Liberty Street, 212-720-6130; www.newyorkfed.org)*, where about a quarter of the world's gold is stored, by calling ahead for tickets at least one month in advance. You can also learn more about the history of Wall Street at the Museum of American Finance

---

WHAT ARE SOME OF THE BEST FREE ACTIVITIES?
New York Public Library *(page 36)* In addition to free tours and all kinds of special events, the enormous marble building is a sight in itself.

Staten Island Ferry *(page 28)* Those with a little imagination know the free, scenic 25-minute ride is a tourist treasure, far more a sightseeing pleasure cruise than weary work trip.

GRAND CENTRAL TERMINAL

(48 Wall Street, at Williams Street, 212-908-4110; www.moaf.org), located in the former headquarters of the Bank of New York. Exhibits include a history of money, a timeline on the credit crisis and more. Next, pay a visit to Trinity Church *(Broadway at Wall Street, 212-602-0800; www.trinitywallstreet.org)* and its sister church, St. Paul's Chapel *(five blocks north on Broadway, 212-233-4164; www.stpaulschapel.org)*, two of the most historic churches in the United States—George Washington worshipped at St. Paul's. The Trinity Courtyard is a lovely patch of green inside the financial district, and where many bankers bring their lunches. Its famous graveyard contains the remains of Alexander Hamilton.

Federal Reserve: Admission: Free. Monday-Friday 9 a.m.-5 p.m. Tours are every hour on the half hour. Last tour is at 3:30 p.m. Museum of American Finance: Admission: adults $8, students and seniors $5, children 6 and under free. Tuesday-Saturday 10 a.m.-4 p.m. (until 6:00 p.m. Wednesday from July-October). Trinity Church: Monday-Friday 7 a.m.-6 p.m., Saturday 8 a.m-4 p.m., Sunday 7 a.m.-4 p.m. Hours for the churchyard vary with the season. During daylight-savings time, the churchyard remains open until 5 p.m., weather permitting; otherwise, it closes at 4 p.m. during the week and at 3 p.m. on weekends. St. Paul's Chapel: Monday-Friday 10 a.m.-6 p.m., Saturday 8 a.m.-3 p.m., Sunday 7 a.m.-3 p.m. Churchyard: Monday-Saturday 10 a.m.-4 p.m. (until 5:30 during daylight savings), Sunday 7 a.m.-3:30 p.m.

WOOLWORTH BUILDING
233 Broadway, Financial District

This Gothic-style skyscraper towering 792 feet above Manhattan's Financial District was built to house the now-defunct five-and-dime's headquarters. Funded completely with cash (lots of nickels and dimes, perhaps?), the building was completed in 1913, and was the tallest in the world until the 927-feet tall 40 Wall Street came along in 1930. Its interior features a cruciform floor plan with vaulted ceilings, and boasts several humorous gargoyles depicting the building's key players including Mr. Woolworth counting his

WHICH ARE THE CITY'S TOP MUSEUMS?

American Museum of Natural History *(page 45)* One of the largest natural history institutions in the world, this enormous Upper West Side museum is famous for its dinosaur exhibits.

Metropolitan Museum of Art *(page 43)* More than two million works of art are housed in this Gothic-Revival building founded in 1870.

Solomon R. Guggenheim Museum *(page 43)* Thousands flock to this contemporary and modern art museum for both its permanent collection (including works by Pablo Picasso, Salvador Dalí and Henri Matisse) and to take in Frank Lloyd Wright's awesome creation.

Whitney Museum of American Art *(page 43)* The museum frequently purchases works from up-and-comers to keep its ever-changing collection fresh.

dimes and architect Cass Gilbert holding a model of the building. Coined the "cathedral of commerce," its opening was celebrated by President Wilson, who pushed a button in the White House to illuminate each floor and the building's façade. Sold by the Woolworth Company in 1998, the building now houses the New York University School of Continuing and Professional Studies' Center for Global Affairs, in addition to other tenants.

GREENWICH VILLAGE/SOHO/WEST VILLAGE

Once the center of New York's bohemian scene, Greenwich Village is a little less counter-culture these days, but no less colorful. It's anchored at the southern tip of Fifth Avenue by Washington Square Park, where street performers intermingle with protestors and chess players. The giant arch at its center is one of New York City's most recognizable symbols. Soho is the neighborhood south of Houston Street, which can be summed up in one word: shopping. Designers such as Anna Sui and John Varvatos mix it up with the likes of the Apple Store and Bloomingdale's, and the crowds never cease. Things are a little more diverse between Sixth Avenue and the Hudson River in the West Village, where the cobblestone streets are lined with bars, bistros and boutiques. The neighborhood has long been famous as a home for artists and writers both real (Dylan Thomas, Charlie Parker) and fictional.

ANGELIKA FILM CENTER & CAFÉ

18 W. Houston St., Soho, 212-995-2000; www.angelikafilmcenter.com
Skip the long lines for big-budget blockbusters and check out the best in independent and foreign fare at Soho's six-screen Angelika Film Center. Its spacious café is a neighborhood favorite where you don't need a ticket stub to get in and enjoy the gourmet pastries and coffee in addition to standard movie-musts like popcorn and Milk Duds. Just be prepared for the rumble—not from the onscreen action, but from the subway tracks running below the theater.
Check Web site for ticket information. Café open from beginning of the first show of the day, to the beginning of the last.

STRAND BOOKSTORE
828 Broadway, Greenwich Village, 212-473-1452;
www.strandbooks.com

Named after the famous London street, this independent bookstore was just one of 48 booksellers occupying New York's famous "Book Row" in the late 1920s. Today, the Strand is the only one left. The shop, which moved to its current location from Fourth Avenue in the 1950s, contains 18 miles of shelves stocked with new and used books, in addition to NYC's largest collection of rare books (such as the first American edition of Alexis de Toqueville's *Democracy in America*). The expansive store also hosts author signings and events.
Monday-Saturday 9:30 a.m.-10:30 p.m., Sunday 11 a.m.-10:30 p.m.

WASHINGTON SQUARE PARK
West Fourth and MacDougal streets, Greenwich Village;
www.nycgovparks.org

This potter's field-turned-park was once home to the public gallows, but today the hanging around is much more leisurely. Located in the heart of Greenwich Village, this green space is not only a popular haunt for sunbathing students from adjacent New York University, but a haven for chess players and street performers. The park's most famous landmark, Washington Arch, an Arc de Triomphe replica, was built between 1890 and 1892 to replace a wooden arch that had been built to commemorate the centennial of George Washington's inauguration. In the 1960s, the park was a popular gathering spot for hippies and artists. Today, it's currently a perfect spot for a little New York City people-watching, particularly at the central fountain.
Daily 6 a.m.-1 a.m.

MIDTOWN/MIDTOWN EAST

Midtown Manhattan is just that—the middle of the island (from 34th to 59th streets), and with all this bit of prime real estate has going on, it may as well be the center of the universe. This is where you'll find the Empire State Building, Chrysler Building, Rockefeller Center and Madison Square Garden. The business district—from the 40s up and along the Avenue of the Americas, a.k.a. Sixth Avenue—is where some of the world's most influential advertising, financial and media companies have their headquarters. Midtown East, between the East River and Madison Avenue, is home to the United Nations and Grand Central Terminal.

BRYANT PARK
Between 40th and 42nd streets and Fifth and Sixth avenues, Midtown;
www.bryantpark.org

The park's central location (just one block from Times Square), free entertainment all summer long and free wireless Internet access makes it very popular with office workers and tourists alike. Entertainment includes concerts and movies on Monday nights after dusk. Bring a blanket and picnic and come early—the lawn starts filling up quickly after 5 p.m. The park also includes four 'wichcraft kiosks, where you can sample some of chef Tom Colicchio's gourmet sandwiches *(page 83)*, soups and salads, or simply grab a coffee, ice cream or hot chocolate. A favorite spot in the park is the Reading Room, an open-air library where you can sit and read books and magazines for free. The Pond is a free ice skating rink in winter.

THE METROPOLITAN MUSEUM OF ART

Daily. January-March, 7 a.m.-7 p.m.; January, until 10 p.m. (while the pond is open); March, until 8 p.m. after Daylight Saving change; April, 7 a.m.-10 p.m.; May-September, 7 a.m.-11 p.m.; October, 7 a.m.-8 p.m.; November-December, 7 a.m.-10 p.m.

CARNEGIE HALL
881 Seventh Ave., Midtown, 212-247-7800; www.carnegiehall.org

If someone asks you how to get to Carnegie Hall, you probably already know the answer: Practice. The answer to one of the city's most tired jokes, this famous Midtown concert hall has played host to some of the most well-practiced classical, pop and jazz musicians of the last century, including Maria Callas, Sergei Rachmaninoff, Bob Dylan, Judy Garland, Frank Sinatra and Billie Holiday. Built by and named after wealthy businessman and philanthropist Andrew Carnegie, this six-story structure with an Italian Renaissance façade of terra cotta and brick boasts not one, but three performance spaces. The Hall faced demolition in 1960 before the city bought it for $5 million. Concert seasons run October through June. Tours are also available during that time.

Box office: September-June, Monday-Saturday 11 a.m.-6 p.m., Sunday noon-6 p.m.; July-August, Monday-Thursday 9 a.m.-6 p.m.

CHRYSLER BUILDING
405 Lexington Ave., Midtown

One of the most iconic examples of Art Deco architecture, the Chrysler Building rises more than 1,000 feet (77 stories) above Lexington Avenue and 42nd Street. Designed to house the motorcar company's offices, architect William Van Alen added automotive accents like metal hubcaps, car fenders and radiator-cap gargoyles to the structure's façade. Briefly the tallest skyscraper in the world, it was soon eclipsed by the taller Empire State Building. The Chrysler is no longer owned or occupied by the automaker; a 90-percent stake in the structure was purchased in 2008 by the Abu Dhabi

Invest Council for $800 million. (Its largest tenants include the law firm Blank Rome LLP and YES Network, the cable television operation of the New York Yankees.) Though there are no guided tours of the edifice, the lobby is open to visitors who wish to gaze at the ceiling fresco dotted with depictions of buildings, airplanes and the Chrysler assembly line.

EMPIRE STATE BUILDING
350 Fifth Ave., Midtown, 212-736-3100; www.esbnyc.com
King Kong perched atop its lofty spire. Cary Grant and Deborah Kerr made the observation deck a quintessential spot for romantics in 1957's *An Affair to Remember*. As New York's tallest—and most famous—skyscraper, it's no wonder many a movie moment has transpired atop this majestic marvel. Constructed shortly after its Art Deco cousin the Chrysler Building, the Empire State Building stands 1,224 feet tall—that's 1,860 steps to the top if you were thinking about climbing it by foot—with a design inspired by the simple pencil. Observatories on the 86th and 102nd floors, open year-round, promise an unparalleled view of the Big Apple.
Admission: adults $22, seniors $16, children 6-12 $20, children 5 and under free. Observatory hours: Daily 8 a.m.-2 a.m.

FAO SCHWARZ
767 Fifth Ave., Midtown, 212-644-9400; www.fao.com
Kids big and small will have a blast at the 50,000-square-foot playland that serves as the flagship for the famous high-end toy giant. (Yes, you can dance on the huge floor piano like Tom Hanks did in the movie *Big*.) The oldest and swankiest toy store in the country moved to its current Fifth Avenue location in 1986, where three floors are stuffed to the rafters with plush stuffed animals, dolls, toy cars and books. Kids can even create their own playthings at toy factories dedicated to Hot Wheels, Madame Alexander Dolls and Barbie.
Monday-Wednesday 10 a.m.-7 p.m., Thursday-Saturday 10 a.m.-8 p.m., Sunday 11 a.m.-6 p.m.

GRAND CENTRAL TERMINAL
87 E. 42nd St., Midtown, 212-340-2347;
www.grandcentralterminal.com
This Beaux Arts-style behemoth is more than just a place to hop a train. Originally constructed in 1871 at the behest of Cornelius Vanderbilt, then rebuilt between 1903 and 1913, Grand Central Terminal is an architectural gem, a bustling transportation center, and a lively retail and dining district. The station's expansive main concourse—with its celestial ceiling (keep

WHAT ARE THE BEST CULTURAL VENUES?
Carnegie Hall *(page 34)* This famous Midtown concert hall has played host to some of the most well-practiced classical, pop and jazz musicians of the last century.

Lincoln Center for the Performing Arts *(page 46)* Some of the Big Apple's most renowned performance groups, including the New York Philharmonic, the New York City Ballet and The Metropolitan Opera make this Upper West Side cultural destination their home.

your eyes peeled for backwards constellations) and acorn and oak-leaf decorations (symbols of the Vanderbilt family)—is by far the building's most iconic section. Whether you're waiting for a train or not, stop in for a drink at the Campbell Apartment *(page 150)*, the private office of 1920's tycoon John W. Campbell, which has been restored and turned into a handsome lounge, or have a bite in one of the many restaurants, including American brasserie Métrazur *(212-687-4600; www.charliepalmer.com)*, the landmark Oyster Bar and Restaurant *(212-490-6650; www.oysterbarny.com)* or Cipriani Dolci *(212-973-0999; www.cipriani.com)*, an outpost of the famous New York restaurant dynasty that invented the Bellini (you can have one here) and which serves tasty beef carpaccio and hearty pastas.

MUSEUM OF MODERN ART (MOMA)
11 W. 53rd St., Midtown, 212-708-9400; www.moma.org
Modern art skeptics should think twice before discounting a visit to this pioneer institution. Since 1929, MoMA has harbored one of the most impressive contemporary art collections in the world. Thanks to a recent $425 million face-lift spearheaded by Yoshio Taniguchi, the museum's exhibition space has nearly doubled in size, allowing for large-scale installations as well as a devoted education and research facility. Famous works lurk around every bend in the museum. You may find yourself gazing at Monet's *Water Lilies* one moment and Van Gogh's *The Starry Night* the next. Opt for a personalized audio tour if you think you'll be lost on the contemporary aesthetic. If modern art still isn't your thing, come for the academic programs, film screenings—there are roughly 22,000 films in house—and the food. A meal at chef Gabriel Kreuther's onsite restaurant The Modern *(page 76)* is a fine finish to an exceptionally avant-garde afternoon.
Admission: adults $20, seniors $16, students $12, children 16 and under free. Sunday-Monday, Wednesday-Thursday, Saturday 10:30 a.m.-5:30 p.m., Friday 10:30 a.m.-8 p.m.

NEW YORK PUBLIC LIBRARY
Fifth Avenue at 42nd Street, Midtown, 917-390-0800; www.nypl.org
It took 500 workers two years to dismantle Fifth Avenue's Croton Reservoir (New York City's main water source), but once they were finished in 1902, the coast was clear for New York's first truly public library. This majestic Beaux Arts-style building (and the largest marble structure constructed in the U.S.) is also known as the Humanities and Social Sciences Library. Guarded by marble lions Patience and Fortitude, the library's initial collections were a conglomerate of materials from John Jacob Astor's and James Lenox's failing libraries. The library now has four major research libraries and 87 branches spread throughout the city. Most of the materials are free to use onsite and there are two free guided tours (Monday-Saturday at 11 a.m. and 2 p.m.) The library also hosts a variety of lectures, author readings and wonderful special exhibitions; check the Web site for a calendar of events.
Monday 11 a.m.-6 p.m., Tuesday-Wednesday 11 a.m.-7:30 p.m., Thursday-Saturday 11 a.m.-6 p.m., Sunday 1 p.m.-5 p.m.

THE PLAZA
Fifth Avenue at Central Park South, Midtown, 212-759-3000;
www.theplaza.com
This famous Beaux Arts hotel—built in 1907 for $12 million—is an iconic

WHAT ARE SOME EXAMPLES OF GREAT ARCHITECTURE IN NEW YORK?

Chrysler Building *(page 34)* Designed to house the motorcar company's offices, architect William Van Alen added automotive accents like metal hubcaps and radiator-cap gargoyles to the structure's façade.

Flatiron Building *(page 40)* One of the city's iconic buildings, this Beaux Arts beauty made of limestone and terra cotta measures an amazingly slim six-and-a-half feet wide at its apex.

Grand Central Terminal *(page 35)* This architectural gem is both a bustling transportation center, and a lively retail and dining district.

The Plaza *(page 116)* The iconic hotel recently underwent a multi-million dollar renovation, while still keeping certain treasures in tact, like the chandelier-dripping lobby where afternoon tea is served.

St. Patrick's Cathedral *(page 38)* The largest gothic-style Catholic cathedral in the United States is well known for its stunning architecture, including altars designed by Tiffany & Co.

Woolworth Building *(page 31)* Coined the "cathedral of commerce," this Gothic-style headquarter's opening was celebrated by President Wilson, who pushed a button in the White House to illuminate each floor.

New York landmark that's played host to a number of movie production sets. The Plaza made its proper film debut in Alfred Hitchcock's *North by Northwest* and has appeared in *The Way We Were* and *The Great Gatsby*. It has also had its share of famous guests; perhaps most famous is the fictional Eloise from the beloved children's books by Kay Thompson. The iconic hotel, located at the picturesque corner of Central Park and Fifth Avenue, recently underwent a staggering $400 million renovation and now boasts 182 condos meant for permanent residence in addition to 282 guest rooms, which come complete with a white-gloved butler on each floor and a touch-screen panel for room customization *(page 116)*. If a stay here isn't an option, don't fret: You can still have afternoon tea in the lovely lobby. The legendary Oak Room also remains.

RADIO CITY MUSIC HALL
1260 Avenue of the Americas, Midtown, 212-307-7171;
www.radiocity.com
This venue drips with stardom, thanks to the many luminaries who have graced the Great Stage (among them the Dalai Lama, Bill Cosby and Frank Sinatra), not to mention those leggy bastions of Americana, the Radio City Rockettes. Some stars show up to perform, others to receive accolades at the Grammys, the Tonys or the MTV Video Music Awards, which have all been held here. The annual *Radio City Christmas Spectacular* starring the Rockettes sells out quickly every year for a reason—it's just plain holiday fun, so buy tickets far in advance if you're in town during Christmas. Check the Web site for performance information.
Tour tickets: adults $18.50, seniors $15, children 12 and under $10. Tours: Daily 11 a.m.-3 p.m. Box office: Monday-Saturday 11:30 a.m.-6 p.m.

LINCOLN CENTER FOR THE PERFORMING ARTS

ROCKEFELLER CENTER
From Fifth Avenue to Seventh Avenue, between 47th and 51st streets, Midtown, 212-632-3975; www.rockefellercenter.com

John D. Rockefeller leased this space in the heart of Midtown from Columbia University in 1928 hoping to create a new home for The Metropolitan Opera. Though his plans were derailed by the Great Depression, today Rockefeller Center is a bustling 19-building complex full of shops, restaurants and offices. Many well-known tenants are housed in the center, including Radio City Music Hall, NBC studios and the famous Rockefeller Center Christmas tree, for which an elaborate lighting ceremony is held and televised to kick off the holiday season each year. (Insider tip: The Top of the Rock observation decks at 30 Rockefeller Center on the 67th, 69th and 70th floors offer expansive views of Manhattan and are often less crowded than the Empire State Building observation deck.) Other popular activities include the NBC Studio Tour (peek backstage at *Saturday Night Live*, *Late Night with Jimmy Fallon* and more), *Today* show tapings and wintertime skating in the plaza's famous ice rink.

Concourse hours: Daily 7 a.m.-midnight. NBC Studio Tour: adults $19.25, children 6-12 and seniors $16.25. Monday-Thursday 8:30 a.m.-4:30 p.m. (departs every 30 minutes), Friday-Saturday 9:30 a.m.-5:30 p.m. (departs every 15 minutes), Sunday 9:30 a.m.-4:30 p.m. (departs every 15 minutes).

ST. PATRICK'S CATHEDRAL
14 E. 51st St., Midtown, 212-753-2261; www.saintpatrickscathedral.org

Opened in 1879, St. Patrick's Cathedral is the largest gothic-style Catholic cathedral in the United States and the seat of the Archbishop of New York. Though a popular tourist attraction (call 212-355-2749, extension 409, to set up a volunteer-guided tour, or just stop in to have a look by yourself), this ornate place of worship still hosts weekly mass services. Located in Midtown and facing Rockefeller Center, the cathedral is well known for its stunning architecture—including its beautiful rose window, a pieta which is three times

the size of Michelangelo's, and altars designed by Tiffany & Co.
Daily 6:30 a.m.-8:45 p.m.

UNITED NATIONS
First Avenue at 46th Street, Midtown East, 212-963-8687; www.un.org
The 18-acre headquarters of this peacekeeping organization isn't technically in New York, but situated atop international territory belonging to all member countries. The complex encompasses four buildings, one of which is the Secretariat, an iconic, 39-story structure with a green-glass-curtained exterior. Tours of the U.N. are available Monday through Friday and take visitors through various council chambers and the General Assembly Hall. Gifts donated by member countries, such as an ivory carving from China and drums from the Caribbean, are also on display.
Tour tickets: adults $12.50, seniors and students $8, children 5-14 $6.50. Tour hours: Monday-Friday 9:45 a.m.-4:45 p.m. (Tours may be limited during debates of the General Assembly from mid-September to mid-October.)

THEATER DISTRICT/TIMES SQUARE
Who hasn't watched—at least on television—the ball drop in Times Square on New Year's Eve? Once a seedy, crime-plagued pocket of peep-shows and adult movie theaters, Times Square is now more family friendly than down-and-out, catering to mobs of tourists visiting the G-rated retail flagships of Hershey, Toys 'R' Us and the like. The adjacent Theater District is where the lights of Broadway theater marquees illuminate what's affectionately known as the Great White Way.

TIMES SQUARE
Broadway and Seventh Avenue, Times Square, 212-768-1560; www.timessquarenyc.org
More than one million people flock to the "crossroads of the world" each year to ring in the New Year by seeing the ball drop. But there's plenty to see and do in this bustling neighborhood the other 364 days of the year. Named in honor of *The New York Times* (the iconic newspaper's offices were once located at the intersection of Seventh Avenue, Broadway and 42nd Street), Times Square is full of non-stop activity, overflowing with shopping, dining, corporate offices (everyone from Morgan Stanley to MTV), television studios (*Good Morning America*) and, of course, theater. Restaurant Row *(West 46th Street between Broadway and Ninth Avenue)* provides eclectic options from Thai to tapas. Then it's just a short walk to one of the dozens of Broadway theaters for a production of *Mamma Mia!*, *The Lion King* or more serious fare, like the 2009 Tony Award-winning play, *Next to Normal*. (Get tickets at the TKTS booth; *page 167).* Nothing beats a late-night stroll under the wash of Times Square's millions of twinkling lights. It may be 4 a.m., but you'll swear it's 4 p.m. (Thanks to a zoning ordinance, businesses must display illuminated signs to move into the area—it's actually against the law not to add that flash.)

TRIBECA/MEATPACKING DISTRICT
Tribeca—an acronym for Triangle Below Canal (Street)—is a downtown neighborhood where industrial warehouses have been converted into pricey loft apartments. The influential Tribeca Film Festival was co-founded by longtime resident Robert De Niro to spur the neighborhood's economy following the September 11 terrorist attacks at the nearby World Trade

Center. Just to the north, the animal carcasses and butchers that once defined the Meatpacking District—which spans from the Hudson River to Hudson Street to the north—have made way in the last decade for pretty people who like to see and be seen at velvet-rope clubs and restaurants.

HIGH LINE
From Gansevoort Street to 34th Street, between 10th and 11th avenues, Meatpacking District, 212-500-6035; www.thehighline.org

Even aging eyesores have potential in the Big Apple—especially if those eyesores include water views and open space. The recently unveiled High Line is Manhattan's newest, and highest, park. Utilizing the original elevated freight train tracks from the 1930s, designers and city planners have transformed the formerly neglected industrial strip into a verdant modern parkway with concrete paths, natural grasses and sleek wooden seating areas. When the project is completed in late 2010, it will stretch one-and-a-half miles up the island's West Side. For now, you can stroll from Gansevoort Street to 20th Street without interruption, 30 feet above the usual fray of horns, crowds and traffic jams.
Daily 7 a.m.-10 p.m.

UNION SQUARE/FLATIRON DISTRICT/GRAMERCY PARK/MURRAY HILL

Union Square is the entry to Greenwich Village and downtown, and is anchored by Union Square Park—a mammoth four-square block plaza that never stops bustling. The park is a popular meeting spot and home to the city's best-known farmers market, a dog run and one of the city's largest subway stations. To the north, the Flatiron District is named for the Flatiron Building, a striking, triangular building at 23rd Street where Broadway and Fifth Avenue converge which was one of the world's earliest steel structures. Gramercy Park is a nearby residential neighborhood lauded for a residents-only private park. Murray Hill is a quiet, no-nonsense eastside neighborhood that lies between 29th and 42nd streets, known for its solidly middle-class inhabitants.

FLATIRON BUILDING
175 Fifth Ave. (between 22nd and 23rd streets), Flatiron District

It's been said that when this iron-shaped wonder was completed in 1902, it caused such irregular wind patterns that women's skirts would blow up as they walked down 23rd Street. Throngs of men crowded the street hoping to catch a glimpse of the show, but they were shooed away by police

---

WHAT ARE SOME TOP ATTRACTIONS THAT LOCALS LOVE?

Angelika Film Center & Café *(page 32)* Check out the best in independent and foreign films at this NYC favorite, where the café serves gourmet pastries and coffee.

Strand Bookstore *(page 33)* Named after the famous London street, this beloved independent bookstore houses New York's largest collection of rare books and hosts regular readings.

Union Square Greenmarket *(page 41)* Locals line up at this downtown outdoor market every Monday, Wednesday, Friday and Saturday to buy fresh produce, bread, jams, cheese and more.

THE NEW YORK BOTANICAL GARDEN

officers giving them what became known as the "23 Skidoo" (a derivative of skedaddle). The structure may not cause such a ruckus nowadays, but it is still considered a jewel of New York's skyline and one of the city's iconic buildings. Designed by famed Chicago architect Daniel Burnham, this Beaux Arts beauty made of limestone and terra cotta measures an amazingly slim six-and-a-half feet wide at its apex.

UNION SQUARE GREENMARKET
17th Street East and Broadway, Flatiron District;
www.cenyc.org/greenmarket
Shop alongside the city's top chefs (who often build their menus based on what's available here) at this year-round farmer's market where everything is local and much of what you'll find is organic. In addition to the best seasonal produce, the market offers all kinds of goods, including hot cider, doughnuts, pretzels and homemade pies. Fill up a bag and then head to Union Square Park to relax and enjoy.
Monday, Wednesday, Friday and Saturday 8 a.m.-6 p.m.

UNION SQUARE PARK
14th Street at Broadway, Flatiron District; www.nycgovparks.org
This European-style piazza brims with all sorts of activity. You might see students from the New York Film Academy honing their craft, home cooks and chefs alike browsing the famous greenmarket, dogs breaking free from apartment life on the narrow dog run, folks protesting (the park has been a location for protests and rallies ever since labor activists gathered here in the 1920s), and kids enjoying the park's three playgrounds. In the days following September 11, the park also became a meeting place for the grieving city. Hotels, restaurants and retail giants line the area. And just what is that large public art installation on the south end? That would be the Metronome, commissioned by the developers of One Union Square South. Puffs of white steam are released throughout the day and a bunch of seemingly random numbers indicates when it's 7:04 a.m. and 36.9 seconds

WHAT'S THE BEST WAY TO SEE NEW YORK IN ONE DAY?

Grab a warm bagel and coffee at Midtown's **H&H Bagels** *(639 W. 46th St., 800-692-2435; www.hhbagels.net)*, which many locals consider the best in the city, before heading to Lower Manhattan to hop a Liberty or Ellis Island-bound ferry from **Castle Clinton National Monument** *(Battery Park, 212-344-7220; www.nps.gov/cacl)*. Spend a few hours searching Ellis Island's immigrant database for information on your ancestors, perusing its artifact-filled museum, or climbing the pedestal of Lady Liberty.

Head back to Manhattan isle and north to the trendy Soho shopping district for a mix of bargain priced (**H&M**, *558 Broadway, 212-343-2722; www.hm.com*) and higher-end designer (**Bloomingdale's**, *504 Broadway, 212-729-5900; www.bloomingdales.com*) goods, plus treats ranging from t-shirts to original pieces of art from street vendors.

Leave enough time to enjoy a nice meal at the ever-popular French bistro **Balthazar** *(page 62)*. You won't go wrong with the steak frites, and be sure to buy a buttery pastry from the bakery before hopping in a cab back to Midtown for a Broadway show. (Check out the **TKTS Discount Booth** in Times Square for same-day show discounts, but plan ahead for the perennially long lines.)

For one last nightcap (or the first of many in the city that never sleeps), take a cab downtown and step into one of the many lounges that fill the gritty streets of the Lower East Side, now one of New York's favorite after-dark destinations. Or join the crowds in the Meatpacking District, where the recently opened **The Standard** hotel *(page 100)* has rejuvenated the nightlife scene. Its beer garden, located under the High Line, is an ideal warm-weather spot, as is the **Standard Grill** *(page 81)*, which serves bistro classics until 4 a.m.

and that there are 16 hours, 55 minutes and 23.1 seconds remaining until midnight. It's easier to figure out what the park's statues are, including an equestrian one of George Washington. (You might wonder what a statue of Mohandas (Mahatma) Gandhi has in common with ones of George Washington and Abraham Lincoln. This was added because of the park's history of social activism.)

UPPER EAST SIDE

Old-money types reside in stunning, sprawling pre-war apartments with Central Park views on the Upper East Side. That's why it's no accident that many of these residences are also just steps away from the high-end boutiques (Michael Kors, Chloé) and department stores (Bergdorf Goodman, Saks Fifth Avenue) along Madison and Fifth avenues. Lots of notable museums make their home here, too, including the Whitney Museum of American Art, the Guggenheim Museum and the Metropolitan Museum of Art. Gracie Mansion, the official residence of the Mayor of New York City, is located in the neighborhood.

CENTRAL PARK
From Central Park South to 110th Street, and from Fifth Avenue to Central Park West, Upper East Side; www.centralparknyc.org
The most frequently visited urban park in the United States, Central Park spans 843 acres in the heart of Manhattan, creating an oasis of towering

trees, tranquil lakes and budding blooms in the midst of New York's concrete jungle. The sprawling green space, designed by famous landscape architects Frederick Law Olmsted and Calvert Vaux in the mid-1800s, is not just an ideal spot for sun-soaked picnics and throwing a Frisbee—it also has a plethora of cultural, architectural and athletic activities *(page 29)*.
Daily 6 a.m.-1 a.m.

THE METROPOLITAN MUSEUM OF ART
1000 Fifth Ave., Upper East Side, 212-535-7710; www.metmuseum.org
Monet, da Vinci, Picasso, van Gogh and Degas—they're all part of the two-million-plus-piece collection at this enormous Gothic-Revival building. Founded in 1870, the museum moved into this building on the eastern edge of Central Park along what's known as Museum Mile. The works here span more than 5,000 years and include the most definitive collection of American art in the world. Arguably the finest Egyptian collection outside of Cairo is here, and the collections from Europe and Asia are equally impressive. Those art history classes you took will pay off when you recognize such works as van Gogh's *Cypresses*, Gauguin's *la Orana Maria* and Degas's *The Dancing Class*.
Suggested admission: adults $20, seniors $15, students $10, children under 12 and members free. Tuesday-Thursday, Sunday 9:30 a.m.-5:30 p.m., Friday-Saturday 9:30 a.m.-9 p.m.

SOLOMON R. GUGGENHEIM MUSEUM
1071 Fifth Ave., Upper East Side, 212-423-3500; www.guggenheim.org
Critics the world over weren't sure what to make of this coiling ivory-colored tower rising from Manhattan's Upper East Side when it was unveiled in 1959. One heralded it "the most beautiful building in America," while another dubbed it "an indigestible hot cross bun." Many argued that its grandiose design overshadowed the art housed within its walls, though its famed architect Frank Lloyd Wright insisted that it perfectly complimented the works, creating an "uninterrupted, beautiful symphony." The building's design seems to bother few nowadays, as thousands flock to this contemporary and modern art museum for both its permanent collection (including works by Pablo Picasso, Marc Chagall, Salvador Dalí and Henri Matisse) and to take in Wright's awesome creation.
Admission: adults $18, students and seniors $15, children under 12 free. Sunday-Wednesday 10 a.m.-5:45 p.m., Friday 10 a.m.-5:45 p.m., Saturday 10 a.m.-7:45 p.m.

WHITNEY MUSEUM OF AMERICAN ART
945 Madison Ave., Upper East Side, 212-570-3600; www.whitney.org
In 1931, Gertrude Vanderbilt Whitney founded the Whitney Museum when she purchased a brownstone at 10 West 8th Street and turned it into the Whitney Studio, an exhibition space and social center for young progressive arts. It began with 700 works of contemporary American art, most from Whitney's own collection. Today, at its current location, the museum houses one of the foremost collections of 20th-century American paintings, sculptures, multimedia installations, photographs and drawings from Edward Hopper, John Sloan, Max Weber and more. Well-known for its annual and biennial exhibits that highlight current artists, the museum frequently purchases works from up-and-comers to keep its collection fresh.
Admission: adults $15, seniors and students $10, New York City public

WHAT'S THE BEST WAY TO SEE NEW YORK IN THREE DAYS?

Start the morning of your second day *(page 42 for suggestions for the first day)* lazing and gazing in lush **Central Park** *(page 42)*; depending on the season and your tastes, you can ice skate, visit the zoo or go for a bike ride before heading to nearby Museum Mile.

Two possibilities: the **American Museum of Natural History** *(page 45)* where you can stroll among the famed dinosaur fossils, or the **Metropolitan Museum of Art** *(page 43)*, which houses some two million works that cover everything from ancient Egyptian artifacts to modern American masterpieces.

Cap off your day with a Ning Sling cocktail (orange vodka mixed with lychee and passion-fruit juices) at The Peninsula Hotel's posh rooftop bar **Salon de Ning** *(page 152)*. For something a little more low-key and substantial, grab a couple of slices at retro-styled **Big Nick's Burger and Pizza Joint** *(2175 Broadway, 212-362-9238; www.bignicksnyc.com)*.

Spend your third day exploring one of New York's outer boroughs. In **Brooklyn**, enjoy a fragrant morning stroll through the 52-acre **Brooklyn Botanic Garden** *(1000 Washington Ave., Brooklyn, 718-623-7200; www. bbg.org)*, where the Cranford Rose Garden has more than 5,000 rosebushes spanning almost 1,200 varieties. Or make friends with Paul Cezanne, Edgar Degas and Georgia O'Keeffe at the **Brooklyn Museum of Art** *(200 Eastern Parkway, Brooklyn, 718-638-5000; www.brooklynmuseum.org)*. It's the second-largest art museum in the city, after the Met. Spend the afternoon catching rays or raising the hairs on the back of your neck at the beaches and amusement parks of **Coney Island** *(page 48)* where you can ride the iconic Cyclone, one of the country's oldest (and most rickety) wooden roller coasters in operation. Then grab a hot dog at the original **Nathan's Famous** *(1310 Surf Ave., Brooklyn, 718-946-2705; www.nathansfamous.com)*.

If you decide to head north from Manhattan and spend the day in the **Bronx**, you can ride a camel or take the Wild Asia Monorail to see tigers, wild horses and elephants at the **Bronx Zoo** *(page 50)*. If you'd rather see fly balls than fur balls, head to New Yankee Stadium *(page 165)* for a baseball game at the Bronx Bomber's brand-new field.

End your trip with dinner on **Arthur Avenue** *(page 50)*, this borough's answer to Manhattan's Little Italy. After a day game, stop by family-run **Mike's Deli** *(2344 Arthur Ave., Bronx, 718-295-5033; www.arthuravenue.com)*, located in the Arthur Avenue Retail Market, for some large and delicious sandwiches, with names such as the Godfather, Michelangelo and Sophia Loren. Or choose from pastas, salads and other platters. One favorite is the eggplant parmigiana. For a heartier meal, bring your culinary imagination because there aren't any menus at **Dominick's Restaurant** *(2335 Arthur Ave., Bronx, 718-733-2807)*—the waiters recite the menu aloud and you order. Or just tell them what you're in the mood for ("How about the catch of the day over some linguini?") and they might bring it out specially made to order.

AMERICAN MUSEUM OF NATURAL HISTORY

school students and children under 12 free. Wednesday-Thursday, Saturday-Sunday 11 a.m.-6 p.m., Friday 1-9 p.m.

UPPER WEST SIDE/COLUMBUS CIRCLE

Cultural bastions including Lincoln Center and the American Museum of Natural History can be found on the Upper West Side, along with thousands of New Yorkers who love the neighborhood's proximity to their Midtown jobs and plethora of shops, restaurants and accessibility to Central Park. Come hungry: New York's legendary H&H Bagels and Zabar's gourmet deli are both here. Columbus Circle, at 59th Street and the southern opening to Central Park, was long-known as nothing more than a super-congested traffic circle before the Time Warner Center—a mixed-use building containing shops, upcscale restaurants, a hotel and music halls—opened here in 2003.

AMERICAN MUSEUM OF NATURAL HISTORY
79th Street and Central Park West, Upper West Side, 212-769-5100; www.amnh.org

One of the largest natural history institutions in the world, this enormous Upper West Side museum is famous for its fossil halls, including two dinosaur halls that are home to more than one million specimens (about 600 are actually on display). Throughout the museum you'll also find life-like dioramas with taxidermied animals like bears, elephants and jaguars in their natural habitats. A few of the stuffed elephants on display in the Hall of African Mammals came courtesy of famous folks like Theodore Roosevelt, who often sent the museum animals he bagged during safaris. The Rose Center for Earth and Space, which was completed in 2000, features a renovated planetarium and exhibit halls covering the 13-billion year history of the universe.

Admission: adults $16, children $9, seniors and students $12, children 1 and under free. Daily 10 a.m.-5:45 p.m.

THE CLOISTERS MUSEUM & GARDENS
99 Margaret Corbin Drive, Upper West Side, 212-923-3700; www.metmuseum.org

An extension of the Metropolitan Museum of Art, the Cloisters house approximately 5,000 pieces of medieval European art dating back to 800 A.D. with emphasis on works from the 12th through 15th centuries. Originally housed in the main branch of the Met, the collection outgrew its digs by 1927. Buoyed by the support of John D. Rockefeller (who not only purchased the extension's plot in Fort Tyron Park but a portion of land directly across the Hudson River to keep the Cloister's view unsullied), the extension was dedicated in 1938. This castle-like edifice incorporates elements from five medieval French cloisters and is a piece of art itself. Inside, you'll find The Cloisters' best-known works: seven wool-and-silk woven tapestries depicting the Hunt of the Unicorn. Many additional tapestries, sculptures, manuscripts and stained glass windows are also on display. The Cloisters' gardens—based on horticulture information gleaned from medieval treatises, poetry and garden documents—are another popular stop.

Admission: adults $20, seniors $15, students $10, children under 12 free. November-February: Tuesday-Sunday 9:30 a.m.-4:45 p.m.; March-October: Tuesday-Sunday 9:30 a.m.-5:15 p.m.

COLUMBUS CIRCLE
Broadway and Central Park South, Columbus Circle

Once nothing more than a traffic nightmare—New York architecture critic Paul Goldberger described Columbus Circle as "a chaotic jumble of streets that can be crossed in about 50 different ways, all of them wrong"—the historic plaza is now a destination for shopping, top-notch dining and general lounging, with traffic thankfully not so much an issue any longer. In the heart of the circle stands a 77-foot granite column topped with a marble sculpture of explorer Christopher Columbus (a gift from the Italian-American community to commemorate the 400-year anniversary of his historic voyage) surrounded by a large fountain where locals and visitors relax. Standing behind this is the Time Warner Center, home to more than 50 shops, the Mandarin Oriental hotel, an enormous Whole Foods Market that locals love (and a great place to pick up a picnic before heading into the park), Jazz at Lincoln Center (where some of the best names perform on a regular basis), and CNN's New York studio. Trump International Hotel and Tower *(page 119)* is also just next door.

LINCOLN CENTER FOR THE PERFORMING ARTS
70 Lincoln Center Plaza, Columbus Avenue and Broadway, Upper West Side, 212-875-5456; www.lincolncenter.org

Some of the Big Apple's most renowned performance groups, including the New York Philharmonic, the New York City Ballet and The Metropolitan Opera make this Upper West Side cultural destination their home. Rising stars frequent the 16-acre complex, too, because it's also the site of the revered Juilliard School (alumni include Robin Williams, Kelsey Grammer and Patti LuPone) and the recently expanded Alice Tully Hall. The surrounding area, known as Lincoln Square, is a bustling restaurant and retail district and the nearby Time Warner Center contains a 1,200-seat theater designed specifically for jazz performances.

Hours vary by building and performance schedules.

WHAT ARE THE BEST PLACES FOR FAMILY FUN?

Radio City Music Hall *(page 37)* Who can resist the Rockettes? Adults and kids alike get a kick out of the popular *Christmas Spectacular* every holiday season, with many making it an annual tradition.

South Street Seaport *(page 28)* This historic landmark has a little something for everyone, including shopping, restaurants, views of the harbor, events and programs, and a museum.

Bronx Zoo *(page 50)* The largest urban wildlife conservation park in the country, the Bronx Zoo is home to more than 4,000 animals to roam, including gorillas, lions and grizzly bears.

FAO Schwarz *(page 35)* Make like Tom Hanks in *Big* and dance on the piano floor at the flagship for the famous high-end toy store.

RIVERSIDE PARK
59th Street to 158th Street along the Hudson River, Upper West Side, 212-408-0264; www.nycgovparks.org
Hugging the banks of the Hudson River, this nearly 330-acre park stretches more than four solid miles. Yet another Frederick Law Olmsted-designed recreational area, the park has basketball courts, baseball and soccer fields, playgrounds, dog runs, a skate park and even a public marina. You'll also find several monuments within the park's borders, including Grant's Tomb—the burial site of President Ulysses S. Grant and his wife Julia which is the largest tomb in North America. Other highlights include a Joan of Arc statue and the Eleanor Roosevelt Monument.

ZABAR'S
2245 Broadway, Upper West Side, 212-787-2000; www.zabars.com
This Upper West Side gourmet grocer is practically a New York institution. As their slogan says, Zabar's really is New York. Started as a simple counter in 1934 by Louis and Lillian Zabar, the market now stretches nearly the length of an entire city block and sees more than 35,000 loyal customers every week. The grocer is known for both its extensive kitchen-gadget selection as well as its high-quality bagels, smoked fish counter, knishes *(page 58)*, olives and cheeses; there is still always a member of the Zabar family in the store. If you're craving something sweet, Zabar's Café also serves native-to-New York desserts such as delicious black-and-white cookies and cheesecake.
Monday-Friday 8 a.m.-7:30 p.m., Saturday 8 a.m.-8 p.m., Sunday 9 a.m.-6 p.m.

BROOKLYN
With 2.6 million residents, Brooklyn is New York City's most populous borough and has a distinct culture all its own. Thanks to its proximity to downtown Manhattan, there is a vibrant arts and cultural scene—writers, painters, designers and restaurateurs migrate to Brooklyn for its less expensive rents and charming neighborhood-centric way of life. The borough is also home to some of the city's most recognized institutions, including the Brooklyn Academy of Music, Brooklyn Botanic Garden, Prospect Park and Coney Island.

PROSPECT PARK

BROOKLYN BRIDGE

Lower Manhattan/Downtown Brooklyn

One of four bridges spanning the East River (the others are the Williamsburg, Manhattan and Queensboro bridges), this 6,016-foot-long wonder connects the boroughs of Manhattan and Brooklyn, and was the longest suspension bridge in the world at the time of its completion in 1883. More than 150,000 people paid one cent to walk across the bridge on opening day (bringing a hog or sheep cost an additional two cents). Today, more than 126,000 vehicles cross the bridge each day, in addition to a steady stream of foot traffic from commuters and tourists looking to get a bit of exercise while enjoying the spectacular views of the river and the Statue of Liberty.

BROOKLYN HEIGHTS PROMENADE

Brooklyn-Queens Expressway, between Joralemon Street and Grace Court

If it's the perfect view you're after, you'll find it at this well-manicured pedestrian walkway above the hum of the Brooklyn-Queens Expressway. Overlooking lower Manhattan, the East River and the Brooklyn Bridge, the esplanade is a popular spot for joggers, Rollerbladers, sightseers, locals looking to relax and film crews coveting the picturesque skyline. (In case you're wondering, the traffic noise from below won't kill the mood.)
Daily 24 hours.

CONEY ISLAND

Surf Avenue between 37th Street and Ocean Parkway, South Brooklyn; www.coneyisland.com

Boardwalks, hot dogs and roller coasters: You'll find them all here. One of the most popular amusement areas of the early 20th century, the south Brooklyn neighborhood (which is actually a peninsula and not an island) feels stuck in a bit of a time warp, with its rickety boardwalks and old-school theme parks. The fate of these amusement parks—most notably the recently shuttered Astroland—has been up in the air for years, but for now some remain open, allowing a new generation to experience vintage rides such as the Cyclone, one of the oldest (and coolest) wooden roller coasters still in operation. Recent additions, including KeySpan Park (home of the minor-league Brooklyn Cyclones) have helped breathe new life into the stagnant neighborhood. But Coney Island is more than just fun in the sun. Indoor entertainment is also available in the form of the New York Aquarium and Coney Island Museum.

Open year-round; amusement parks open Easter-Labor Day.

PROSPECT PARK
95 Prospect Park West, Brooklyn, 718-965-8951;
www.prospectpark.org

Central Park may be New York's most famous, but ask any Brooklynite about their favorite green space, and they'll be quick to sing the praises of this 585-acre park in the heart of their beloved borough. Designed by Central Park architects Frederick Law Olmsted and Calvert Vaux, Prospect Park features a 90-acre spread of grass aptly name the Long Meadow, plus Brooklyn's only forest and a zoo with nearly 400 animals. In the park's boathouse, you can visit the first urban Audubon Center for hands-on nature exhibits. The park is also home to an antique carousel, frequent concerts and performances.

Daily 5 a.m.-1 a.m.

THE BRONX

The Bronx is the northernmost of New York City's five boroughs and the only part attached to North American mainland. It is most famous as the home of the New York Yankees (a.k.a., Bronx Bombers, who have a brand

WHAT ARE THE BEST PLACES FOR SPORTS FUN?
Chelsea Piers *(page 24)* This 28-acre sports and entertainment complex boasts a 40-lane bowling alley, golf club, ice skating rinks, rock climbing wall, swimming pool, restaurants and spa.

Central Park *(pages 29, 42)* Each weekend, hords of joggers join the packs circling the park's closed-to-traffic roads. Besides being New York's favorite runner's destination, Central Park is also a great spot for trail riding (there are three bridle paths; tours are available through Riverdale Equestrian Center, *www.riverdaleriding.com*), inline skating, playing baseball, basketball and countless other sports.

USTA Billie Jean King National Tennis Center The courts where champions are made each September at the U.S. Open are open daily to the public. Rates for court time at the National Tennis Center *(www.usta.com)* in Queens start as low as $20 per hour, and reservations can be made up to two days in advance. To put some polish on your game, sign up for a group or private lesson with one of the center's professional instructors.

New Yankee Stadium *(page 165)* Take a tour of the new home of the New York Yankees, where you'll see tributes to the team's top stars, including Lou Gehrig, Mickey Mantle, Joe DiMaggio and Babe Ruth. Fans can make a day (or night) of it by also adding lunch or dinner at one of the stadium's new dining venues.

new stadium here just like the Mets) and the Bronx Zoo, the largest nature preserve in the United states, spanning 265 acres and containing more than 4,500 animals.

ARTHUR AVENUE
Arthur Avenue, Bronx; www.arthuravenue.com
Pay a visit to the real Little Italy of New York. Italians made the area of Belmont their home at the turn of the century, and many made their living by selling food items from pushcarts on Arthur Avenue. In 1940, Mayor Fiorello LaGuardia greenlighted construction of an indoor market where they could sell their goods. Seventy years later, the passion for artisanal foods and wines continues. Visit the European market *(2344 Arthur Ave.)* and you'll be overtaken by the smell of freshly baked breads, aromatic cheeses and house-cured meats. Beyond the market, there is also an abundance of restaurants, pizza parlors and pastry shops—some dating to the 1920s. At Roberto's *(632 E. 186th St., 718-733-9503)*, everyone orders from the blackboard list of specials and waiters spoon heaps of fresh pasta on your plate. Calandra Cheese *(2314 Arthur Ave., 718-365-7572)* sells fresh mozarella and other cheeses, while the bread sold at Terranova Bakery *(691 E. 187th St., 718-733-3827)* is a feast in itself.

BRONX ZOO
2300 Southern Blvd., Bronx, 718-220-5100; www.bronxzoo.com
The Bronx Zoo boasts 265-acres for more than 4,000 animals to roam, making it the largest urban wildlife conservation park in the country, Much of the zoo's land has been made into special habitats suited for its diverse variety of animals, including gorillas, lions, gibbons and grizzly bears. Take a 20-minute monorail ride along the Bronx River and take in the surroundings of the Wild Asia portion of the zoo with tigers, elephants and rhinos roaming nearby. An interactive children's zoo lets kids check out animal homes, try on simulated claws and paws, and get their picture taken with chickens. There are also several indoor exhibits to explore, including the Butterfly Garden, Monkey House and World of Birds.
Admission: adults $15, seniors $13, children 3-12 $11. April-October, Monday-Friday 10 a.m.-5 p.m., Saturday-Sunday 10 a.m.-5:30 p.m.; November-March, daily 10 a.m.-4:30 p.m.

THE NEW YORK BOTANICAL GARDEN
200th Street and Kazimiroff Blvd., Bronx, 718-817-8700;
www.nybg.org
With more than one million plants, this is one of the largest and oldest (founded in 1891) botanical gardens in the country. It consists of 250

WHAT ARE THE BEST MARKETS IN NEW YORK?
Chelsea Market *(page 23)* Chelsea Market encompasses an entire city block and houses gourmet-goods shops, drool-worthy restaurants and a few TV studios.

Union Square Greenmarket *(page 41)* Shop alongside the city's top chefs at this year-round farmer's market where, besides the freshest produce, you'll find all kind of treats, including hot cider, doughnuts and pies.

Zabar's *(page 47)* As their slogan says, Zabar's really is New York, much loved for its knishes, cheeses and cookies.

UNITED NATIONS

landscaped acres and 50 curated gardens. The property also contains the last 50 acres of native forest that once covered New York City. The Enid A. Haupt Conservatory has 11 distinct plant environments with changing exhibits and permanent displays, including the Fern Forest, Palm Court and Rose Garden. There is a great emphasis on education, with programs on horticulture and science. For the kids, there is the Everett Children's Adventure Garden, a 12-acre space that offers a boulder maze and giant animal topiaries. The botanical garden is one of the best ways to "get out of the city" without leaving its borders.

Admission: adults $6, seniors and students $3, children 2-12 $1, children under 2 free. Free Wednesday, 10 a.m.-noon Saturday. April-mid-January, Tuesday-Sunday 10 a.m.-6 p.m., mid-January-March 10 a.m.-5 p.m.

HARLEM

Harlem is arguably the cultural epicenter of African-American arts and culture. The landmark Apollo Theater is credited with launching the careers of James Brown, Michael Jackson, Stevie Wonder and countless other singers and musicians, while Sylvia's Soul Food *(page 93)* has long attracted a mix of locals and visiting celebs—especially politicians on the stump. The historic brownstones that line many of the neighborhood's residential streets have become some of the city's most coveted real estate in recent years.

APOLLO THEATER
253 W. 125th St., Harlem, 212-663-0499; www.apollotheater.org
The famous Apollo Theater first opened its doors in 1914. In 1934, Ralph Cooper, Sr. commenced his ever-popular Amateur Nite Hour, an extension of his already prominent radio show. That same year, Ella Fitzgerald and Benny Carter launched their careers by participating in Amateur Night. The rest is music history. Apollo Theater quickly became known for jump-starting the careers of many performing artists, including Stevie Wonder, Michael Jackson, Billie Holiday, James Brown and Lauren Hill. Amateur Night still exposes fresh talent every Wednesday night. Tours are offered to groups

of 20 people or more (smaller groups or individuals can join a tour if one is scheduled when you'd like to go).
Amateur night: Wednesday, 7:30 p.m. Prices vary.

QUEENS

Most visitors to New York City know Queens as the part of the city they fly into—it's where John F. Kennedy and LaGuardia airports are located. The borough is also one of the most diverse places in all of the United States—it's home to New York's Greektown (in Astoria), the city's second Chinatown (in Flushing) a "Little Guyana" (Richmond Hill) and a bevy of other ethnic pockets. The New York Mets play in brand-new Citi Field in Flushing Meadows, and right next door you can check out the unofficial symbol of Queens, the 12-story high Unisphere—a massive globe structure commissioned for the 1964-1965 World's Fair, which took place here.

ASTORIA

Just a few stops from Manhattan is where you'll find the prominent Queens borough of Astoria. It is an eclectic community, largely populated by Greeks. However, with the bountiful parkland and culture that abounds here, it has attracted people from around the world, and is also popular with recent grads and artists, as the rental properties offer more for less. Astoria's main promenades include 30th Avenue, Steinway, Ditmars and Broadway. Along 30th Avenue and Broadway between 31st and Steinway streets, you'll find many of its classic Greek restaurants, markets and bakeries, which are known to be the best in Queens. On 24th Avenue, grab a seat at Bohemian Hall *(29-19 24th Ave., 718-274-4925; www.bohemianhall.com)*, one of the city's oldest beer halls and gardens built in 1910. Steinway Street is best known for its shopping. Astoria Park *(19th St., www.nycgovparks.org)*, which includes more than 65 acres of natural space, is located between the Hell Gate and Triborough Bridges, and has the largest public pool in New York City. The American Museum of the Moving Image *(34-12 36th St., 718-784-4520; www.movingimage.us)* is also nearby. Astoria was once the site of the Astoria Studios, which cultivated screen legends such as Rudolph Valentino and Gloria Swanson; renovated and reopened in the late 1970s, the studios are now known as the Kaufman Astoria Studios.

QUEENS JAZZ TRAIL
Queens; www.flushingtownhall.org
While jazz music has been claimed by the likes of New Orleans, Chicago, Harlem and others, many consider Queens to be the rightful "Home of Jazz." If you're a fan, tour the history of jazz that is ever present in this borough by visiting its cultural institutions, famous homes, local museums and archives. Make sure to include Flushing Town Hall *(13735 Northern Blvd., Flushing, 718-463-7700; www.flushingtownhall.org)* the area's center for culture and the arts; The Louis Armstrong House Museum *(34-56 107th St., Corona, 718-478-8274; www.louisarmstronghouse.org)*, which includes a tour of Armstrong's home and an assortment of audio clips; and Addisleigh Park *(St. Albans; www.addisleighpark.org)* where you'll be able to find the former Tudor-style residences of many of jazz's late greats.

BRONX ZOO

STATEN ISLAND

Staten Island feels more like a suburb than one of the five boroughs with its wealth of (by New York City standards) sprawling homes with backyards and pools, as well as strip malls and chain restaurants. Separated from the other boroughs by New York Bay, Staten Island is the only part of the city not serviced by its subway system. One of the best tourist attractions in town is a round-trip ride between here and Manhattan on the free Staten Island Ferry, which offers breathtaking views of New York Harbor and the Statue of Liberty.

THE GREENBELT
700 Rockland Ave., Staten Island, 718-351-3450;
www.sigreenbelt.org

In the heart of Staten Island exists this 2,800-acre nature preserve. The Greenbelt is made up of wetlands, forestry and miles of rolling meadows. Spend an afternoon hiking the numerous trails and discovering the natural land that spreads over this city island. Trek up Moses Mountain for a view of the sprawling woodlands and the Atlantic Ocean beyond. Within The Greenbelt are several traditional parks that offer many outdoor recreation opportunities, such as bird watching, archery and baseball. These parks include LaTourette, Willowbrook and High Rock. At Willowbrook, there is a traditional carousel with 51 hand-carved animals. There is also the 260-acre William T. Davis Wildlife Refuge with an observation deck and woodland trails, home to the first Audubon Center in New York City. For more information, stop by the Greenbelt Nature Center before hitting the trails.

Admission: free. Nature Center: April-October, Tuesday-Sunday 10 a.m.-5 p.m.; November-March, Wednesday-Sunday 11 a.m.-5 p.m. Preserve: Daily.

STATEN ISLAND MUSEUM
75 Stuyvesant Place, Staten Island, 718-727-1135;
www.statenislandmuseum.org

If you're planning to take a cruise on the Staten Island Ferry, schedule time to check out the Staten Island Museum, located just two blocks from the ferry terminal. This museum was founded in 1881 and was established to recognize the arts, natural sciences and history of Staten Island. Its current collections contain pieces that date back to 12,000 years, with more than two million artifacts from pre-history to present day, including the region's most inclusive representation of New York's early Native Americans. Recent temporary exhibits have included one on the history of the ferry.

Admission: adults $2, seniors and students $1, children under 12 free. Monday-Friday 12 p.m.-5 p.m., Saturday 10 a.m.-5 p.m., Sunday 12 p.m.-5 p.m.

STATEN ISLAND ZOO
614 Broadway, Staten Island, 718-442-3100;
www.statenislandzoo.org

First opened in 1933, the Staten Island Zoo was organized and is now operated by the Staten Island Zoological Society. Achieving the Society's mission: "to disseminate a knowledge of zoology and an appreciation of animal life," the museum offers frequent educational programs and activities. Popular events include "Breakfast with the Beasts," and "Dinosaurs and More," which includes prehistoric fossils and 3-D models. The zoo has a large and internationally recognized collection of native and exotic reptiles and numerous species of rattlesnakes (one of the largest collections in the United States), amphibians, marine reef fish, mammals and birds. The Staten Island Zoo is also famous for "Staten Island Chuck," the city's famous groundhog that predicts the fate of the winter each Groundhog Day. The event is an entertaining spectacle if you'll be in town on February 2nd.

Admission: adults $8, seniors $6, children 3-14 $5, children under 3 free. Free on Wednesday after 2 p.m. Daily 10 a.m.-4:45 p.m.

WHERE TO EAT

ADOUR ALAIN DUCASSE

THE CITY THAT ALWAYS EATS

What's not to love about New York dining? There's the depth, breadth and height of the many, many options, from $400 dinners in a glassy skyscraper at Masa in Columbus Circle to the $6.75 burger on a paper plate at the West Village's Corner Bistro. There's the longevity—restaurants like Le Bernardin and Gotham Bar and Grill that wowed in the 1980s and continue to impress. There are ethnic eats and underground supper clubs *(page 63)*, global-fusion flavors, dark and moody dining rooms (Allen & Delancey) and fluorescently lit delis (Barney Greengrass). There's the trend toward farmers market fare—any chef worth his or her (artisanal or kosher) salt cooks with the seasons in mind and uses local purveyors to do so. And the personalities of the star chefs and knowing that for every statesman-like award-magnet like Per Se's Thomas Keller, there's a talented, young go-getter like David Chang of Momofuku striving to be the Next Big Thing. We're losing count. There's just so much to adore, consume and explore New York City.

CHELSEA/HELL'S KITCHEN/GARMENT DISTRICT

★★★★DEL POSTO

85 Tenth Ave., Chelsea, 212-497-8090; www.delposto.com

If you're looking for checkered tablecloths and the quaint fare of typical red-sauce joints, keep moving. The ambitious, sprawling Del Posto reflects the bold, larger-than-life persona of its famous owner-partner, Mario Batali. At 24,000 square feet, with soaring columns and enough mahogany to give environmentalists palpitations, this high-end Italian restaurant dwarfs its competition in size and style, but still pays attention to tiny details like purse stools for the ladies. Sliced jalapeño peppers in the spaghetti rotti with Dungeness crab will have you reaching for ChapStick to cool your lips. That's the kind of bold touch one expects from Batali, as is serving whole fish dramatically and expertly portioned tableside by attentive servers. Dinner here is wildly expensive and may leave you wondering how on earth pasta strands made of flour, eggs and water can cost so much ($30 for panzotti, or pasta pockets filled with rabbit). But one taste of dishes like that and the remarkably flaky torta Carotina—sliced and served tableside with cool, creamy gelato—will quickly quell your doubts about whether the meal was worth every penny.

Italian. Lunch (Wednesday-Friday), dinner. Reservations recommended. $36-85

★★THE RED CAT

227 Tenth Ave., Chelsea, 212-242-1122; www.theredcat.com

Folksy but also art-house cool, the Red Cat is the kind of unpretentious restaurant that leaves you wondering why there simply aren't more places like it. With its art-adorned barn walls, warm red banquettes and hanging iron lanterns, this neighborhood Mediterranean-American charmer is frequented by horn-rimmed-glasses-wearing professionals who sit solo at the bar, tearing into the thick double-cut pork chop and sipping a glass of peppery pinot noir. The vegetables are so fresh and thoughtfully prepared—rapini comes sautéed in garlic and chili flakes—that you'll wonder whether there really is a farm out back from which the chef is plucking his ingredients.

Contemporary American. Lunch (Tuesday-Saturday), dinner. $16-35

JEAN GEORGES

★★★SCARPETTA
355 W. 14th St., Chelsea, 212-691-0555; www.scarpettanyc.com
It's all about the pasta at this unassuming Italian spot on the edge of the Meat packing District. Located within a rehabbed Greek revival townhouse, the restaurant is modern, yet cozy with dim lighting and exposed brick walls. Executive chef Scott Conant has created a menu that offers impressive dishes like fennel-crusted lamb loin with mint and pecorino and imported turbot over white asparagus in a mustard-riesling emulsion. But it's the simple spaghetti with tomato and basil that will have your tastebuds buzzing. The pasta is cooked al dente and piled high on the plate, coated with a fresh, sweet tomato sauce and just the right balance of basil. Forgo dessert for the cheese plate; the ricotta di bufala with truffle honey satisfies any after-dinner sweet tooth.
Italian. Dinner. Outdoor seating. Reservations recommended. Bar. $36-85

CHINATOWN/LITTLE ITALY/NOLITA
★JING FONG
20 Elizabeth St., Chinatown, 212-964-5256
If the New York Stock Exchange trading floor were a restaurant, Jing Fong would be it. This Hong Kong-style dim sum banquet hall is never without frenzy. Gesturing diners vie for the attention of jacketed waiters wheeling carts heaped high with plates of steamed pork buns, sticky rice with pork in lotus leaf and other traditional dim sum goodies. Get your game face on: The competition can get stiff between diners battling over that last basket of dumplings.
Chinese. Breakfast, lunch, dinner. $16-35

EAST VILLAGE/LOWER EAST SIDE
★★★ALLEN & DELANCEY
115 Allen St., Lower East Side, 212-253-5400;
www.allenanddelancey.net
Named after the Lower East Side intersection where it's located, this restaurant brings a little more boho chic to the Lower East Side. Thick

WHICH FOODS ARE QUINTESSENTIALLY NEW YORK?

Some foods are as synonymous with the city as yellow cabs and the Empire State Building. From bagels to thin-crust pizza, there are some foods that say New York like nothing else.

BAGELS Many New Yorkers bemoan the demise of the bagel, which they rail is supposed to be dense and chewy *not* airy and fluffy. Nothing ignites more debate, but **H+H Bagels** *(2239 Broadway, at 80th Street, 212-595-8000, 800-692-2435; www.hhbagels.com)* is often cited as the best New York bagel (though detractors maintain they're too sweet). If you're looking for bagel sandwiches—or even cream cheese—you can fuggetaboutit; H+H sells bagels and bagels only. For all the fixings, try **Ess-a-Bagel** *(359 First Ave., at 21st Street, 212-260-2252; www.ess-a-bagel.com)* or **Murray's Bagels** *(500 Avenue of the Americas, at 13th Street, 212-462-2830; www.murraysbagels.com)*.

PIZZA BY THE SLICE Pizza in New York must be thin and foldable, oozing with cheese and light on the sauce. The pizza cognoscenti all have their own opinions, but the most popular place for a slice (especially late night) is at a **Ray's**. You'll find them all around the city, each with a slightly different name, "Ray's Original," "Ray's Famous Original," "Famous Ray's Pizza." None of them are actually related but they all offer the same New-York style pizza that, at least after a few drinks, appeals to slice hounds all over the city.

HOT DOGS You can buy one from any street cart, but there are two places for classic dogs: **Gray's Papaya** *(2090 Broadway, 212-799-0243)* and **Papaya King** *(179 E. 86th St., between Third and Lexington avenues, 212-369-0648; www.papayaking.com)*. Both serve the same crispy-on-the-outside grilled hot dogs and frothy papaya drinks that may just be the city's best cheap eats.

BLACK AND WHITE COOKIE These cakelike cookies with half-moons of black and vanilla icing are a New York staple. You can buy them in practically every deli or bakery in the city, but the people at **Glaser's Bake Shop** *(1670 First Ave., between 87th and 88th streets, 212-289-2562; www.glasersbakeshop.com)* have been making them since 1902.

PASTRAMI ON RYE For this classic New York deli sandwich, pastrami is sliced and served warm on rye bread. Some claim the best is found at **Katz's Deli** *(205 E. Houston St., 212-254-2246; www.katzdeli.com)*. Others claim **Second Avenue Deli** *(162 E. 33rd St., 212-689-9000; www.2ndavedeli.com)* is the best Jewish (and kosher) deli for pastrami, as well as brisket, matzah ball soup, hot dogs and everything else.

KNISHES You can find them at delis all over the city but for the real deal Yiddish snack that consists of mashed potatoes, ground beef and other fillings covered in fried or baked dough, head to **Zabar's** *(2245 Broadway, at 80th Street, 212-787-2000; www.zabars.com)*, the famous Upper West Side market that's as New York as you can get.

FROZEN YOGURT New Yorkers' love of fro-yo goes back way before **Pinkberry** and all those other natural yogurt franchises. It's actually not even yogurt, but the most popular alternative for ice cream in New York was and is **Tasti D Lite** *(www.tastidlite.com)*. After eating this made-from-milk treat, you'll most certainly ask, Can it really only be 80 calories (per serving)? It is, which makes ordering up a large serving an easy indulgence.

PER SE

red-velvet drapes and candles dripping with wax on bookshelves make this seductive gastropub feel like a brothel-like foodie haven. Forget bangers and mash—the kitchen makes normally cringe-worthy animal parts (is that a lamb's neck on your plate?) something to crave. The dining room is so dark you might need a pocket flashlight just to read the menu, so memorize a few signature items just in case, such as the divine porchetta and morcilla with riesling-braised cabbage, hazelnuts and violet mustard, or the poached halibut with Italian olives, artichoke barigoule and roasted tomato. It's hard to resist tossing in a side of the Jerusalem artichokes and bacon for the table.

Contemporary American. Dinner. Reservations recommended. $16-35

★★DBGB KITCHEN & BAR
299 Bowery, East Village, 212-933-5300; www.danielnyc.com
It seems that anything Daniel Boulud touches turns to culinary gold, and DBGB Kitchen & Bar is proving no exception. Boulud's newest downtown venture is a more casual approach to French brasserie fare with sausage leading the charge. There are more than a dozen links to choose from including standouts such as the Berliner, German currywurst alongside turnip confit, and the Tunisienne, lamb and mint merguez with harissa, lemon-braised spinach and chickpeas. But the menu highlights extend beyond encased meat. The lemon and rosemary roasted chicken is moist and flavorful, and the Frenchie burger is a fun play on a traditional burger with pork belly, arugula and morbier cheese on a peppered brioche bun. Floor-to-ceiling open shelves stocked with glassware, copper pots and dry goods tastefully salute the restaurant's Bowery location, which long stood as New York's industrial restaurant supply district. In case you forget you're dining in a Boulud restaurant, the chef's favorite culinary quotes line the mirrors around the bar.

French, German. Lunch, dinner. Bar. $16-35

★★THE MERMAID INN
96 Second Ave., East Village, 212-674-5870; 568 Amsterdam Ave., Upper West Side, 212-799-7400; www.themermaidnyc.com
This seafood eatery boasts a well-stocked raw bar and is decked out with framed maritime maps and fish prints, plus dishes of goldfish pretzels on the bar. A double-cut pork chop (East Village location) and a grilled hanger steak (Upper West Side location) infiltrate the otherwise exclusively seafood menu, and the short-but-well-chosen wine list complements the ocean fare. A lobster sandwich bears chunks of celery and comes heaped on a buttery brioche roll with a side of Old Bay-seasoned fries, and complimentary chocolate pudding served in a demitasse cup rounds out the night. The dark wooden tables are placed liberally throughout the dining room, back garden and front patio, so it never gets too noisy.
Seafood. Dinner, Saturday-Sunday brunch (Upper West Side location). Outdoor seating. $16-35

★★MOMOFUKU SSÄM BAR
207 Second Ave., East Village, 212-254-3500; www.momofuku.com
Star chef David Chang dabbles in pork the way great artists work in clay or watercolor. His steamed pork belly buns (also available at nearby Momofuku Noodle Bar), regional country ham selections and crispy pig's head torchon make Chang New York's reigning prince of pork. The jewel in his crown is bo ssäm—a hefty roasted Boston pork butt that takes six to eight hours to prepare. (Ordering this dish in advance for a party of at least six is the only way to get a reservation.) It's served with Chang's interpretation of traditional accoutrements: kimchi, oysters, Korean rice and bibb lettuce. Communal tables keep the mood here light and fun, and the hipster staff is blissfully helpful. If you're craving more of a challenge, try getting a table at sister property and restaurant-of-the-moment Ko; the ultra-strict reservation policy may be frustrating, but if you get in, it doesn't take long to see what all the fuss is about.
Asian. Lunch, dinner. $16-35

★★OTTO ENOTECA PIZZERIA
1 Fifth Ave., East Village, 212-995-9559; www.ottopizzeria.com
Mario Batali's bustling pizza joint near Washington Square Park is one of the few spots in the city where a large group can dine really well and not break the bank. Thin pizzas (like the memorable pane frattau, made with tomato and pecorino romano and topped with a velvety sunny side up egg) are crisped on a griddle, while $9 pastas (spaghetti alla carbonara, rigatoni with escarole and Italian sausage) are hearty and satisfying. It's the housemade gelato that's out of this world, especially the fruity and unexpected olive-oil flavor. The staff is highly knowledgeable about wine—no small feat, as there are more than 700 Italian bottles on the menu.
Italian. Lunch, dinner. $15 and under

★★PRUNE
54 E. First St., East Village, 212-677-6221; www.prunerestaurant.com
A place that serves 10 different kinds of Bloody Marys (like the Caesar, served with Boodles gin, clam juice and a pickled egg) obviously knows a thing or two about brunch. That's why you'll wait north of 90 minutes on weekend mornings for a seat in the snug-though-charming dining room. If you tough it out, your prize is delicious fare like roasted marrow bones with

WHAT ARE THE BEST OVERALL RESTAURANTS IN NEW YORK?

Jean Georges (page 90) Chef Jean-Georges Vongerichten is a master at layering flavor, making each bite a hit parade of taste.

Le Bernardin (page 75) A sure thing since it opened in 1986, Le Bernardin has really hit its stride under chef Eric Ripert, who continues the restaurant's tradition of serving luxurious French seafood.

Masa (page 90) Put yourself entirely in the hands of chef Masa Takayama and you're guaranteed to have a dining experience like no other.

Per Se (page 90) This lavish restaurant in the Time Warner Center offers the fine-dining indulgences for which fans worship chef Thomas Keller.

sea salt and parsley salad or grilled mackerel atop pickled beets and saffron aioli. Don't skimp on the vegetable sides, which include artichokes bathed in tarragon butter and escarole with Merquez sausage. Lunch and dinner offerings are equally innovative and consistently sensational, and service is pleasantly cheery.
Contemporary American. Lunch (Monday-Friday), dinner, Saturday-Sunday brunch. $16-35

★★★WD-50
50 Clinton St., Lower East Side, 212-477-2900; www.wd-50.com
Dining at WD-50 is part feast and part science experiment, thanks to heralded chef Wylie Dufresne's cutting-edge techniques. Here, even mayonnaise goes from plain-Jane to wow as Dufresne fries it and serves it in a neat row of white pellets alongside calf's tongue. The restaurant also serves squab with carob and cream soda, a combination that you likely won't find anywhere else. Even the carb-averse can dive into a plate of noodles, which are actually made of ground shrimp. The food here intrigues, but more important, it's delicious. Pack your sense of adventure and be prepared to spend—the 12-course tasting menu costs $215 with wine pairings.
Contemporary American. Dinner. Closed Monday-Tuesday. Reservations recommended. $36-85

GREENWICH VILLAGE/SOHO/WEST VILLAGE
★★★BABBO
110 Waverly Place, Greenwich Village, 212-777-0303;
www.babbonyc.com
Mario Batali is the rock 'n' roll bad boy of the restaurant world. He's got a notorious temper, a ragtag wardrobe and a cameo in a Bloodsugars' music video to his credit along with all those fabulous restaurants. It's at Babbo where he lets his rebel personality shine; a close friend of R.E.M.'s Michael Stipe, Batali understandably skips Old Blue Eyes and plays whatever he wants over the dining room sound system at this traditional-with-a-twist Italian restaurant. So rock out while tucking into Batali's creative dishes like "mint love letters"—delicate pasta pockets of spicy lamb sausage with just a hint of mint to cool your palette—and melt-in-your-mouth beef cheek ravioli with rich squab liver and black truffles. A $125 "traditional" tasting menu with wine is a song compared to similar menus at other restaurants—and you can bet those places won't likely have that rustic, rock combo all rolled into one.
Italian. Dinner. $36-85

L'ATELIER DE JOËL ROBUCHON

★★★BALTHAZAR

80 Spring St., Soho, 212-965-1414; www.balthazarny.com

This warm, noisy French bistro—a hot spot of the '90s and now a reliable standby—is a transporting experience, from the sunshine-yellow walls to the European crowd devouring steak au poivre, duck confit and other "I-must-be-in-Paris" staples. The brunch is among the best in town; the smartest calls are the pillowy brioche French toast and baskets of baked goods—but don't eat that entire croissant or you might not fit between the snugly packed tables when you get up to leave. The late-night menu keeps Balthazar bustling until after midnight seven days a week. No time for a full meal? Stop at the adjacent bakery for one of the city's best baguettes or a crisp, buttery chocolate chip cookie before hitting the Soho shopping circuit.

French. Breakfast, lunch (Monday-Friday), dinner, Saturday-Sunday brunch. $16-35

★★★BLUE HILL

75 Washington Place, West Village, 212-539-1776;
www.bluehillnyc.com

Chef Dan Barber is one of New York's masters of farm-to-table cuisine, using ingredients sustainably grown at the Stone Barns Center for Food and Agriculture, a farm and educational center 30 miles away in the Hudson Valley. (A country-chic dining experience is available at the farm, too.) Much of the produce, from the pickled ramps in the martinis to the shiitake mushrooms in the warm asparagus soup, is grown on the farm. Other ingredients like guinea hen, goat cheese and veal are from local purveyors, and you can taste their freshness. The below-street-level dining room is calm, warm and elegant.

Contemporary American. Dinner. $36-85

WHAT ARE THE CITY'S UNDERGROUND SUPPER CLUBS?

The first rule of underground supper clubs is that no one talks about underground supper clubs. Got it? Sometimes called "secret restaurants" or "speakeasies," underground supper clubs have been taking place around the city, where professional chefs looking for a creative outlet churn out restaurant-quality fare for groups of about 12 to 25 people in apartments all over town.

Cooks get to pursue their culinary dreams while avoiding city health department restrictions and high overhead costs associated with opening and operating an actual restaurant. Foodies dig the thrill of a stealth adventure in a secret location, usually for about 40 bucks. Getting in on the secret is easy: Consult the Web sites below for a list of upcoming events, then e-mail for reservations. Because most supper clubs are held in private apartments and intended to be intimate, you boost your chances of snagging a spot by responding as soon as something's posted and keeping the size of your group small (one to four people). The point of supper clubs is to meet new people, not just chat with those you came with. No need to bring beverages—cocktails and wine are included in the price.

The Whisk & Ladle *(www.thewhiskandladle.com)* is the most popular of these clubs, hosting a cocktail hour and five-course dinner for $40 in a former factory loft in Williamsburg, Brooklyn. Rotating works of local artists adorn the loft walls and musicians or DJs provide entertainment while you sip wine and enjoy dishes like beet and gorgonzola risotto prepared by a trio of twenty-somethings who met on Craigslist looking for like-minded cooks. The waiting list for this bimonthly experience is long, so make your reservation request stand out. A simple "Reservation for two, please," won't cut it with this creative crew, which is looking for the same in its guests.

Named after TV food personality Ted Allen and actress Amy Sedaris, **Ted & Amy's** *(www.karamasi.com/supperclub)* supper club in Fort Greene, Brooklyn, is actually run by foodie friends Adam Quirk and Kara Masi. Dinners for 8 to 12 are held once or twice a month in Kara's apartment and cost $30 to $35 a head. The fare is seasonal—seared scallops with summer corn from a local farm in summertime, and pumpkin ravioli and spiced pork tenderloin when the temperatures drop—and guests can hang out in the kitchen while dinner is prepared.

Even die-hard carnivores will enjoy chef Matteo Silverman's vegetables-only **Four Course Vegan** *(www.4coursevegan.com)* supper club. Held Saturdays at his off-the-beaten-path Williamsburg loft, dinners for 14 people feature imaginative dishes such as Thai eggplant roll with oyster mushrooms and tamarind chile sauce and spinach dumplings with fennel relish and chanterelle cream. You'll finish the $40 dinner with sweets like dark chocolate mousse studded with black raspberries. Sign up for the online mailing list so you can respond A.S.A.P. to upcoming dinners as they're announced, typically a week or two in advance.

Sunday Night Dinner *(www.oneasskitchen.blogspot.com)* feels like you're eating at the home of a friend—albeit one with serious cooking chops. Wine consultant and caterer Tamara Reynolds and travel writer Zora O'Neill cook for up to 20 people in their Astoria, Queens apartment. These multi-course dinners are typically $35 and include wine. A summer dinner might be hosted at their long, backyard picnic table, heaped with grilled chicken or lamb burgers, black-eyed peas or rice pilaf dotted with cherries and fennel, and grilled peaches with crème anglaise for dessert.

DANIEL

★★BLUE RIBBON BRASSERIE
97 Sullivan St., Soho, 212-274-0404; 280 Fifth Ave., Park Slope, Brooklyn, 718-840-0404; www.blueribbonrestaurants.com
Blue Ribbon is everything a good brasserie should be—woody and warm, with a menu that leans heavily on upgraded comfort classics like strip steak and fried chicken but expertly folds in worldly touches like paella. The candlelit eatery (the crown jewel of the local empire that includes Blue Ribbon Sushi and Blue Ribbon Bakery) excels with its always-fresh raw bar and juicy bomb of a burger. Tip for the chef-obsessed: With a kitchen that serves until 4 a.m. (at the Soho location), Blue Ribbon has long been a favorite late-night hangout for the toqued set after they finish shifts at nearby restaurants.
Contemporary American. Dinner. $36-85

★★★BRAEBURN
117 Sullivan St., West Village, 212-255-0696;
www.braeburnrestaurant.com
Eating at Braeburn is like wrapping yourself up in a cashmere blanket: warm, comforting and exquisite. Diners hug small handcrafted mesquite tabletops while digging into dishes such as crab ravioli and butter poached lobster with sweet corn, bacon and bittersweet onion sauce. Daily specials include buttermilk fried chicken and braised St. Louis ribs. Or you can try the comfort menu for only $30, which may inclue heirloom tomatoes, pork tenderloin with local peach and apricot relish and an ice cream sundae or chocolate pudding for dessert. Chef Brian Bistrong, who honed his skills at Bouley and The Harrison, among other restaurants, before finally opening up his own restaurant with Braeburn, simply knows how to elevate comfort food. And it's worth surrounding yourself with his perfect dishes every time.
Contemporary American. Dinner, brunch. $36-85

★CORNER BISTRO
331 W. Fourth St., West Village, 212-242-9502
Nothing about this former speakeasy is fancy—the kitchen is the size of a

WHAT ARE THE TOP CLASSIC RESTAURANTS?

'21' Club *(page 69)* This classic institution, a former speakeasy with a hidden wine vault, still attracts a who's who of celebrities and power brokers.

Daniel *(page 86)* Chef Daniel Boulud attention to detail—like the perfectly suspended flower petals in the ice cubes—is what has kept Daniel firmly moored among New York's most elite and elegant restaurants.

Four Seasons Restaurant *(page 73)* It doesn't get more New York than the Four Seasons Resturant. Editors, socialites and financial types all dine here on a regular basis. The Pool Room is anchored by Mies van der Rohe's legendary white marble pool and surrounded by trees that change with the seasons.

Gramercy Tavern *(page 84)* Charming Gramercy Tavern is a favorite upscale dining choice for everyone from expense-account suits to fashionistas and serious foodies who come here for the wonderful season cuisine.

Le Cirque *(page 76)* Owner Sirio Maccioni still presides over his restaurant each night, greeting guests and exhorting them to *manga! manga!*

La Grenouille *(page 75)* New York's elite have been dining on the French classics at this sumptuous, flower-filled room since 1962.

closet, the bar is dark and food comes on either paper or plastic plates—but everything is memorable. The small pub menu is posted on the wall, but skip it and just order the bar's namesake, the legendary Bistro Burger (eight ounces of broiled beef topped with bacon, cheese, onions, lettuce and tomato) and a side of fries. You'll still have money left to plug the jukebox and get a mug or two of $2.50 drafts. But get here early—the line for one of the precious few tables gets long and frustrating, particularly on weekend nights.
American. Lunch, dinner. $15 and under

★★★CRU
24 Fifth Ave., West Village, 212-529-1700; www.cru-nyc.com
The elegantly restrained décor at this Village restaurant oozes wealth in that subtly showy old-money kind of way, and service is warm and proper. The ever-changing menu demands attention with its global influences and creative combinations. East Coast cod packs a Latin punch with chorizo crust and piquillo-blood orange compote, while chilled foie gras over white chocolate and basil elevates the concept of sweet and savory to a new level. An award-winning wine list—it's the size of a phone book and has two volumes, one for whites and one for reds—will make you gasp. Cru boasts an astounding 150,000 bottles from the private collection of its owner, Roy Welland, and sways toward French wines from Burgundy.
Contemporary European. Dinner. Closed Sunday-Monday. $36-85

★★★★GOTHAM BAR AND GRILL
12 E. 12th Street, West Village, 212-620-4020;
www.gothambarandgrill.com
Gotham Bar and Grill opened in 1984 and proves that, just like bangs and skinny jeans, some holdovers from the '80s just get trendier with age. Acclaimed chef Alfred Portale is a perfectionist who pioneered architecturally-inspired food presentation. His edible compositions—the roasted Maine lobster is presented with lobster claws wrapped around the

WHICH PLACES HAVE THE BEST PIZZA?

CO *230 Ninth Avenue, Chelsea, 212-243-1105; www.co-pane.com*
What started as a half-baked test-case from a mobile pizza truck at the Union Square Greenmarket has evolved into one of the hottest pie shrines in Manhattan. Jim Lahey of Sullivan St. Bakery fame serves up thin-crusted—is there any other kind in New York?—Neapolitan pizzas with top-of-the-line toppings such as shaved black truffles, veal meatballs and béchamel. The menu says it best: "Our pies are not always round." But their free-form shape and often charred crust only augment the complimentary blend of ingredients. Adventurous sorts should try the fennel and sausage pie, sprinkled with red onions and chilis, or the bird's nest, a generous mix of raschera, tome de savoie, shaved asparagus, quail eggs and parmesan. The 54-seat space is both modern and casual, and rarely has a seat to spare. So come early, or prepare to wait for your little slice of heaven.
Pizza. Lunch, dinner. Reservations recommended. $36-85

Franny's *295 Flatbush Ave., Park Slope, Brooklyn, 718-230-0221; www.frannysbrooklyn.com*
Tree-huggers rejoice. With recycled paper menus, organic ingredients, renewable energy, and biodegradable to-go containers, Franny's is as environmentally-friendly as they come. The fact that the Italian fare coming from the kitchen actually tastes good is a bonus. And what a bonus it is. The menu is small and centers around thinner-than-thin Neapolitan pizzas, though there are a number of farm-fresh appetizers and a few pasta dishes. Order one of the pies that incorporates the buffalo mozzarella. More adventurous sorts can try the pizza with clams, chilies and parsley. Located in Brooklyn's chic Park Slope, there is no lack of good restaurants to try. But how many of them can say they convert kitchen grease to biodiesel fuel?
Pizza. Lunch, dinner. $15 and under

Keste' Pizza and Vino *271 Bleecker St., West Village, 212-243-1500; www.kestepizzeria.com*
Roberto Caporuscio knows good pizza. After spending years as an Italian cheese salesman, Caporuscio has made it his mission to bring authentic Neapolitan pizza to Manhattan, and he is confident in his ability to do so. (After all, Caporuscio is president of the Association Pizzaiuoli Napoletani, which schools others in the art of Neapolitan pizza making.) The menu is packed with nearly 20 varieties of pizza—a good thing since Caporuscio refuses to add or omit ingredients from any of his pies. Purists should stick to the margherita, which offers just the right ratio of sauce to cheese. Otherwise, try the pizza del papa with butternut squash cream, smoked mozzarella and artichoke or the pizza del re with prosciutto di parma and truffle spread. While the wood-burning oven churns out pies quickly, it is no match for the number of hungry diners, so expect a wait.
Pizza. Lunch, dinner. $16-35

tail which sit atop spaghetti squash along with potato purée and toasted brussels sprout halves—are the stuff of true epicurean delight. Bright and airy with stylish, silk-draped lighting and not a hint of vanity, this landmark feels like a comfortable pair of jeans, albeit with a high-end designer label.
Contemporary American. Lunch (Monday-Friday), dinner. $36-85

GOTHAM BAR AND GRILL

★★INO
21 Bedford Street, West Village, 212-989-5769; www.cafeino.com

Ten years ago, the concept of Italian-style grilled sandwiches was groundbreaking (and inspired copies everywhere). Today, this panini pioneer is still as good as ever. The tiny (25-seat) restaurant has everything you could ask for: wonderful wines and cheese, hot and crispy panini in combinations such as Italian sausage with butternut squash mustard, rucola and fontina, and wonderfully satisfying breakfast options, including an Italian BLT (pancetta, tomato, arugula and lemon mayo) and a truffled egg toast that you'll crave afterward. Best of all, Ino serves until 2 a.m., making it the perfect spot for a casual breakfast, lunch or a late-night snack.
Italian. Lunch, dinner, late-night. $16-35

★★HOME RESTAURANT
20 Cornelia St., West Village, 212-243-9579;
www.homerestaurantnyc.com

Like many New York City apartments, Home Restaurant is tiny. The understated wood dining room is small. The tables are small (some generously-sized diners think too small). Even the menu is small with only a handful of dishes offered. But what Home lacks in size, it makes up in flavor. Every dish is made from local farm-fresh, sustainable products. Even the wines come from regional vineyards in the Hudson Valley, Finger Lakes and North Fork of Long Island. The mac and cheese, with or without chorizo, is gooey and delightful, while the coriander-crusted double cut pork chop caters to a more sophisticated appetite. Don't leave Home without trying the butterscotch pudding. There's an adorable outdoor garden too, if you can find an open table.
Contemporary American. Lunch, dinner. $16-35

★★PEARL OYSTER BAR
18 Cornelia St., West Village, 212-691-8211; www.pearloysterbar.com

This New England clamshack by way of the West Village has many outstanding seafood options, from briny raw oysters and clam chowder with smoky bacon to whole-grilled fish and bouillabaisse. Really, there's only one item you need to think about: the lobster roll. The one here will bring you to your knees. A toasted, buttery hot dog bun cradles chunks of sweet lobster and shares the plate with a nest of shoestring fries. It's a perfect mix of sweet, salty, crunchy and creamy. The secret's long been out on the food here, so expect a wait despite a long-overdue expansion a few years back.
American, seafood. Lunch (Monday-Friday), dinner. Closed Sunday. $16-35

★★RAOUL'S
180 Prince St., Soho, 212-966-3518; www.raouls.com
Cramped quarters and a rushed waitstaff are part of the charm of this downtown bistro mainstay. Opened in the 1970s by the Alsatian Raoul brothers, the restaurant has grown from a struggling neighborhood eatery to a bustling Manhattan hotspot for scene-seeking locals and tourists in the know. Tightly packed tables provide a bustling atmosphere, especially in the main dining room. (For a quieter dining experience, request a table in the covered garden behind the kitchen or in the upstairs loftspace—don't mind the clairvoyant.) Signature dishes include the artichoke vinaigrette soaked in Raoul's famous dressing and extra peppery steak au poivre with French fries. Portions are generous, but it's worth leaving a bit on your plate in order to save room for the profiteroles.
French. Lunch, dinner. $16-35

★★★SAVOY
70 Prince St., Soho, 212-219-8570; www.savoynyc.com
Located on two floors of a Soho townhouse, Savoy embodies the art of organic, seasonal cuisine. In fact, chef Peter Hoffman can be seen loading up his bike with the freshest finds from the Union Square farmers market early in the morning to prepare the day's menu. The beauty of Savoy is that produce is allowed to shine on its own with little adornment. Asparagus

---

WHICH RESTAURANTS HAVE STOOD THE TEST OF TIME?
Odeon *(page 81)* In New York, restaurants come and go. Odeon has managed to stick around for 20 plus years by preparing simple dishes well (the strong martinis don't hurt, either).

Picholine *(page 91)* Chef Terrance Brennan's French-Mediterranean cuisine continues to impress at Picholine, which gets more distinguished with age.

Union Square Café *(page 85)* One of New York's most revered restaurants, Union Square Café set a new standard for seasonal greenmarket cuisine when it opened nearly 25 years ago, and it continues to be a go-to spot.

WHICH RESTAURANTS HAVE THE BEST VIEWS?
Asiate *(page 88)* The sweeping views of Central Park, courtesy of the 16-foot-high windows, invite diners to linger over dessert and coffee (or more wine).

The Modern *(page 76)* Most seats afford great views of the MoMA sculpture garden next door, so don't be surprised to catch glimpses of a Miró and Picasso's pieces as you dine.

might be simply grilled and topped with sea salt and shaved Parmesan, and entrées typically have no more than five main ingredients. Savoy can be this side of precious (check out the honey from Hoffman's rooftop hives), but the freshness and high quality of the food can't be beat. The fireplace makes this charming setting a must in winter, while heavy wooden beams overhead and warm walls surrounding the small dining room give Savoy a country-in-the-city feel.

Contemporary American. Lunch (Monday-Saturday), dinner. $36-85

★★★STRIP HOUSE
13 East 12th St., Greenwich Village, 212-328-0000;
www.striphouse.com

From the neon sign out front to the loungy interior with burgundy banquettes, red velvet walls and pictures of semi-nude burlesque girls on the walls, this is a far cry from Steak 'n' Shake, or even Peter Lugers. Many a business deal is made over plump shrimp cocktail and thick bone-in strip steak or dry aged ribeye. Don't skimp on the sides; the truffled creamed spinach tops the list, but the mashed potatoes are a close second. It's no surprise at this machismo palace that the portions are huge, and the theme carries through to dessert where a single slice of chocolate cake is enough to feed a family of five.

Steak. Lunch, dinner. $36-85

MIDTOWN/MIDTOWN EAST/MIDTOWN WEST
★★★'21' CLUB
21 W. 52nd St., Midtown West, 212-582-7200; www.21club.com

This classic institution, a former speakeasy with a hidden wine vault, is a place where suited men sip tumblers of Scotch with the guys in the downstairs Bar Room while digging into medium-rare steaks and inflating stories about business and broads. Is this the '50s, or 50-plus years later? That's precisely the beauty of '21' Club, where time seems to have stopped and a who's who of celebrities and power brokers (George Clooney, Bill Gates) eating burgers and Caesar salads provides more noteworthy decoration than the hanging model airplanes downstairs, or the murals and chandeliers in the upstairs dining rooms.

American menu. Lunch (Monday-Friday), dinner. Closed Sunday. $86 and up

★★★★ADOUR ALAIN DUCASSE
The St. Regis New York, 2 E. 55th St., Midtown, 212-710-2277;
www.adour-stregis.com

Legendary chef Alain Ducasse's Adour is a dramatic leap from the French master's previous endeavor, Alain Ducasse at the Essex House. Where the Essex House scared away diners with a French elegance rarely seen stateside, Ducasse's Adour is meant to be a subdued yet elegant wine bar. Draped in warm burgundy and gold with a corridor outfitted in leather and walls lined with well-stocked wine coolers and grape vines, the space is a perfectly warm setting for chef Joel Dennis' straightforward but expertly prepared and sophisticated French comfort food. Adour's dishes range from simple and straight-from-the-farm to quietly stunning and intricate. Start off with delicate foie gras or ricotta gnocchi and follow it with an expertly prepared duck breast or the braised wild striped bass. Adour's wine list is among the city's best, and the desserts, created by pastry chef Sandro

Micheli, rank accordingly—they include a luxuriously rich dark chocolate sorbet and pear with roasted pecans.
Contemporary French. Dinner. $36-85

★★★ANTHOS

36 W. 52nd St., 212-582-6900; www.anthosnyc.com

Expense-account businessmen now have a new place to lunch, and a new cuisine to lunch on. Chef-of-the-moment Michael Psilakis's newest endeavor, Anthos, carries the modernized Greek food that he is known for to a sophisticated upscale, if sterile, space in Midtown. The atmosphere is simple with white walls, pale pink and chocolate brown accents and images of cherry blossoms throughout (anthos is Greek for "blossom"). The menu rings far more complex. Olive oil-poached chicken with eggplant and rapini and arctic char with cracked bulgur, roasted grapes and moschofilero fondue are highlights. Psilakis also plays into the burger trend with a juicy lamb burger, accompanied by feta, spicy pepper purée and French fries. The small bar up front serves intricate and potent cocktails—and ouzo, of course—which makes returning to the office after lunch a challenge.
Greek. Lunch (Monday-Friday), dinner. Closed Sunday. Reservations recommended. $36-85

★★★AQUAVIT

65 E. 55th St., Midtown East, 212-307-7311; www.aquavit.org

The Scandinavian cuisine at Marcus Samuelsson's Midtown eatery is a far cry from the café at IKEA. The super-modern dining room is bright and minimal with angular booths, and the bar has stylish egg-shaped chairs reflecting a sharp Scandinavian aesthetic. The menu emphasizes traditional seafood and game, but with a sophisticated twist (foie gras ganache with quail egg, pickled tomato and mustard; duck atop parsley spätzle, radicchio and root vegetables). The onsite Aquavit Café features a more casual menu of Scandinavian staples including six different kinds of herring, beef Rydberg and, yes, Swedish meatballs. Then there are the dozen-plus housemade aquavits; we recommend both the horseradish and the mango, lime and chili pepper-combo flavors. A great way to try it all: The Sunday smorgasbord ($48 including a Danish Mary) is stocked with herring and hot potatoes, Swedish cheese, gravlax with mustard sauce and, of course, Swedish meatballs.
Scandinavian. Lunch (Monday-Friday), dinner, Sunday brunch. $36-85

★★★★AUREOLE

135 W 42nd St., Midtown, 212-319-1660;
www.aureolerestaurant.com

Owned by Charlie Palmer, Aureole specializes in the kind of stylish yet comfortable fine-dining experience completely devoid of pretension—here, it really is about the food and not a celebrity chef. Aureole now inhabits the famous Bank of America building under the kitchen leadership of executive chef Christopher Lee. Diners receive star treatment from courteous staff doling out hearty dishes such as veal tenderloin and sweetbreads, Australian rack of lamb or crispy black sea bass with French white asparagus. If you crave lighter fare, sit in the bar room where you will see more casual options such as the Aureole grilled burger or the diver sea scallop sandwich. A wine list heavy on European and California labels also includes the restaurant's own sparkling wine, Aureole Cuvée—no doubt a popular choice for the marrying kind of guests that you frequently see here on bended knee,

popping the question before dessert.
Contemporary American. Lunch (Monday-Saturday), dinner. Bar. Reservations recommended. $36-85

★★★BLT MARKET

The Ritz-Carlton New York, 1430 Sixth Ave., Midtown West, 212-521-6125; www.bltmarket.com

Laurent Tourondel's BLT (Bistro Laurent Tourondel) Market in the Ritz-Carlton hotel is a valentine to all things local and seasonal and another star in Tourondel's constellation of restaurants, which includes BLT Steak and BLT Prime. Diners feast on peak-season ingredients, like spring's pea and ricotta ravioli with spicy sausage, mint and pea shoots. The soft shell crab comes from Maryland, while Jamison Farm provides the lamb, and nearly all of the vegetables come from farms nearby. No matter where it hails from, the food is delicious.

Contemporary American. Breakfast, dinner. Closed Sunday-Monday. Reservations recommended. $36-85

★★★BLT STEAK

106 E. 57th St., 212-752-7470; www.bltsteak.com

It's a choose-your-own-adventure Laurent Tourondel-style at this Midtown steak emporium. First, pick the cut: hanger, filet, New York strip, ribeye, porterhouse, double sirloin. Next, the sauce: béarnaise, peppercorn, red wine, mustard, blue cheese, horseradish, barbecue. And finally, the sides: oversized onion rings, creamed spinach, hash browns, stuffed mushroom caps, potato gratin, to name a few. Fish and chicken options are available for those not in a beef mood, and there are enough sides to be a meal unto themselves. The backlit bar is a nice spot to sip a drink while waiting for a table, and the main dining room is pleasantly light and airy, a welcome change from the standard steak joint.

Steak. Lunch, dinner. $36-85

DEL POSTO

★CARNEGIE DELI

854 Seventh Ave., Midtown West, 800-334-5606;
www.carnegiedeli.com

This is a Jewish deli on steroids—heaps of deliciously fatty pastrami piled between soft slices of rye bread are enough for at least two meals, and mile-high cheesecake wedges could double as door stops. Nothing says American excess like this New York institution, which boasts a personality as large as its portions. Try creatively named sandwiches like Carnegie Haul (pastrami, tongue and salami with relish) or Bacon Whoopee (chicken salad BLT)—and enjoy these hulking sandwiches or a big bowl of matzo ball soup while gazing at the celebrity headshots lining the walls.

American. Breakfast, lunch, dinner. $16-35

★★★CONVIVIO

45 Tudor City Place, Midtown East, 212-599-5045;
www.convivionyc.com

If the aging socialites of NYC can get facelifts to increase their appeal, why can't a restaurant? That's exactly what restaurateur Chris Cannon and chef

---

WHAT ARE THE BEST STEAKHOUSES?

BLT Steak *(page 71)* Create your perfect meal at Laurent Tourondel's Midtown steak emporium: choose the cut, the sauce and the sides. Any combination you choose is sure to be a winner.

Sparks Steak House *(page 77)* There may be a surprisingly small array of beef cuts, but what is available is excellent (the New York sirloin is the signature dish) and the wine list is hefty.

Strip House *(page 69)* Many a business deal is made over plump shrimp cocktail, thick bone-in strip steak or dry-aged ribeye and delicious sides such as the truffled creamed spinach.

Michael White asked themselves before trading stuffy-and-serious L'Impero for a more casual, food-focused endeavor in the same locale. The result: a bright new star in Tudor City—about as far east as you can be in Manhattan without swimming in the East River—where the pasta sings and the price is palatable. The $59 four-course prix fixe dinner includes winners such as stracciatella (creamy cheese curd, tangy tomato and basil), maccheroni alla carbonara (pillowy pasta laced with pancetta, egg and pecorino) and scottadito di agnello (perfectly-grilled lamb chops over escarole in a sizzling salsa verde). Don't be put off by the buttoned-up clientele that frequent the place; as one of the few decent eateries neighboring the United Nations, it gets its share of foreign diplomats on expense accounts.
Southern Italian. Lunch (Monday-Friday), dinner. $36-85

★★★THE FOUR SEASONS RESTAURANT
99 E. 52nd St., Midtown, 212-754-9494;
www.fourseasonsrestaurant.com

A sports jacket isn't the only thing you need when dining here. An expense account comes in handy as well, with a menu that charges $45 for Maryland crab cakes and $65 for a rack of lamb with mint jus. Chances are you can find an equally good meal for less elsewhere in Manhattan, but you'll be hard pressed to find a better dining room in which to enjoy it. Both the Grill Room and Pool Room are considered prized destinations among New York's dining elite. The Grill Room hosted JFK's 45th birthday party and boasts walnut-paneled walls and soaring two-story windows. It doesn't get more New York than the Four Seasons Resturant. On the opposite end of the restaurant, the Pool Room is anchored by Mies van der Rohe's legendary white marble pool and surrounded by trees that change with the seasons. Widely spaced tables and exemplary service make either room a good choice for a private affair.
Contemporary American. Lunch, dinner. $86 and up

★★★★GILT
The New York Palace Hotel, 455 Madison Ave., Midtown East, 212-891-8100; www.giltnewyork.com

Located in the Villard Mansion within the New York Palace Hotel, Gilt has been rejuvenated with new chef Justin Bogle and a constantly changing menu that spotlights seasonal flavors (lamb tartare with rhubarb, buckwheat and sorrel, and tandoori-spiced black cod with roasted eggplant, mustard greens and toasted coconut) in three-, five- and seven-course tasting menus. An impressive wine list features 1,400 bottles, including 50 selections under $50. Tippling not your thing? Gilt has assembled an extensive list of nearly 40 teas (like the rare, aged High Mountain oolong tea from Taiwan) chosen with seasonality in mind. The wood-paneled, library-esque 52-seat dining room in this historic mansion is straight out of a Brontë novel, while the contrasting slick bar with futuristic décor suggests a modern club setting, perfect if you're looking for a more casual à la carte dining option. Or slip outside to the Palace Gate, a new seasonal seating area that serves up bar menu favorites amidst the melee of Midtown.
Contemporary American. Dinner (Tuesday-Saturday). Bar (open seven days). Reservations recommended. $86 and up

★★★★GORDON RAMSAY AT THE LONDON

The London NYC, 151 W. 54th St., Midtown West, 212-468-8888;
www.gordonramsay.com

The somewhat hushed, polished dining room decorated in a muted palette contrasts starkly with the salty, fiery chef and namesake of this celebrated 45-seat Manhattan restaurant in the London NYC hotel. You won't see TV cameras or hear Gordon Ramsay dropping "F" bombs at a skittish staff like he does on the reality TV shows *Hell's Kitchen* and *Kitchen Nightmares*. But you might utter an expletive in amazement at the innovative and expertly prepared cuisine here, including caramelized duck breast, roasted foie gras and ginger poached lobster. A three-tiered "Bon Bon trolley" weighed down with confections—think peanut brittle, salted caramels and handmade chocolates—provides a playful and sweet finale.

Contemporary European. Dinner. Closed Sunday-Monday. Reservations recommended. $86 and up

★★★★L'ATELIER DE JOËL ROBUCHON

Four Seasons Hotel New York, 57 E. 57th St., Midtown East,
212-829-3844; www.joel-robuchon.com

This is lauded chef Joël Robuchon's fourth outpost of L'Atelier worldwide, and he further establishes his talented flair for flavor with an ambitious small-plate French menu by way of Asia. "L'Atelier," which means "workshop" in French, offers a dizzying array of small-tasting portions on the regular menu, making your choices—from frog's legs croquettes to crispy langoustines—a bit overwhelming. But that's like saying a lottery jackpot is too big. The restaurant offers a mixture of table and counter seating similar to that of a sushi restaurant; if you're more inclined to keep tabs on the open kitchen rather than your dining companion, opt for a spot at the v-shaped bar.

French. Dinner. Reservations recommended. Bar. $86 and up

WHICH RESTAURANTS HAVE THE MOST BEAUTIFUL DÉCOR?

Bouley *(page 79)* David Bouley's new Tribeca headquarters resembles a pretty French countryside restaurant with vaulted gold-leafed ceilings, shelves of apples, tapered candles and large Impressionist-style paintings framed in velvet.

Daniel *(page 86)* The redesigned space marries neo-classical sophistication and organic playfulness: archways and balustrades are bisected by vine-like wrought iron sconces, Limoges chandeliers drape the dining room in warm light and understated leafy table arrangements stand out against otherwise neutral tones.

Gilt *(page 73)* The wood-paneled, library-esque 52-seat dining room in this historic mansion is straight out of a Brontë novel, while the contrasting slick bar with futuristic décor suggests a modern club setting.

Eleven Madison Park *(page 84)* The Art Deco room with soaring ceilings (at least two stories high), marble floors and windows that look out onto lovely Madison Square Park is simply radiant.

La Grenouille *(page 75)* Overflowing with fresh flowers, this timeless New York restaurant with its large picture windows and charming awning out front is a lovely transporting space.

GRAMERCY TAVERN

★★★★LA GRENOUILLE

3 E. 52nd St., Midtown East, 212-752-1495; www.la-grenouille.com

Decked out with more flowers than a royal wedding, this lovely and luxurious French restaurant is the kind of place where you'll want to dress up and carry a French phrase book so you can converse with the waiter. La Grenouille— which means "frog" in French, though this is actually a prince of a place—is where the most glittery and powerful personalities (Truman Capote in years past, Martha Stewart today) have dined since 1962, enjoying the polished service that is the pinnacle of attentiveness. Just as the cashmere twin set and diamond studs worn by the socialite at the next table will never go out of style, neither will the French classics on the menu here, from frog's legs to Dover sole. Notoriously pricey, La Grenouille has added an affordable $49 theater menu (before 6:30 p.m. and after 9 p.m.), making it—at last!—a upscale dining option even for those on a budget.

French. Lunch (Tuesday-Friday), dinner. Closed Sunday. Jacket required. Bar. $86 and up

★★★★★LE BERNARDIN

155 W. 51st St., Midtown West, 212-554-1515; www.le-bernardin.com

It's hard to keep food in your mouth when your jaw keeps dropping in awe. And awestruck you'll be at chef Eric Ripert's skilled transformation of everything that swims into his pristine dishes. A sure thing since it opened in 1986, Le Bernardin has really hit its stride under perfectionist Ripert. Since he succeeded chef Gilbert Le Coze in 1995, Ripert has continued Le Bernardin's tradition of serving luxurious French seafood with a modern and international flavor (yuzu in the fluke marinade, and salmon served with a jalapeño emulsion). Ripert has divided the menu into playfully named sections: "Almost Raw" (oysters, kampachi), "Barely Touched" (poached white tuna, warm lobster carpaccio) and "Lightly Cooked" (pan-roasted monkfish, poached halibut). A handful of meat dishes available upon request—like seared Kobe beef and pan-roasted squab—will make carnivores sit up and take notice,

WHAT ARE THE BEST PLACES FOR BRUNCH?

Balthazar *(page 62)* The brunch is among the best in town, and the smartest calls are the pillowy brioche French toast and baskets of baked goods.

Prune *(page 60)* A place that serves 10 different kinds of Bloody Marys obviously knows a thing or two about brunch. It's worth the wait for delicious fare like roasted marrow bones with sea salt and parsley salad.

Sarabeth's *(page 92)* New Yorkers wait up to an hour or more for the other-worldly ricotta lemon pancakes and at this brunch institution.

too. With its butterscotch leather chairs and beige fabric-covered walls, Le Bernardin feels a bit like a corporate dining room, but enormous sprays of seasonal, twiggy flowers soften the décor. The prix fixe dinner menu is $109; the tasting menu with wine is $220.

French. Lunch (Monday-Friday), dinner. Closed Sunday. Reservations recommended. $86 and up

★★★★LE CIRQUE
151 E. 58th St., Midtown, 212-644-0202; www.lecirque.com

This venerable New York City mainstay of haute cuisine reincarnated itself in 2006 when it moved from its old digs at the New York Palace Hotel to the Bloomberg Tower in Midtown. Toss in a new chef, Craig Hopson, and a revitalized menu and you've got a winning combination. Plump foie gras ravioli is a standout appetizer, while lamb served with flaky eggplant in filo, goat cheese and a red pepper purée seals the deal for the entrées. Le Cirque's impresario-owner, Sirio Maccioni, presides over his creation each night, looking over a more subdued dining room compared to the outlandish previous space—there's no longer a baroque-carnival feel, but more of an Upper East Side party atmosphere, albeit encased in a gold tent. The new futuristic glass and steel space is more suited to Midtown's business crowd and the sometimes-cold Le Cirque service. But a towering napoleon dessert can make up for any missteps you may encounter from your waiter.

Contemporary French, Italian. Lunch (Monday-Friday), dinner. Closed Sunday. Reservations recommended. Jacket required. $36-85

★★★★THE MODERN
Museum of Modern Art, 9 W. 53rd St., Midtown, 212-333-1220; www.themodernnyc.com

The Modern, an elegant sun-lit Midtown addition to restaurateur Danny Meyer's dense portfolio (which includes Blue Smoke, Gramercy Tavern and Union Square Café) is really two restaurants in one—the sophisticated Dining Room and a less-formal Bar Room. Split up into two rooms separated by frosted glass, both restaurants reside in The Museum of Modern Art, one of the most elegant buildings in New York. In fact, most seats afford great views of the MoMA sculpture garden next door, so don't be surprised to catch glimpses of a Miró or a Picasso as you dine. Still, chef Gabriel Kreuther—who took home the James Beard Award for Best Chef: New York City in 2009—tries his darndest to take your attention from the masterpieces outside to those on your plate with his bold, flavorful food, and he succeeds. The romantic, 85-seat Dining Room offers more elegant dishes like chorizo-crusted codfish with white cocoa bean purée and harissa oil; roasted

CORTON

lobster with chanterelles, heart of palm and chamomile blossom nage; and a Pennsylvania duck breast with a black trumpet marmalade, fleischschneke and banyuls jus. In the less-formal Bar Room, you can find an earthy menu emphasizing small plates with big tastes, such as a pasta dish elevated by chewy, salty escargots and fragrant wild mushrooms. A not-to-miss dessert is the pistachio dark-chocolate dome with pistachio ice cream and amaretto gelée. It's essentially edible art.

French, Contemporary American. Lunch (Monday-Friday), dinner. Closed Sunday. $36-85

★★★MONKEY BAR

60 East 54th St., Midtown, 212-207-9085; www.theglaziergroup.com

If it seems like everyone dining here has been plucked straight from the pages of *Vanity Fair*, it's because there is a good chance that they have. Monkey Bar is co-owned by Graydon Carter, editor of the trend-centric publication, and the dining clientele is predictably beautiful. From the doorman who greets you upon arrival to the doting waitstaff, service is impeccable—and it should be considering the prices. The menu is a mixed bag, offering everything from scrambled eggs to burgers to chicken paillard. Your best bet is to stick with the classics. The fish n' chips is surprisingly light and flavorful. Or just come for the cocktails, which include a very tasty (and potent) mango mojito. The interior is Art Deco cool with murals throughout and comfortable banquettes. Monkey Bar won't serve you the best meal of your life, but you may have the time of your life people-watching.

Contemporary American. Lunch, dinner. $36-85.

★★★SPARKS STEAK HOUSE

210 E. 46th St., Midtown East, 212-687-4855;
www.sparkssteakhouse.com

A Manhattan mainstay since 1966, Sparks delivers the boys club style and brisk service often associated with old-school steak joints. Give or take the décor, this midtown behemoth delivers on flavor. The menu encompasses all

WHICH RESTAURANTS SERVE THE BEST BURGERS?

Burger Joint *(Le Parker Meridien, Midtown, 118 W. 57th St., 212-245-5000; www.parkermeridien.com)* If you can find this tiny wood-paneled hole-in-the-wall (it lurks behind a shroud of drapes off Le Parker Meridien's lobby), you're in for a comfort treat. Burgers come topped with lettuce, tomatoes, onions, pickles, mustard, ketchup and mayo, and brown-bagged fries are hot and salty. The best part is that this juicy patty will run you only $7, which beats the $20 burger on the room service menu.

Shake Shack *(Madison Square Park, Madison Avenue and E. 23rd St., Lower East Side, 212-889-6600; www.shakeshack.com)* This tiny Madison Square Park burger stand may have "sold out" by opening outlets on the Upper West Side and Citi Field, but the freshly ground blend of sirloin and brisket patties still get people to wait in line for hours. A griddled potato bun and special shack sauce are the only accoutrements you'll need (in addition to a hand-spun chocolate shake, of course).

JG Melon *(1291 Third Ave., Upper East Side, 212-650-1310)* Around since 1972, this old-style pub still packs them in, thanks in larger part to the meaty hamburgers it churns out daily. The buns are on the small side and toppings are slim to none (unless you consider a few pickles and onions well-dressed), but the burgers are charred to perfection and juicy. Don't waste the calories on the mediocre cottage fries, and remember to hit the ATM before you indulge. JG Melon only takes cash.

Zaitzeff *(72 Nassau St., Financial District, 18 Avenue B, Lower East Side, 212-571-7272; www.zaitzeffnyc.com)* This Financial District mainstay keeps it simple, sort of—sirloin or Kobe beef, quarter- or half-pounder, Portuguese muffin or sourdough roll, cheese or no cheese. The secret here, apart from the fact that fast and fresh lunch options in the neighborhood are minimal, is the juiciness of the meat and the speed of the service. The hand-cut sweet potato fries aren't bad either.

Five Napkin Burger *(630 Ninth Ave., Theater District, 212-757-2277; www.5napkinburger.com)* Though there are seven burgers to choose from, the Original 5 Napkin Burger is the only real choice for burger aficionados—10 ounces of ground chuck beef, comte cheese, warm caramelized onions and a dollop of rosemary aioli on a white bread bun.

Minetta Tavern *(113 MacDougal St., West Village, 212-475-3850; www.minettatavernny.com)* The newest kid on the burger-crawl block isn't wasting any time on basics. The Black Angus burger—all $26 worth—blends dry aged New York strip, skirt steak and brisket into an eight-ounce patty that cooks on a griddle covered in grapeseed oil, while clarified butter is drizzled on top to form a charred crust. Toss in a homemade brioche bun, a stack of caramelized onions and some skinny fries and you've found nirvana.

The Little Owl *(90 Bedford St., 212-741-4695; www.thelittleowlnyc.com)* The bacon cheeseburger at the Little Owl, with its mix of brisket and short ribs, maple-smoked bacon, Gus's brined pickles and slightly sweet homemade bun, is worth every single delicious calorie—or whatever wait you experience to get into this wonderful restaurant.

the steakhouse standards: shrimp cocktail, creamed spinach, hash brown potatoes, and a surprisingly small array of beef cuts. (Don't come craving a ribeye.) But what is on the meat menu is excellent. The New York sirloin is the signature dish, slightly charred and salty on the outside, but still rare. No need for steak sauce, which is a good thing since the waitstaff doesn't take kindly to the request. The wine list is hefty and offers a nice range of vintages and prices.
Steak. Lunch, dinner. $36-85

★★★★SUGIYAMA
251 W. 55th St., Midtown West, 212-956-0670;
www.sugiyama-nyc.com
This may be the closest you'll get to Japan without hopping on a plane. The minimalist Sugiyama (tiny bamboo lanterns offer minimal sparkle to an otherwise spartan, booth-filled space) offers innovative and interesting takes on traditional Japanese food that you won't find elsewhere in the city. It specializes in kaiseki, three-, five- or eight-course seasonal tasting menus that emphasize harmony in flavor, texture, color and shape. The menu typically progresses from cold dishes (mixed greens with Japanese mushrooms) to hot (beef tenderloin grilled on a hot stone), producing a taste bud-pleasing medley of flavors and sensations. A chef's choice kaiseki menu (called omakase) is also available.
Japanese. Dinner. Closed Sunday-Monday. $36-85

TRIBECA/MEATPACKING DISTRICT
★★★★BOULEY
163 Duane St., Tribeca, 212-964-2525; www.davidbouley.com
David Bouley recently moved his acclaimed restaurant to a new Tribeca headquarters and the results are impressive. The dining room's vaulted gold-leafed ceiling is bold, his determination to serve high-end ingredients is fierce, and freebies like a lemon tea cake for ladies to take home for the next morning's breakfast are a godsend. You won't be able to restrain your glee at Bouley's classic-yet-unconventional French fare, like rosemary-crusted rack of lamb in a pool of zucchini-mint purée, and seafood dishes adorned with yuzu and Japanese pickles. The over-the-top mantra doesn't stop at the entrées: The Chocolate Frivolous dessert is an exercise in excess—a plate piled high with chocolate brûlée, chocolate parfait, chocolate-walnut spice bread, orange-cointreau ganache and a generous scoop of chocolate ice cream. You'll be on a sugar rush all evening.
French. Lunch, dinner. Reservations recommended. $86 and up

★★★CORTON
239 W. Broadway, Tribeca, 212-219-2777; www.cortonnyc.com
White on white is the new black at this trendy Tribeca restaurant. The windowless space epitomizes modern simplicity with lightly stenciled whitewashed walls, white linen tablecloths and white Bernardeaud china. Such sophistication is par for the course with old school chef Paul Liebrandt, who works his magic in a state-of-the-art kitchen visible from the dining room through a narrow slit in the wall. The three-course prix fixe menu ($85) may appear fussy at first glance—think foie gras with sour cherries, chioggia beet and marcona almonds, and Montauk cod over razor clam risotto and arugula chantilly—but Liebrandt delivers with exceptionally delicate flavors and farm fresh ingredients. Dessert keeps the culinary bar held high with French treats

such as the black cherry clafoutis with sour plum and lemon verbena. At a time when Manhattan foodies are turning their attention toward cheap burger joints and casual no-nonsense menus, Corton proves that exceptional food is always in vogue. Good luck getting a reservation less than a month in advance, but once you're in, you'll be very glad you came.

French. Dinner. Closed Sunday. Reservations recommended. $86 and up

★★★THE HARRISON
355 Greenwich St., Tribeca, 212-274-9310; www.theharrison.com
Since chef Amanda Freitag took the reins in January 2008, she has infused new life into The Harrison, whose sister restaurant, Chelsea's The Red Cat *(page 56)*, also has that Mediterranean-American thing down pat. Freitag's menu is both familiar and imaginative—traditional offerings like lamb chops get punched up with anchovy and rosemary, and the seasonal salmon will clear your sinuses thanks to the horseradish crust and red mustard greens. Fries cooked in duck fat are both indulgent and addictive. The candlelit tables are a little too close for comfort, but the reliable food more than makes up for the tight surroundings. Sidewalk seating out front is ideal for enjoying a warm evening and fabulous people-watching in eternally trendy Tribeca.

Contemporary American. Dinner. $36-85

★★★LOCANDA VERDE
377 Greenwich St., Tribeca, 212-925-3797;
www.locandaverdenyc.com
The newest incarnation in Robert De Niro's trendy Greenwich Hotel, Locanda Verde is a refreshingly casual and affordable eatery in a neighborhood of heavy hitters. The once cavernous space has become intimate with warm

WHAT ARE THE BEST CELEBRITY CHEF RESTAURANTS?

Craft *(page 83)* Tom Colicchio of TV's *Top Chef* obviously knows food, and it shows at his hyper-seasonal restaurant where diners build their own meals.

Babbo *(page 61)* Mario Batali is the bad boy of the restaurant world and it's at Babbo where he lets his rebel personality shine with dishes like the melt-in-your-mouth beef cheek ravioli with rich squab liver and black truffles.

Daniel *(page 86)* Chef Daniel Boulud is fastidious about details—like the clarity of his veal stock, the flower petals suspended in ice cubes in some of the cocktails and the complimentary warm madeleines at meal's end.

Jean Georges *(page 90)* The novelty may have worn off, but Jean Georges is still as good as it was when it opened back in 1997. Today, the chef has countless other restaurants, but you can always count on a consistently wonderful experience at his flagship.

L'Atelier de Joël Robuchon *(page 74)* This is lauded chef Joël Robuchon's fourth outpost of L'Atelier worldwide, and he further establishes his talented flair for flavor with an ambitious small-plate French menu.

Masa *(page 90)* There are no menus at Masa, but no matter. It's best to put your yourself entirely in the hands of chef Masa Takayama, who bases his menu on the best ingredients he can find that day, or purely on whim.

lighting, a charming granite bar and soaring French doors that open onto the sidewalk. The open kitchen allows diners to keep tabs on chef Andrew Carmellini, a disciple of Daniel Boulud, as he churns out family-style Italian fare with little fluff and lots of taste. Small plates, known as cicchettis, start the evening off well. The blue crab crostino with jalapeño and tomato, and the sheep's milk ricotta are both excellent. The small theme carries throughout the menu with portion sizes ringing in well below average. Luckily, size has nothing to do with flavor, the orecchiette with rabbit sausage, sweet peas and fiore sardo will have you wishing you lived next door.
Italian. Lunch, dinner. $36-85

★★★NOBU
105 Hudson St., Tribeca, 212-219-0500;
www.myriadrestaurantgroup.com
Chef Nobuyuki Matsuhisa solidified his darling status here when he opened this, the first of his New York City eateries, in 1994. The sleek restaurant backed by Robert De Niro broke traditional sushi rules with its pioneering Japanese-South American style, serving concoctions like scallops drizzled with hot pepper sauce and slivers of velvety yellowtail studded with rounds of jalapeño. Nobu's miso-marinated black cod has inspired countless imitations, but it's gotten easier to try the real deal now that there are 17 Nobu restaurants around the world, from Miami to Milan. If you can't get a table at Nobu here in New York, try its sister spot Nobu Next Door *(212-334-4445)* one door down, where the menu is almost exactly the same but the no-reservations policy (except for dinner parties of five or more) makes it a good last-minute option.
Japanese. Lunch (Monday-Friday), dinner. $36-85

★★ODEON
145 W. Broadway, Tribeca, 212-233-0507;
www.theodeonrestaurant.com
Hot spots come and go but the crowds eventually come home to Odeon, the original hipster restaurant in Tribeca (which used to serve the likes of Andy Warhol back in the day). Odeon is refreshingly simple and straighforward, offering well-executed bistro classics such as a rich and crispy croque monsieur, a thick and juicy hamburger with cheese and bacon, and a nice omelet with fries. Order one of the potent martinis and you pretty much have a meal that is guaranteed to hit the spot.
Contemporary American. Lunch, dinner, late night. $16-35

★★★THE STANDARD GRILL
848 Washington St., Meatpacking District, 212-645-4100;
www.thestandardgrill.com
Nestled under the High Line in the euro-chic Standard Hotel, The Standard Grill is sexy, showy, and anything but, yes, standard. The kitchen is open from 7 a.m. to 4 a.m., catering to both neighborhood early birds and the party-hardy night owls. Four separately managed dining rooms keep the madness under control, but the atmosphere is still loud and slightly frenetic; if you can get a table in the expansive outdoor garden, do so. Popular dishes include a green bean salad accompanied by cinnamon and crispy shallots; a perfectly seasoned Berkshire pork chop; and duck fat smashed potatoes. The cocktails are as strong a draw as the food. Bartenders work at ludicrous speeds to pour out inventive potables like the penny drop (a vodka and

ginger zinger) and the housemade limoncello.
Contemporary American. Breakfast, lunch, dinner, late night. $16-35

UNION SQUARE/FLATIRON DISTRICT/GRAMERCY PARK/MURRAY HILL

★★ARTISANAL FROMAGERIE & BISTRO
2 Park Ave., Murray Hill, 212-725-8585; www.artisanalbistro.com
If you love cheese, then you've found your paradise in this sprawling, dimly lit bistro with buttercream yellow walls and red-checkered floors. Couples nibble on baskets of airy gougères at the bar while cheese-savvy servers hustle pots of gooey fondue to tightly packed wooden tables. It's the quality of the French-style food, from hearty leg of lamb to charred hanger steak, that salvages Artisanal from becoming a kitschy fondue joint and instead makes it a delightful restaurant you will want to return to again and again. Weekend brunch isn't for the cholesterol conscious—the cinnamon sugar dusted beignets are impossible to refuse.
French. Lunch (Monday-Friday), dinner, Saturday-Sunday brunch. $16-35

★★BLUE SMOKE
116 E. 27th St., Murray Hill, 212-447-7733; www.bluesmoke.com
The smell of smoking meat wafts through the entire spacious, airy restaurant, priming your appetite for its stick-to-your-ribs food. Many regional barbecue styles are served here—so expect the likes of saucy Kansas City ribs and dry-rubbed Texas-style fare. While the barbecued ribs and brisket hit the spot, the side dishes are stars in their own right. Gooey macaroni and cheese, smoky baked beans and braised collard greens with bacon will have you licking your plate clean. The burger here is a double-fister, and it can be topped with smoked bacon. The jazz club downstairs and a late-night menu keep this place jumping past midnight.
American. Lunch, dinner. $16-35

★CITY BAKERY

3 W. 18th St., Flatiron District, 212-366-1414; www.thecitybakery.com

Every neighborhood should have a City Bakery, where imaginative salads make vegetables exciting, soups are silky and flavorful, and chocoholics rejoice at the creamy, dreamy hot chocolate with homemade marshmallows. The caramelized French toast (available only on weekends) and pretzel croissant have legions of fans, as do the array of sweet baked treats. Seating in the boisterous, high-ceilinged café is limited, so if you're not the patient type, take your goods to go and sit in nearby Union Square to munch alfresco.

American. Breakfast, lunch. $15 and under

★★★★COUNTRY

The Carlton Hotel, 90 Madison Ave., Murray Hill, 212-889-7100;
www.countryinnewyork.com

While swooning over a meal in the opulent dining room is no longer an option—the space is now only for private parties—the downstairs cafe has taken up the helm, offering three square meals a day amidst a sleek atmosphere of leather chesterfields and dark wood moldings. Chef-owner Geoffrey Zakarian, who also runs Country's sister restaurant, Town, is known for his expert execution of dishes that might not necessarily be novel—like bison tenderloin, succulent chicken for two and classic burgers—but nevertheless delight in their perfect marriage of texture and harmonious flavors. It's hard to ignore the four-sided zinc bar anchored in the center of the 28-foot space, and even harder to dismiss seasonal sparkling-wine cocktails such as Sicilian—a blend of white crème de menthe mixed with lime purée, muddled mint leaves, bitters and sparking wine.

Contemporary American. Breakfast, lunch (Monday-Friday), dinner, Saturday-Sunday brunch. $36-85

★★★CRAFT

43 E. 19th St., Flatiron District, 212-780-0880;
www.craftrestaurant.com

Tom Colicchio of *Top Chef*—the sexiest bald head on TV since Kojak—obviously knows food. It shows at his restaurant Craft (part of the Craft chain that includes Craftsteak, Craftbar and 'wichcraft), which emphasizes fresh ingredients and cooking methods as so many other restaurants do, but does so like no other. Diners build their own meals—an exciting or daunting experience, depending on your sense of adventure and food curiosity. First,

---

WHICH RESTAURANTS ARE BEST FOR LARGE GROUPS?

Blue Smoke *(page 82)* This lively barbecue joint (there's a jazz club downstairs) has a roll up your sleeves and eat atmosphere, and offers many different styles of ribs, gooey sides and spacious red booths.

Mesa Grill *(page 85)* This Bobby Flay restaurant offers a three course prix fixe menu for parties of 12or more; larger groups of up to 50 can reserve the private balcony overlooking the restaurant.

OTTO Enoteca Pizzeria *(page 60)* Mario Batali's bustling pizza joint is one of the few spots in the city where a large group can dine really well and not break the bank.

select a preparation method (roasting, braising, raw), and then the ingredient (halibut, sweetbreads, oysters) for the table. Servers bring plates for everyone in the group to share. The diver scallops and braised short ribs are standouts, while the restaurant's desserts have a deserved cult following—the homemade Boston crème doughnuts with blueberry compote, chocolate malted milk and cheesecake ice cream will not disappoint. The elegantly industrial dining room emulates the menu's work-in-progress theme, with dangling filament light bulbs and exposed brick and iron.
Contemporary American. Dinner. $36-85

★★★★ELEVEN MADISON PARK
11 Madison Ave., Flatiron District, 212-889-0905;
www.elevenmadisonpark.com
The large scale of the Art Deco dining room—think high ceilings volumous floral arrangements, hulking light fixtures—contrasts with the modestly-sized food portions. But what does adorn the plate is so thoughtfully conceived, gorgeously executed and alive with flavor that you won't mind. The French-influenced greenmarket cuisine includes such dishes as Muscovy duck glazed with lavender honey, and foie gras terrine with plums, umeboshi and bitter almonds. Here, the trolley really does go ding ding—a mobile martini cart means a cocktail can be prepared at your table. The boozy treats are served with a dish of olives, a small dish of Marcona almonds and a fancy toothpick.
Contemporary American. Lunch (Monday-Friday), dinner. Closed Sunday. $86 and up

★★★★GRAMERCY TAVERN
42 E. 20th St., Flatiron District, 212-477-0777;
www.gramercytavern.com
Charming Gramercy Tavern is self-assured without being flashy and comfortable without being dull, making it a favorite upscale dining choice for everyone from expense-account suits to serious foodies wondering if the Chioggia beets came from the farmers market down the street (they probably did). Chef Michael Anthony has filled the big toque left behind by Tom Colicchio, and he has infused the classic menu with creative flourishes—from the hazelnut yogurt sauce and red cabbage complementing the halibut to the apple chutney on the foie gras custard—that keep you on your toes just when you think you've got the place pegged. Try a specialty such as

---

WHAT ARE THE BEST ITALIAN RESTAURANTS?
Al Di Là *(page 94)* You'll think you hear gondoliers singing outside when you tuck into the authentic Northern Italian dishes at this charming Brooklyn spot.

'Cesca *(page 89)* Dependably delicious and cozy, this rustic Italian restaurant is a favorite of Upper West Siders.

Convivio *(page 72)* This bright new star in Tudor City by Chris Cannon and chef Michael White has pasta that sings and great prices.

Del Posto *(page 56)* Dinner here is wildly expensive and may leave you wondering how on earth pasta strands made of flour, eggs and water can cost so much, but rest assured, its worth every bite.

the shrimp salad with grapefruit or rack of pork and braised belly, and for dessert, warm chocolate bread pudding. The long bar is a perfect perch from which to enjoy the à la carte menu, plates of cheese and wines by the glass.

Contemporary American. Lunch (Monday-Friday), dinner. Reservations recommended. $86 and up

★★MESA GRILL
102 Fifth Ave., Flatiron District, 212-807-7400; www.mesagrill.com
Food Network fans know chef Bobby Flay as the red-haired chef who is a master of the grill. Today, he's practially an empire, with multiple restaurants under his helm, cookbooks and numerous television appearances. But Mesa Grill, which opened in 1991, was his first restaurant, and above all else, Flay is the king of all things spicy. Dishes like the shrimp and roasted garlic corn tamales, New Mexican spice-rubbed pork tenderloin with crushed pecan butter, and sixteen-spice duck breast with carrot-habanero sauce and a chorizo-goat cheese tamale with thyme, prove that his food keeps getting better and better. The service can be clunky, but your focus will be on the food.

Southwestern. Lunch (Monday-Friday), dinner, brunch (Saturday-Sunday). $35-85

★★★TABLA
11 Madison Ave., Flatiron District, 212-889-0667; www.tablany.com
Much like the mixed cuisine that it serves, Tabla is two restaurants in one. The main dining room occupies a sophisticated balcony-level space with crisp white tablecloths, warm candlelight and golden mosaics on the walls, and serves new American cuisine accented by Indian spices and flavors. Downstairs, the Bread Bar includes an outdoor patio and caters to a more casual crowd with home-style Indian cuisine. No matter where you choose to dine, views of Madison Square Park and the Flatiron building are yours for the taking. The menu changes daily, but standouts include the Tabla crab cakes, blended with papadum and served alongside avocado salad and tamarind chutney, slow-cooked wild striped bass, and the roasted skate with coconut and steamed south Indian rice noodles. For a quick bite, nothing beats the pulled lamb and mustard-mashed potato naanini sandwich (be sure to grab an extra napkin or two).

Contemporary Indian. Lunch, dinner. $36-85

★★★UNION SQUARE CAFÉ
21 E. 16th St., Union Square, 212-243-4020; www.unionsquarecafe.com
One of New York's most revered restaurants, Union Square Café set a new standard for seasonal greenmarket cuisine when it opened nearly 25 years ago, and it continues to be a go-to spot for everyone from tourists to trendoids. The menu hasn't changed much since the start, but why mess with a good thing? Plus, the dishes feel timeless rather than dated due to the ever-changing seasonal touches on the menu, like sugar snap pea salad tagliatini and pan-roasted chicken atop asparagus bread pudding. The restaurant's creamy walls and warm wood floors and chairs are so comfortable that you might feel like you're eating at an old friend's house. And in many ways, you are.

Contemporary American. Lunch, dinner. Reservations recommended. $36-85

GORDON RAMSAY AT THE LONDON

★★★VERITAS

43 East 20th St., Flatiron District, 212-353-3700; www.veritas-nyc.com
Wine, wine and more wine. With a list more than 192,000 bottles deep, thanks
mainly to the Park B. Smith wine collection becoming available, wine is the
keystone of any meal at Veritas. And what better accompaniment to award-
winning wine than gourmet French fare? Black truffles, foie gras and frogs
legs all play a part in chef Gregory Pugin's sophisticated menu. The Wagyu
filet with béarnaise croquets and shishito peppers in a bordelaise sauce is
perhaps the most memorable dish on the menu. Sidestep the sweets for the
ever-changing assortment of cheeses. The interior is neutral and modern,
leaving the focus entirely on the food and wine. After all, in vino veritas.
French. Lunch, dinner. $36-85.

UPPER EAST SIDE
★★★CAFÉ BOULUD

20 E. 76th St., Upper East Side, 212-772-2600; www.danielnyc.com
The look of the dining room may have changed, thanks to a cosmetic
renovation in 2009, but the same exceptional French cuisine continues to flow
from the kitchen under the command of chef Gavin Kaysen. Daniel Boulud's
more casual eatery, Café Boulud is reminiscent of a buzzing neighborhood
brasserie with high ceilings, tightly packed tables and mirrors lining the
walls. The menu is divided into categorical themes: tradition, season, garden
and world cuisine. It's hard to resist getting traditional with the foie gras au
torchon, or dipping into the summer season with Maine peekytoe crab over
a carrot purée. For a good smattering of each, opt for the prix fixe lunch.
Café Boulud is a popular destination for brunch as well. One look at the
viennoiseries basket of pastries and you'll understand why.
French. Lunch, dinner. $36-85

★★★★DANIEL

60 E. 65th St., Upper East Side, 212-288-0033; www.danielnyc.com
Chef Daniel Boulud is fastidious about details—like the clarity of his veal

stock, the flower petals suspended in ice cubes in some of the cocktails and the complimentary basket of warm madeleines at meal's end. But this is what's kept Daniel firmly moored among New York's most elite and elegant restaurants. After a massive redesign in 2008 under the command of famed designer Adam Tihany, the space marries neo-classical sophistication and organic playfulness. Archways and balustrades are bisected by vine-like wrought iron sconces, Limoges chandeliers drape the dining room in warm light and understated leafy table arrangements stand out against otherwise neutral tones. Eating here, you'll happily part with stacks of greenbacks just to dig a fork into his legendary potato-coated sea bass or a dish of succulent veal prepared three ways. The very attentive staff is a highlight, expertly helping well-heeled diners navigate the 1,500-bottle wine list and graciously amending tasting menus to fit your preferences. Choose between three-course prix fixe and six- or eight-course tasting menus, or dine à la carte in the lounge.

French. Dinner. Closed Sunday. Reservations recommened. $86 and up

★★JOJO
160 E. 64th St., Upper East Side, 212-223-5656;
www.jean-georges.com

Dining at Jojo's is more akin to a meal at a friend's apartment than a restaurant—as long as that friend has a palatial Upper East Side townhouse, a knack for cooking flawless French cuisine and goes by the name Jean-Georges. The interior can waver on prissy and overdone, but one bite of the ricotta ravioli with spring vegetables, and you'll hardly care. The poached lobster is unique with a tangy lemon risotto and caramelized fennel, while the duck is perfectly cooked in sweet and sour shallots. Desserts are extraordinary. Raspberry crisp, gooey chocolate cake, poached peaches, warm madeleines. Take your pick; they're all rich and satisfying.

French. Lunch, dinner. $36-85

★★★★KAI
822 Madison Ave., Upper East Side, 212-988-7277;
www.itoen.com/kai/

To reach this serene Japanese restaurant, you must first pass through the tea shop Ito En downstairs, which makes Kai seem like a hidden gem of some sort—and actually, it is. The atmosphere is hushed and the décor sleek and minimalist, right down to the single flower on each table. Kai specializes in kaiseki, a Japanese multicourse seasonal tasting menu, for $85, while a prix fixe omakase (chef's choice) menu is $150-$200 per person, while the Kagoshima Wagyu steak is $16 per ounce with a five-ounce minimum. If the kaiseki has you parched, opt for hot or cold sake or one of more than a dozen teas on hand—you are above a tea shop after all.

Japanese. Lunch, dinner. Closed Sunday-Monday. $86 and up

WHAT ARE THE BEST DELIS?
Carnegie Deli *(page 34)* Nothing says American excess like this New York institution, which boasts a personality as large as its portions.

Barney Greengrass *(page 89)* Traditional fare such as sturgeon, herring, sable and whitefish salad have made this no-frills Formica haven with its surly counter staff a go-to eatery for generations of New Yorkers.

WHAT ARE THE BEST SPOTS FOR A CASUAL LUNCH?

City Bakery *(page 83)* Every neighborhood should have a City Bakery, where imaginative salads make vegetables exciting, soups are silky and flavorful, and the hot chocolate has homemade marshmallows.

Ino *(page 67)* This panini pioneer is still as good as ever, serving wonderful panini, a nice selection of breakfast items including a divine truffled egg toast, and a nice selection of wines. In a word: perfection.

Home Restaurant *(page 67)* Home only offers a handful of dishes but each is made from local farm-fresh, sustainable products, and prove that it's quality and not quantity that matters. The wines are local and the butterscotch pudding is wonderfully nostalgic.

Pearl Oyster Bar *(page 67)* This New England clamshack by way of the West Village has many outstanding seafood options, the best of which is the to-die-for lobster roll.

★SERENDIPITY 3
225 E. 60th St., Upper East Side, 212-838-3531;
www.serendipity3.com
Don't let the crush of people ogling knickknacks for sale dampen your desire to indulge in a signature frozen hot chocolate or three-scoop "drugstore" sundae at this Upper East Side sweet shop. There are few places in New York as playful as Serendipity, where both kids and kids-at-heart can unabashedly worship at the altar of sweets. Serendipity feels like an Alice in Wonderland tea party come to life, complete with multicolored Tiffany lamps (some of them real), a tiny space and larger-than-you-can-imagine sticky treats. "Serious" food is available, too, from burgers and hot dogs to meatloaf and pasta.
American, dessert. Lunch, dinner. $16-35

★★★SHUN LEE PALACE
155 E. 55th St., Upper East Side, 212-371-8844;
www.shunleepalace.com
A favorite choice for Chinese-food-loving New Yorkers who want something a little more refined than some of the places in Chinatown, Shun Lee specializes in Hunan, Cantonese and Szechuan classics. Its following is not unfounded: The food here is flavorful and light, with many authentic, time-intensive dishes you won't find at neighborhood Chinese spots. The Beggar's Chicken, for example, is a vegetable-, pork- and seafood-stuffed chicken wrapped in lotus leaves and packed in clay soil before baking for several hours. Vegetarians who wrestle with the carnivore-crave—particularly the Peking duck variety—will find salvation in the Veggie Duck Pie, a tofu take on the famous delicacy, pancake, hoisin sauce and all. Shun Lee's sister restaurant, Shun Lee on the Upper West Side *(43 W. 65th St., 212-595-8895)*, serves similar food and is a popular choice with the Lincoln Center crowd.
Chinese. Lunch, dinner. $16-35

UPPER WEST SIDE
★★★★ASIATE
Mandarin Oriental, New York, 80 Columbus Circle, Upper West Side,
212-805-8881; www.mandarinoriental.com
French-Asian fare is nothing new—hello, 20th century Vietnam—but it sure

is something to write home about if it comes from this restaurant inside the Mandarin Oriental hotel. Asiate offers thoughtful, well-executed East-meets-West fare, like roasted foie gras and glazed eel atop braised daikon in an anise-pineapple broth, and black sea bass with stir-fried Asian vegetables in a ginger-lemongrass consommé. Indeed, everything about this restaurant is noteworthy, from the sweeping views of Central Park, courtesy of the 16-foot-high windows, to the glittering tree-branch sculpture hanging from the ceiling, to the beautiful china on your table and the wine collection, which fills up an entire wall. The chocolate fondant with raspberry granite is the perfect complement to your evening.

French-Asian. Breakfast, lunch (Monday-Friday), dinner (Monday-Saturday), Saturday-Sunday brunch. $86 and up

★BARNEY GREENGRASS
541 Amsterdam Ave., Upper West Side, 212-724-4707; www.barneygreengrass.com

If you like your restaurants with a schmear of character and history, look no further than the 100-year-old Barney Greengrass. Known affectionately as "The Sturgeon King," this appetizing Jewish deli (which moved from its original Harlem location to its current spot in 1929) takes the nickname seriously: Sturgeon and velvety lox top bagels and bialys, and weave through fluffy scrambled eggs with onions for one of the most popular breakfasts on the Upper West Side. Other traditional fare such as herring, sable and whitefish salad have also understandably made this no-frills Formica haven with its surly counter staff a go-to eatery for generations of New Yorkers. Expect a long wait, especially on weekends, when you might bump elbows with the likes of Jerry Seinfeld.

Deli. Breakfast, lunch. Closed Monday. $16-35

★★★'CESCA
164 W. 75th St., Upper West Side, 212-787-6300; www.cescanyc.com

Dependably delicious and cozy, the rustic Italian restaurant 'Cesca has been a favorite of Upper West Siders since it opened in 2003. Stenciled white walls, soft lighting and large, circular booths keep the mood relaxed. The open kitchen churns out hits such as parmesan and prosciutto fritters dusted with a surprising kick of cayenne, and orecchiette with crumbled pork sausage and broccoli rabe. A three-course pre-theater menu is available before 6:30 p.m. for crowds catching a show at nearby Lincoln Center. If you need a kickstart before the performance, swing by the long, granite-topped bar for a Tuscan Maple Sidecar with maple syrup and Grand Marnier or a tangy Via Veneto Spritz, bubbling over with Prosecco, Aperol and lemon.

Italian. Dinner, Sunday brunch. $36-85

★★★DOVETAIL
103 West 77th St., Upper West Side, 212-362-3800; www.dovetailnyc.com

Neighboring the American Museum of Natural History, Central Park and Lincoln Center, Dovetail is a welcome addition to a tourist heavy, and restaurant slim, locale. Chef John Fraser honors fresh, local ingredients with simple dishes that emphasize flavor over fuss. The pistachio crusted duck with daikon, water greens and sweet and sour plums is succulent and tangy with an even balance of salty and sweet, while the truffle gnocchi alongside Serrano ham and chanterelles is light and airy. Come for the famed Sunday

Suppa, an affordable prix fixe menu, or head down to the sherry cellar to watch the magic in the kitchen while you dine. The interior is sleek without being pretentious and modern without being uncomfortable. Brick columns and muslin-covered walls give the space a casual urban vibe, perfect for the Upper West Siders who frequent it.

Contemporary American. Dinner. $36-85

★★★★★JEAN GEORGES
1 Central Park West (near Columbus Circle), Upper West Side, 212-299-3900; www.jean-georges.com

So this is what fabulous looks and tastes like. The minimalist dining room is Grade-A sexy—it resembles an extra-large egg, thanks to the curved white seating, soft round lighting, pale white walls and sheer drapes. The soaring ceiling and windows and the dainty Spiegelau stemware contribute to the delicate, airy feeling, but that's as far as your attention will veer from the real star of the show: Jean-Georges Vongerichten's ethereal Asian-influenced French cuisine (roasted sweetbreads with pickled white asparagus and coriander; young garlic soup with frog's legs). Vongerichten is a master at layering flavor, making each bite a hit parade of taste—striking you first with smoky squab, chasing it with poignantly sweet summer peas, then following with a refreshing hint of peppermint. Savor his flawless technique in a three-course meal ($98) or a seven-course procession of signature dishes ($148). For a more casual rendezvous with Jean Georges' tantalizing cuisine, settle for a table at the outdoor Terrace or neighboring Nougatine.

French. Lunch (Monday-Friday), dinner. Closed Sunday. Reservations recommended. $86 and up

★★★★★MASA
Time Warner Center, 10 Columbus Circle, Upper West Side, 212-823-9800; www.masanyc.com

When you surrender this much cash (at least $450 a head—or more, depending upon availability of ingredients—before drinks and tip) and power (the chef decides what you'll eat), the food better be flawless. Luckily, chef Masa Takayama's creations are, and when you put yourself entirely in his expert hands, he'll regale you with an array of five to six appetizers, 20 to 25 different types of fresh seafood and a dessert course. The chef is infatuated with high-end, luxury ingredients such as truffles (white truffle tempura; black truffles on oysters), caviar (a generous scoop of which tops tuna belly), Ohmi beef and foie gras. Seafood is flown in daily from Japan. There are just 26 seats; ask if you can sit at the sushi counter, composed of a single slab of Japanese cypress Hinoki wood, so you can watch Takayama and his team of chefs at work.

Japanese. Lunch (Tuesday-Friday), dinner. Closed Sunday. Reservations recommended. $86 and up

★★★★★PER SE
Time Warner Center, 10 Columbus Circle, Upper West Side, 212-823-9335; www.perseny.com

Per Se bears the same blue front doors as French Laundry (its country cousin in Napa Valley) and has similar high-end flourishes like nine varieties of salt, plus chef Thomas Keller's legendary "oysters and pearls" dish of Island Creek oysters, creamy tapioca and caviar. But the 64-seat Per Se in the Time Warner Center, with its neutral brown palette and silver accents, feels more cosmopolitan and overtly ambitious in ways the pastoral French Laundry is not. Yet at its heart, Per Se offers the fine-dining indulgences fans worship Keller for (artisanal butter; a fierce focus on fresh ingredients), and it'll still take you five hours to stuff yourself silly on foie gras and truffles as a cavalcade of servers fawn over you. (The daily-changing nine-course tasting menu—vegetarian option available—is $275, and a $175 five-course lunch menu is available Friday through Sunday.) So what if the East Coast setting is a bit more buttoned-up? You won't miss the original a bit.

Contemporary American. Lunch (Friday-Sunday), dinner. Jacket required. Reservations recommended. $86 and up

★★★★PICHOLINE
35 W. 64th St., Upper West Side, 212-724-8585;
www.picholinenyc.com
Chef Terrance Brennan's French-Mediterranean cuisine continues to impress at Picholine, which opened in 1993 and seems to get more distinguished with age. The refined menu lacks the fussiness of some French restaurants—you

WHAT ARE THE BEST BARBECUE PLACES?
Hill Country
30 W. 26th St., 212-691-0507; www.hillcountryny.com
If you don't know where Hill Country is—think long horns and George W.—, you're sure to learn upon stepping inside this soaring Manhattan namesake. It is all about Texas barbecue here, where an enormous silver lone star hangs over the bar, photographs of deserted dusty roads decorate the walls and beef is what's for dinner (although you can get pork and chicken, too). Reminiscent of legendary Kreuz Market, Hill Country serves its dry-rubbed brisket, sausage and ribs by the pound cafeteria-style, each wrapped in authentic butcher paper. Opt for the marvelously tender brisket, choosing either lean or moist (fatty), and don't skimp on the sides. The sweet potato bourbon mash acts as a nice flavor contrast to the barbecue, while the green bean casserole ensures that you're getting your daily serving of greens. Two full bars and a live music stage draw a lively, and refreshingly casual, nightlife crowd for Chelsea.
Barbecue. Lunch, dinner. $16-35

Daisy May's
623 11th Ave., 212-977-1500; www.daisymaysbbq.com
After earning its stripes for it's affordable and juicy pulled pork sandwiches served fresh from a midtown lunch cart, Daisy May's has enjoyed rock star status in New York City's barbecue circuit. The counter service and cafeteria atmosphere of its Hell's Kitchen homebase may not seem like a huge step up from sidewalk service, but there is a certain charm to the place—Big Ten pennants, beer signs, counter service and all. Touting authentic Southern barbecue, the menu is a carnivore's dream. Stick to the specials: Oklahoma jumbo beef ribs, Kansas City sweet pork ribs, and beef brisket. Of course any self-respecting barbecue joint is just as serious about its sides as its meat. The brown sugar sweet potatoes are a dream. The prices have slowly risen in recent years, but so have the portion sizes. Worth its weight in barbecue sauce? You decide.
Barbecue. Lunch, dinner. $15 and under

WHAT ARE NEW YORK'S BEST BISTROS?

Artisanal Fromagerie & Bistro *(page 82)* Couples nibble on baskets of airy gougères at the bar while cheese-savvy servers hustle pots of gooey fondue to tightly packed wooden.

Balthazar *(page 62)* This warm, noisy French bistro is a transporting experience, from the sunshine-yellow walls to the European crowd devouring steak au poivre and duck confit.

Blue Ribbon Brasserie *(page 64)* Blue Ribbon is everything a good brasserie should be—woody and warm, with a menu that leans heavily on upgraded comfort classics like strip steak and fried chicken.

Locanda Verde *(page 80)* Located in the trendy Greenwich Hotel, Locanda Verde is a refreshingly casual and affordable eatery that offers crowd-pleasing specials such as buttermilk fried chicken.

The Red Cat *(page 56)* From the moment you enter the warm red and white dining room to the moment you leave feeling perfectly satisifed from your dinner of chicken with garlicky soy beans or steak and potatoes, you will be happy.

won't find overly rich sauces and heavy, buttery entrées here—but it doesn't skimp on elegance. The fare is simple, seasonally driven and clean in construction: Hearty rabbit comes with fresh tagliatelle and wild snails, while wild striped bass is served with corn chorizo and chanterelle escabéche. Pull up to the bar and try the cheese flights, which are organized by country of origin, and make a good pre- or post-theater treat. The service is poised in the windowless lavender dining room, which gets its sparkle from an enormous chandelier overhead.

French. Dinner. Closed Sunday-Monday. Reservations recommended. $86 and up

★★SARABETH'S

423 Amsterdam Ave., 212-496-6280; 1295 Madison Ave., Upper East Side, 212-410-7335; Whitney Museum of American Art, 945 Madison Ave., Upper East Side, 212-570-3670; 40 Central Park South, Midtown West, 212-826-5959; Lord & Taylor, 424 Fifth Ave., 212-827-5068; www.sarabeths.com

During the nearly inevitable hour-long wait for a table on Sunday mornings, you may wonder if pancakes and eggs are worth it. The answer? Absolutely. This brunch mainstay is favored by a J.Crew-clad, preppy set seeking otherworldly ricotta lemon pancakes and three-egg omelets in a faux-country setting. If you can't bear the wait, pick up a selection of scones, muffins and a jar of jewel-toned homemade jam (we like strawberry peach, mixed berry or plum cherry) from the bakery counter. Lunch and dinner offerings like chicken pot pie are just what you'd expect—hearty and homey.

American. Breakfast, lunch, dinner. Whitney Museum location: lunch only (closed Monday). Lord & Taylor location: lunch only. $16-35

THE GROCERY

★★TAVERN ON THE GREEN
Central Park West at 67th Street, Upper West Side, 212-873-3200;
www.tavernonthegreen.com
Tavern is a bit like the Hummer of restaurants—showy, too expensive and
a so-called remodeled classic that's really just a clunky novelty beneath
its shiny veneer. No amount of murals, over-the-top topiaries or twinkling
lights can disguise what can often be an uneven dining experience amid
mobs of tourists. That said, there will always be hordes of visitors revving up
their credit cards to enjoy pricey classics such as lobster bisque and prime
rib just for the privilege of eating in beautiful Central Park near the urban-
yet-bucolic Sheep Meadow. Afternoon tea service is a nice alternative to
the pomp and pageantry of dinner, and the warm scones with sweet jam
and Devonshire cream make an ideal four o'clock snack. At press time, the
future of the restaurant was uncertain. So call ahead before heading out.
*American. Lunch (Monday-Friday), dinner, Saturday-Sunday brunch.
Reservations recommended. $36-85*

HARLEM
★★★SYLVIA'S
328 Lenox Ave., Harlem, 212-996-0660; www.sylviasrestaurant.com
Critics may say that Sylvia's has lost some of its soul since it spawned
cookbooks and a line of food products including canned black-eyed peas
and jarred "Sassy Sauce." But this legendary Harlem soul-food eatery—which
Sylvia Woods opened with her husband Herbert in 1962 in a luncheonette
where she had formerly waitressed—is still a go-to spot for everything fried,
smothered and sauced in the Southern comfort tradition. All of the usual
faves are here: catfish, chicken livers, ribs, waffles and fried chicken, grits,
collard greens, coconut cake, banana pudding—we could go on. President
Barack Obama has been seen dropping in for fried chicken, as has former
President Bill Clinton. Don't miss the Sunday gospel brunch; you'll leave with
a spring in your step and your belly full.

American, Southern. Breakfast, lunch (Monday-Saturday), dinner, Sunday brunch. $16-35

BROOKLYN

★★AL DI LÀ

248 Fifth Ave., Park Slope, Brooklyn, 718-783-4565;
www.aldilatrattoria.com

Past the crush of hungry waiting diners and thick velvet drapes at the door lies a cozy dining room where a glassy chandelier suspends from the ceiling. You'll think you can hear gondoliers singing outside when you tuck into the authentic Northern Italian dishes like creamy cuttlefish risotto, braised rabbit and pillowy squash ravioli sautéed in brown butter and sage. Years of positive reviews and a no-reservations policy create painfully long waits on weekends, but the restaurant's wine bar around the corner is a colorful and comfortable spot to happily spend your wait.

Northern Italian. Dinner. Closed Tuesday. $36-85

★GRIMALDI'S PIZZERIA

19 Old Fulton St., Dumbo, Brooklyn, 718-858-4300;
www.grimaldispizza.com

If the line snaking down the sidewalk for a red-and-white-checkered-table cloth-topped table doesn't tip you off, then we'll spell it out: The coal-oven pizzas here are sublime, from the creamy ricotta cheese topping down to the blistered crust underneath. A large pie is just $15 and toppings add a few dollars more, so if you can't get a table, order one to go—this pizza tastes just as good when you're eating it sitting on the stoop outside. Grimaldi's is near the base of the Brooklyn Bridge, in fashionable Dumbo, making the walk over the bridge and back to Manhattan easy as pie.

Pizza. Lunch, dinner. $15 and under.

★★★THE GROCERY

288 Smith St., Carroll Gardens, Brooklyn, 718-596-3335;
www.thegroceryrestaurant.com

Located about 20 minutes from Manhattan in this pretty Brooklyn neighborhood, the Grocery is an unassuming-yet-overachieving eatery specializing in exceptional farmers market fare (roasted beets with goat cheese ravioli, slow-rendered duck breast with kasha) churned out by chefs Charles Kiely and Sharon Pachter, a low-key husband-and-wife team. The 30-seat restaurant feels quaint—with the chefs sometimes even serving the food. There's a positively lovely garden out back and sage-green walls inside, so anywhere you dine is a delight. But the prices ($130 for a six-course tasting menu with wine) remind you that Brooklyn is just a stone's throw from Manhattan.

Contemporary American. Dinner. Closed Sunday-Monday. $16-35

★★MOTORINO

319 Graham Ave., Williamsburg, Brooklyn, 718-599-8899;
www.motorinopizza.com

Located on a quiet neighborhood street in Williamsburg, Brooklyn, Motorino has a lot of things going for it. The lines are never too long, the service is friendly and the atmosphere is casual and fun. The outdoor garden is tight, but a nice alternative to the dining room, which can get toasty thanks to an outdated air conditioning unit. The menu includes salads, cured meats and

an impressive selection of cheeses, but you're just as well skipping straight to those steaming Neapolitan pies. Purists will enjoy the simple goodness of the margherita, though the crust can edge on charred. The soppressata piccante is another good choice with tomatoes, spicy soppressata, garlic and chili oil. The dessert offerings are limited, but the gelati works wonders to soothe the roofs of any burnt mouths (especially the coconut).
Italian. Lunch, dinner. $16-$35

★★★PETER LUGER STEAK HOUSE
178 Broadway, Williamsburg, Brooklyn, 718-387-7400;
www.peterluger.com
Just over the East River in a somewhat-sketchy part of Brooklyn near the Williamsburg Bridge is the legendary Peter Luger's, whose dining room can only be described as beer-hall chic—weathered wooden tables, a few beer steins on the shelves and somewhat surly servers who seem like they've been here since the restaurant opened in 1887. The Forman family, which owns the venerable steakhouse, personally selects the prime beef and then dry ages it onsite, resulting in tasty cuts that go unrivaled by other steakhouses. Our advice: Skip the menu and simply explain whether you want steak for one, for two and so on. Sides are simple classics, like German fried potatoes and creamed spinach, intended to keep the buttery broiled porterhouse the deserved star of the meal. Unless you have a Peter Luger credit card (apply online at the restaurant's Web site), you must pay cash or risk the wrath of a crusty, bow-tied waiter.
Steak. Lunch, dinner. $36-85

WHERE TO STAY

NEW YORK CITY ★ WHERE TO STAY

SLEEP AND THE CITY

New York City may never sleep, but at some point, you have to. You'll find everything from white glove butler service to cutting edge interior design at New York's
hundreds of hotels, which means you can choose one that seems almost tailor
made for your tastes. Rooms in Manhattan might be small, and bathrooms even
smaller, but this city also has some of the most storied, trend-setting, luxurious
hotels in the world. Who hasn't dreamed of living at The Plaza (like Eloise) or
thirsted to mingle with the in-crowd in one of the city's top hotels? Just try to get
at least some sleep while you're in town.

EAST VILLAGE/LOWER EAST SIDE
★★★THE BOWERY HOTEL
335 Bowery, East Village, 212-505-9100; www.theboweryhotel.com

This boutique spot in the Bowery—an area once home to legendary punk bar
CBGB and long known for being more gritty than pretty—embodies the area's
continuing gentrification. A short walk from Nolita, the East Village, Lower
East Side and Soho, the latest venture for hoteliers Eric Goode and Sean
MacPherson (Waverly Inn, Maritime Hotel), has a dimly lit lobby with leather-
and velvet-upholstered furniture that feels old and cozy, minus any mustiness.
The lounge, with its velvet banquettes, dark wood walls and fireplace, draws
a cocktail-seeking crowd as do the outdoor patio and small back bar known
for its absinthe-based concoctions. Guest suites have wood-slatted floors,
marble bathrooms and floor-to-ceiling paned factory windows that overlook
the neighboring tenements just to remind you that—despite the HD television, iPod stereo system and docking station, this isn't the Upper West Side.
The location may be too rough around the edges for some, but the beautiful
lounges, rustic restaurant and free copies of the *New York Post* will make you
feel right at home.
135 rooms. Restaurant, bar. Business center. Pets accepted. $351 and up

★★★HOTEL ON RIVINGTON
107 Rivington St., Lower East Side, 212-475-2600;
www.hotelonrivington.com

The super-modern steel-and-glass Hotel On Rivington offers 21 stories of hip
and luxurious guest rooms. All have floor-to-ceiling windows for sweeping
Manhattan views, and most include balconies. Sensuous details range from
velvet sofas and chairs in the living spaces, bathrooms constructed with glitzy
Bisazza tiles and glass-enclosed showers with skyline views, to Swedish
Tempur-Pedic mattresses and Frette linens. The hotel sits in the heart of
the rapidly gentrifying Lower East Side, where there's no shortage of trendy
boutiques, hip restaurants and popular local watering holes, including the
1,500-square-foot onsite lounge, 105 Riv.
*110 rooms. Complimentary breakfast. Restaurant, bar. Fitness center. Business
center. Pets accepted. $351 and up*

FINANCIAL DISTRICT/BATTERY PARK CITY
★★★MILLENIUM HILTON
55 Church St., Financial District, 212-693-2001; www.hilton.com

This Financial District hotel is a good choice for business travelers who need
proximity to Wall Street as well as vacationers who want to be near popular
spots like Battery Park, Greenwich Village, Tribeca and Soho. The ho-hum

WHAT ARE THE MOST LUXURIOUS HOTELS?

The St. Regis New York *(page 110)* For over-the-top pampering and white glove servce, this Fifth Avenue hotel is the one to choose.

Mandarin Oriental, New York *(page 118)* If you crave luxury but prefer your surroundings on the sleek side rather than stuffy, this modern tower rising over Central Park delivers top-notch service with Asian flair. This super chic addition to the luxury hotel landscape in New York has jaw-dropping views, super-luxe amenities and a convenient location in Columbus Circle.

The Peninsula New York *(page 109)* A new Shanghai-style rooftop bar and gorgeously revamped spa up the luxury factor at this New York standby. But it's the personalized service (you might find yourself wondering how everyone from the doorman to the waiter at breakfast knows you by name) that makes a stay here special.

The Ritz-Carlton New York, Central Park *(page 109)* Probably one of the best Ritz-Carlton hotels anywhere, this Uptown classic whispers luxury, with its exclusive, formal butler service available to cater to whatever you need, whenever you need it. Rooms are bathed in buttery tones and luxe touches such as cashmere throws.

guestrooms in the 55-story skyscraper aren't anything special in terms of décor, but they do have 42-inch flat-screen televisions, high-speed Internet access, personalized voicemail and Hilton's "Serenity Bed" with plush down pillows. Request a room with views of the Statue of Liberty or East River, with its iconic bridges. Fitness facilities are top-notch and include a heated indoor pool.

569 rooms. Restaurant, bar. Fitness center. Pool. Business center. Pets accepted. $351 and up

★★★NEW YORK MARRIOTT DOWNTOWN
85 West St., Financial District, 212-385-4900;
www.marriott.com

This Financial District hotel has great access to Wall Street, and the South Street Seaport. Guest rooms in the 38-floor building were renovated in spring 2008, and include 32-inch flat-screen TVs, marble bathrooms, beds with 300-thread-count linens and down comforters. There's an indoor pool, too, but be sure to request the hotel's best perk, if it's available: a room with a view of New York Harbor and the Statue of Liberty.

497 rooms. Restaurant, bar. Fitness center. Pool. $351 and up

★★★★THE RITZ-CARLTON, BATTERY PARK
2 West St., Battery Park, 212-344-0800; www.ritzcarlton.com

Top-notch views of the Statue of Liberty, Ellis Island, New York Harbor and the downtown skyline make the Ritz's quieter downtown, waterfront location on the southwestern tip of Manhattan a great excuse to avoid the chaotic Midtown hotel scene. Harborside rooms are equipped with telescopes, and all the rooms have the typically plush Ritz-style amenities. Bulgari toiletries are in the marble bathrooms, and feather-beds come with 400-thread-count Frette linens, feather duvets and goose-down pillows. If that's not enough to lull you to sleep, a deep-tissue or hot-stone massage at the Prada Beauty Spa should do the trick.

MANDARIN ORIENTAL, NEW YORK

298 rooms. Restaurant, bar. Fitness center. Spa. Business center. Pets accepted. $351 and up

GREENWICH VILLAGE/SOHO/WEST VILLAGE

★★★60 THOMPSON

60 Thompson St., Soho, 877-431-0400; www.60thompson.com

Beautiful is the operative term here. Opened in 2001, this boutique hotel's clientele and staff are just as attractive and stylish as the trendy rooms designed by Thomas O'Brien and Aero Studios. Sferra linens cover the dark-wood beds, products by Fresh stock the marble bathrooms and gourmet Dean & DeLuca goods fill the mini-bars. To top it all off, literally, the A60 rooftop lounge—with great downtown views that include water-tower topped lofts and the distant Empire State Building—is open only to members and hotel guests. More exclusive still is the "Thompson Loft"—a two-story penthouse with a marble fireplace and its own private rooftop terrace. Privacy in New York—now that's a beautiful thing.

100 rooms. Restaurant, bar. Fitness center. $351 and up

★★★THE MERCER

147 Mercer St., Soho, 212-966-6060; www.mercerhotel.com

Housed in a landmark Romanesque revival building, this is a see-and-be-seen hotel that's all about modern luxury. All rooms have sleek Christian Liaigre interiors that artfully mix soothing neutral colors, hardwood floors and rich materials like leather upholstery and 400-count Egyptian-cotton linens. Bathrooms are just as inviting, with oversized marble tubs big enough for two and bath products from Swedish company FACE. Too tired to unpack? No problem—the staff can take care of that. Need a private trainer or an in-room massage? They've got that (and plenty of other personalized services) available, too. If all that weren't enough, Jean-Georges Vongerichten's American-Provençal restaurant, Mercer Kitchen, is onsite.

75 rooms. Restaurant, bar. $351 and up

★★★SOHO GRAND HOTEL
310 West Broadway, Soho, 212-965-3000; www.sohogrand.com

Still one of just a handful of hotels in Soho, this property was the first to open in the neighborhood in more than a century when it came on the scene in 1996, and it has been a hipster mainstay ever since. The lobby's glass-bottle-paved staircase, cast-iron accents and concrete pillars were designed by William Sofield to mimic the neighborhood's characteristic warehouse lofts. Rooms are downtown-chic, with walls of massive windows, neutral color schemes, leather touches, iPod docks and even a pet goldfish upon request. You can bring along your cat or dog, too—the hotel is owned by pet-products company Hartz Mountain Industries, and offers everything from room service for your pet to on-call veterinarians and even a special pet-limo service. The hotel's Grand Bar & Lounge (a.k.a. "Soho's Living Room") is a good place to start exploring New York nightlife—it has long been popular with both New York's celeb set (Uma Thurman, Kevin Spacey and Heidi Klum) and out-of-towners. The adjoining Yard, open May through September, is a great place to get margaritas and light summer fare under the city sky.

363 rooms. Restaurant, bar. Fitness center. Business center. $351 and up

★★★THE STANDARD
848 Washington St., Meatpacking District, 212-645-4646; www.standardhotels.com/new-york-city

Possibly one of the last new hotels to open before 2009's recession put a stop to new building construction in New York, the Standard, sister to L.A.'s sleek and modern boutique hotel, made its way east last year to New York's Meatpacking District. The hotel resides in two newly constructed Modernist towers that literally straddle one of New York's greatest new attractions, the High Line elevated parkway. The same sleek, spare and stylish design seen in Andre Balazs's other properties can be seen here, with rooms featuring minimalist furnishings, luxury linens and spacious baths, and cutting edge tech toys such as oversized high-def TVs and iPod-friendly sound systems. The fully stocked gym is open 24 hours, and the onsite restaurant, the Standard Grill serves bistro favorites late into the night.

337 rooms. Restaurant, bar. Fitness center. $251-350

JUST OPENED
CROSBY STREET HOTEL
79 Crosby St., Soho, 212-226-6400; www.firmdale.com

Opened in fall 2009, this boutique hotel is the first U.S. offering by British hoteliers Tim and Kit Kemp, whose six London hostelries are known for their style and intimate scales. This Stateside version boasts the same eclectic English country-meets-modernist design as its London sisters (think layers and layers of fabrics and textures). It also boasts a 90-seat screening room, ample fitness room and the spacious street-level Crosby Bar. Rooms are cozy and colorful, with flat-screen TVs, iPod docking stations and marble bathrooms.

86 rooms. Bar. Fitness center. $351 and up

MIDTOWN/MIDTOWN EAST
★★★THE ALEX HOTEL
205 E. 45th St., Midtown East, 212-867-5100; www.thealexhotel.com

This 33-story hotel near the Chrysler Building whisks you away from New York's constant bustle to a serene oasis where David Rockwell's minimalist décor proves instantly soothing. Clutter-free guest rooms are awash in a palette of whites, creams and earth tones, while limestone bathrooms have Frette towels and products by Frédéric Fekkai. If you have to stay in the city for more than a quick visit—or just hate to say goodbye—extended-stay suites make your time here comfortable with luxury Poggenpohl-fitted kitchens sporting everything from Sub-Zero refrigerators to Miele dishwashers.

203 rooms. Restaurant, bar. Fitness center. Business center. Pets accepted. $351 and up

★★ALGONQUIN HOTEL
59 W. 44th St., Midtown, 212-840-6800; www.algonquinhotel.com

Since 1902 the Algonquin has been popular with theatrical and literary glitterati, most notably members of the legendary Round Table luncheons: The exclusive group of creative types, including Dorothy Parker, Edna Ferber and Harpo Marx, met at the hotel almost daily during the decade following World War II to exchange ideas and barbs (financing for *The New Yorker* magazine was secured here). Today, it's still loaded with character, from the antique furniture to its most popular current resident, Matilda the cat—the latest in a long line of felines that have called the hotel home since a wayward feline first wandered in and ended up staying in the 1930s. Rooms have recently been remodeled and include comfortable pillow-top beds, duvets and modern amenities like flat-screen TVs. For a special treat, make a reservation for dinner and a cabaret show at the famous Oak Room Supper Club, the hotel's dark-wood paneled restaurant where crooners like Harry Connick, Jr. and Diana Krall got their starts.

174 rooms. Restaurant, bar. Fitness center. Pets accepted. $251-350

★★★BRYANT PARK HOTEL
40 W. 40th St., Midtown, 212-869-0100; www.bryantparkhotel.com

For years, this hotel has attracted a who's-who list of designers, media bigwigs and celebs during New York's Fall and Spring Fashion Weeks, thanks to its proximity to the tents erected to host the runway shows across the street. The shows are moving to Lincoln Center this year, but no matter: many of the same fashionistas frequent this boutique property all year round anyway. They enjoy the amenities in the mod rooms (leather chairs, Tibetan rugs and Travertine marble bathrooms) such as high-definition flat-screen televisions, BOSE Wave music systems and Obus Forme sound therapy machines which

---

WHICH HOTELS HAVE THE BEST VIEWS?

Mandarin Oriental, New York *(page 118)* Occupying the top floors of the Time Warner Center in Columbus Circle, you can see almost all of Central Park from the beautiful Asian-inspired rooms. Be sure to ask for an east-facing room on a high floor to get the best possible vistas.

The Ritz-Carlton, Battery Park *(page 98)* You have no chance of forgetting where you are when you wake up to views of the Statue of Liberty and Ellis Island. This downtown hotel delivers, with floor-to-ceiling views of the harbor and beyond.

Trump International Hotel & Tower New York *(page 119)* No other building stands in the way of Trump New York and its location directly overlooking Central Park, and no other New York hotel delivers so spectacularly with its vistas. Because the hotel is housed in a modern tower, each room has floor-to-ceiling windows to make the most of those views.

FOUR SEASONS HOTEL NEW YORK

lull them to sleep with gentle waterfall sounds and wakes them with chirping birds. There's also a loft meeting space that's popular for sample sales, a 70-seat theater-style screening room and "entertainment planner" (really just a clever title for the concierge) at guests' disposal. Japanese restaurant Koi and the large underground Cellar Bar are always packed with the young and fashionable. Book one of the 10 rooms that face the park—these come with terraces to enjoy the lovely views and all the activity that is always going on in Bryant Park.

129 rooms. Restaurant, bar. Fitness center. $351 and up

★★★THE CARLTON ON MADISON AVENUE
88 Madison Ave., Midtown, 212-532-4100; www.carltonhotelny.com
It wasn't long ago that this now-stunning 1904 Beaux Arts building was a run down property that seemed destined for decay. But a $60 million, five-year renovation project headed by architect David Rock-well breathed brand-new life into the hotel. Today, the three-story lobby and lounge areas are bathed in opulent golds and creams, and the sound of the cascading waterfall here serves as a soothing background soundtrack. Rooms are all about what's plush and new, with Frette bedding, free wireless, and iHome systems. Preserving the hotel's original décor is important, too: An ornate 28-foot Tiffany stained-glass dome, discovered during renovations under such thick layers of dirt and tobacco tar that it was thought to be painted black, has been restored. The main downside: no spa or fitness center.

316 rooms. Restaurant, bar. Business center. Pets accepted. $351 and up

★★★CHAMBERS HOTEL
15 W. 56th St., Midtown, 212-974-5656; www.chambershotel.com
From the large front door made from woven walnut wood to the more than 500 pieces of artwork by everyone from John Waters to Do-Ho Suh, the Chambers Hotel feels like a chic downtown gallery that's plopped down into the middle of New York's Midtown retail hub. In addition to the paintings that line the walls of the guest rooms, hallways and other public spaces, the hotel uses

WHICH HOTELS HAVE THE BEST ROOFTOP BARS?

60 Thompson *(page 99)* A stay here gets you private access to the super-exclusive Morroccan-inspired rooftop bar a60. The downtown views and celeb spottings will make you want to linger.

Dream Hotel New York *(page 103)* Step out onto the terrace at this swank cocktail lounge and you get a magnificent view of Times Square.

The Peninsula New York *(page 109)* Having a drink at Salon de Ning is like stepping back into 1930s Shanghai, except that you're overlooking Fifth Avenue. The concept recreates the look and feel of a socialite of that era's personal salon, including ladylike libations such as the "Ning Sling", made with lychee and passion fruit juices.

WHICH HOTELS ARE BEST FOR A LIVELY SCENE?

Bryant Park Hotel *(page 101)* The fashion crowd comes here to visit the onsite loft that is frequently used for sample sales; a screening room, and 24-hour gym provide plenty of non-shopping options.

The Mercer *(page 99)* The Mercer is a home away from home for celebrities and trendsetters (Marc Jacobs has a regular room). Jean-Georges Vongerichten's Mercer Kitchen also draws an A-list.

Soho Grand Hotel *(page 100)* NYC's glamorous set can be seen lounging in the Grand Bar & Lounge, otherwise known as "Soho's Living Room."

Gramercy Park Hotel *(page 114)* In the '70s, this hotel was the preferred address of visiting rock stars. The recent Ian Schrager-led renovation smartened up the place and stayed true to its roots with décor by artist Julien Schnabel and art by Andy Warhol. The Rose Bar maintains a tough-to-cross velvet rope and sexy cocktail hour crowd.

warm shades of brown throughout, and the rooms have a loft-like feel with large windows, sleek furniture and mini-bars stocked with Dean and Deluca goods. Massage therapists, babysitters and even personal shoppers from Henri Bendel are a phone call away.

77 rooms. Restaurant, bar. Pets accepted. $351 and up

★★★DREAM HOTEL NEW YORK

210 W. 55th St., Midtown, 212-247-2000, 866-437-3266; www.dreamny.com
Vikram Chatwal, the brains behind Time Hotel, turned the former Majestic Hotel into this slumber-themed property in 2004. You'll feel like you've walked into a trippy dream the moment you hit the lobby, where a two-story aquarium and gold Catherine the Great statue are part of the eclectic design mix. The restaurant here is an outpost of the Serafina chain of northern Italian spots known all over town for their specialty pizzas. An Ayurvedic spa was designed by Deepak Chopra to allow guests to massage and meditate their way to peacefulness before turning in for the night in the minimalist rooms, outfitted with feather beds and 300 thread-count Egyptian sheets, and awash in blue lights that create a twilight feel. If a nightcap is more your style, take the elevator up to the Ava Lounge, which offers a seasonal rooftop garden that sits high above the city with views of Times Square and Columbus Circle.

220 rooms. Restaurant, bar. Fitness center. Spa. Pets accepted. $351 and up

TRUMP INTERNATIONAL HOTEL & TOWER

★★★DYLAN HOTEL

52 E. 41st St., Midtown, 212-338-0500; www.dylanhotel.com

This 16-story 1903 Beaux Arts structure was once home to the Chemist's Club of New York, which explains the insignia over the stone entryway. The microscopes and test tubes are long gone, but designer Jeffrey Beers experiments with amber lightboxes suspended from the lobby ceiling, and in a nod to its origins, the hotel provides beakers in place of bathroom cups. Rooms are open and airy spaces, with 11-foot ceilings and large windows, and accented with a mix of muted shades, jewel-toned materials and American walnut furniture; bathrooms are outfitted with Carrara marble. If you're feeling experimental, check yourself into the Alchemy Suite, which was once a Gothic chamber created to replicate a medieval alchemist's lab. It still has the original stained-glass windows and vaulted ceilings.

107 rooms. Restaurant, bar. Fitness center. Business center. $351 and up

★★★★★FOUR SEASONS HOTEL NEW YORK

57 E. 57th St., Midtown East, 212-758-5700; www.fourseasons.com

Well-heeled travelers kick off their shoes in the 52-story Midtown outpost of this luxe hotel chain, appropriately located steps from shopping-mecca Fifth Avenue. Designed by I.M. Pei, its jaw-dropper is the 33-foot-high backlit onyx ceiling in the lobby (which led Jacqueline Kennedy Onassis to nickname it "The Cathedral.") Sweeping views of Central Park and other parts of the city are part of the allure of the guest rooms, which range in size from 500 to 800 square feet—larger than many New York City apartments—with roomy seating areas (some have furnished terraces, too). Other treats include big marble bathrooms with soaking tubs, and silk drapes that you can control bedside to open or close on those views. Plenty of celebrities have stayed here because they can't get enough of the Four Seasons' signature top-notch service, luxurious spa and fine dining establishments, including L'Atelier de Joël Rubuchon *(page 74)*.

368 rooms. Restaurant, bar. Fitness center. Spa. Business center. Pets accepted. $351 and up

WHAT ARE NEW YORK'S TOP BOUTIQUE HOTELS?

60 Thompson *(page 99)* This fashionable property's clientele and staff are just as beautiful and stylish as the rooms designed by Thomas O'Brien. The Soho location is steps from some of the city's best shopping, and the rooftop bar is still a stylish place for cocktails.

The Bowery Hotel *(page 97)* It may be located on the gritty Lower East Side, but gorgeous Old World décor and excellent bar areas make this boutique hotel one of the best recent additions to the city.

The Greenwich Hotel *(page 113)* Each of the 88 guest rooms here is unique, and adorned with global influences such as Parisian antiques, Moroccan tilework, Tibetan rugs and repurposed Japanese lumber.

Royalton Hotel *(page 110)* These days, boutique hotels are as ubiquitous as Best Westerns. The Royalton was the first, and it's still as cool as ever—a renovation in 2009 gave the space rich, dark and clubby décor and tech toys such as high-def plasma TVs.

WHICH HOTELS ARE BEST FOR FAMILIES?

Hotel Beacon *(page 117)* This former apartment building has spacious rooms with kitchenettes (suites have sofa beds) and its location near Central Park and the American Museum of Natural History makes it easy to explore the city's attractions.

The New York Palace *(page 108)* Parents with daughters know that a visit to American Girl Place, the multi-storied doll emporium, is a New York City must-see. The New York Palace offers one of the closest locations to the Fifth Avenue store, and makes the most of it with special rates for American Girl fans, as well as complimentary beds for the dolls and custom-made chocolate lollipops for their owners.

★★★HOTEL ELYSÉE
60 E. 54th St., Midtown, 212-753-1066; www.elyseehotel.com
Built in 1926 and named after one of the best French restaurants of that time, the Hotel Elysée combines the charm of an intimate bed and breakfast with the service and style of an upscale boutique hotel. The lobby is elegantly decked out with marble floors and mahogany walls, while the guest rooms are styled in French country décor. Stop by the Club Room for complimentary wine and hors d'oeuvres on weekday evenings and pick up free daily guest passes to the local branch of New York Sports Club at the front desk. Be sure to check out the famous Monkey Bar, littered with statues, pictures and paintings of its name-sake animal. It was once a haunt for celebs like Ava Gardner, Marlon Brando and 15-year hotel resident Tennessee Williams, who lived here until his death in 1983.
103 rooms. Complimentary breakfast. Restaurant. Business center. $351 and up

★★★HÔTEL PLAZA ATHÉNÉE
37 E. 64th St., Midtown East, 212-734-9100; www.plaza-athenee.com
The Hôtel Plaza Athénée sits on a strip of prime real estate in Manhattan: a tranquil, tree-lined street just a few blocks from Central Park. The lobby is awash in marble and crystal, but also has a modern feel thanks to wireless Internet access. Rooms have rich cherry furniture and jewel-toned color schemes like maroon and gold, plus nice extras such as Belgian linens and

complimentary morning coffee. Some suites boast indoor atriums and outdoor balconies. The nearly 2,449-square-foot Penthouse Duplex suite on the 16th and 17th floors includes two bedrooms, a decorative fireplace, formal dining for 12 and a private terrace running half the hotel's length. If that's your style, you'll probably also love that Barneys New York and the other high-end shops along Fifth Avenue are just steps away.

149 rooms. Restaurant, bar. Fitness center. Business center. Pets accepted. $351 and up

★★HOTEL ROGER WILLIAMS

131 Madison Ave., Midtown, 212-448-7000; www.hotelrogerwilliams.com
The name's a bit lackluster, but we can assure you that there's nothing drab about this recentlly renovated 16-story hotel named for Rhode Island's founder. The modern rooms range from the simple, single-bed superior rooms and Japanese-inspired doubles where furnishings include shoji screens, to garden terrace rooms that have landscaped patios and great city views. All have special touches, whether it's a colorful quilt on the bed or a bright-blue armchair and orange bench in the corner. The unique Help Yourself Breakfast Pantry is a casual, buffet-style service where you can choose from New York specialties like croissants from Balthazar, bagels from H&H or just a complimentary newspaper in the morning. The Mezzanine Lounge is a little more formal, with a menu that changes as the day progresses.

193 rooms. Complimentary breakfast. Restaurant, bar. Fitness center. Business center. $251-350

★★★JUMEIRAH ESSEX HOUSE ON CENTRAL PARK

160 Central Park South, Midtown, 212-247-0300;
www.jumeirahessexhouse.com
Opened in 1931, this landmark hotel sits on Central Park and recently underwent a two-year, $90 million refurbishment. Rooms come with custom-designed furniture and other special touches including amber-colored glass sinks, red leather-framed mirrors and wall-to-wall cabinetry for extra storage space. Not everything is a throwback to the mid-20th century, however. Modern touches include touchscreen controls for lighting and music, flat-panel TVs and lighted footpaths to the bathrooms. If you're in need of a little restoration of your own, the in-house spa features a steam bath, sauna and a host of treatments like massages and facials.

515 rooms. Restaurant, bar. Fitness center. Spa. Pets accepted. $351 and up

★★★LE PARKER MERIDIEN

118 W. 57th St., Midtown, 212-245-5000; www.parkermeridien.com
Business-minded types will appreciate the ergonomic touches at this Midtown hotel: built-in 6-foot-long workstations with adjustable Herman Miller Aeron chairs, 32-inch TVs set back in swiveling consoles and roll-away storage compartments for luggage. Junior suites add luxury in the form of two-person, cedar-lined baths and showers. There's a weight room, and both basketball and racquetball courts, but it's the rooftop pool that's a longtime-favorite of locals and tourists alike. Same goes for Norma's, one of three onsite restaurants, which caters to a mix of natives and visitors with popular breakfast items including the "Zillion Dollar Lobster Frittata" and "Artychoked Benedict." The hotel is also famous for it's excellent burger joint *(page 78)*.

731 rooms. Restaurant. Fitness center. Pool. Business center. Pets accepted. $351 and up

★★★LIBRARY HOTEL
299 Madison Ave., Midtown, 212-983-4500; www.libraryhotel.com

Bookworms will get a kick out of this concept hotel, located steps from the New York Public and Pierpont Morgan Libraries on what's known as "Library Way." Rooms are identified by one of 10 Dewey Decimal System categories, and 6,000-plus books are shelved throughout the hotel. Whether you're mad for math or hungry for literature, you can choose a room based on more than 60 themes. The rooms are pleasantly unstuffy, thanks to a décor that's heavy on creams, whites and other light colors. Social readers should check out the mahogany-paneled Writers' Den, which has a cozy fireplace and greenhouse.
60 rooms. Complimentary breakfast. Restaurant, bar. $251-350

★★★THE LONDON NYC
151 W. 54th St., Midtown, 212-307-5000; www.thelondonnyc.com

Anglophiles will love this Midtown luxury hotel which offers the finest elements of British sophistication and understatement. The 500-square-foot London Suites, with bed chamber and separate parlor, were conceptualized by British interior architect David Collins, and are decorated with parquet flooring, custom-woven banquettes and embossed-leather desks, plus tech pleasures like iHome players and Mitel touchscreen phones. If the biggest and best is what you're after, book the 2,500-square-foot penthouse, which is spread out on two floors with 180-degree views that include Central Park and the George Washington Bridge. It also offers a dining room that seats eight and access to the Chef's Table in the hot-and-hyped onsite restaurant Gordon Ramsay at the London *(page 74)*. The hotel partners with Quintessentially, a luxury concierge service famous for pulling strings and doing the impossible, like scoring same-night seats to the most popular Broadway shows or chartering a private jet on a moment's notice. If you'd rather stay in, calls across the pond are on the house eight hours a day.
561 rooms. Restaurant, bar. Fitness center. Business center. $351 and up

★★MANSFIELD
12 W. 44th St., Midtown, 212-277-8700; www.mansfieldhotel.com

In contrast to the elegant, classic lobby with its original fireplaces, the small rooms at the century-old Mansfield are decidedly modern thanks to recent re-dos. The ebony-stained hardwood floors are complemented by shades of white and tan throughout the spaces. Comfortable beds have pillow-top mattresses and 300-count linens, while bathrooms are stocked with Aveda products. You won't get much in the way of views here, but you'll find comfort in the hotel's M Bar—an intimate lounge with a domed skylight and mahogany bookshelves, as well as the beautifully restored Beaux Arts library, where you can kick back with a book or chess match by the fire. If you can't sleep or just need a quick pick-me-up, there's complimentary cappuccino, espresso, coffee and tea service around the clock in the lobby.
126 rooms. Bar. Fitness center. Business center. Pets accepted. $351 and up

★★★MILLENNIUM U.N. PLAZA HOTEL
1 United Nations Plaza, Midtown East, 212-758-1234;
www.millenniumhotels.com

Diplomats, business travelers and a few guests from the *Rachael Ray* show (the show's official hotel) all find something to like about this Midtown East hotel located next to the United Nations. Plenty of meeting and banquet space is available, including a fitness center, pool and even indoor tennis courts. The

THE PENINSULA NEW YORK

rooms are sparsely decorated and have a calm, neutral pallete, allowing the sweeping views of the U.N. and the rest of the city to take center stage instead. Unbothered by looming skyscraper neighbors (guest rooms start on the 28th floor), the hotel has some of the best panoramic views of the city—making the rooms feel more like private penthouses than part of a hotel. The only con here: The property is pretty far east, so you'll have to walk several avenues over to catch the subway at Grand Central Station.

427 rooms. Restaurant, bar. Fitness center. Pool. Business center. Pets accepted. Tennis. $251-350

★★★★THE NEW YORK PALACE
455 Madison Ave., Midtown East, 212-888-7000;
www.newyorkpalace.com
The moment you step through the Madison Avenue gates of the Villard Mansion and walk down the grand staircase, this hotel's motto, "Old World Elegance—New World Opulence," clicks into place. First built as a luxury apartment building in 1882, the structure was transformed into a hotel in 1980. The spacious and sumptuously appointed rooms throughout the 55-story tower include marble bathrooms, comfortable seating, work desks and large cozy beds. If you're looking to splurge, Triplex Suites are up to 5,000 square feet and boast Art Deco décor and unforgettable views from their 18-foot windows and private rooftop terraces.

892 rooms. Restaurant, bar. Fitness center. Spa. Business center. Pets accepted. $351 and up

★★★OMNI BERKSHIRE PLACE
21 E. 52nd St., Midtown, 212-753-5800; www.omnihotels.com
Pillow-top mattresses and feather pillows in all the rooms should make it easy to get a good night's sleep amid the never-ending frenzy outside this Midtown luxury hotel. Rooms range in size from a 271-square-foot deluxe—with options for one king-size or two double beds up to the 1,000-square-foot Rodgers &

Hammerstein Suite, lavishly appointed with a wraparound terrace, fireplace and spa tub. There's also a sundeck and fitness center on the 17th floor.
396 rooms. Restaurant, bar. Fitness center. Pets accepted. $351 and up

★★★★★THE PENINSULA NEW YORK
700 Fifth Ave., Midtown East, 212-956-2888;
www.newyork.peninsula.com

Rising 23 stories above some of the best shopping in New York, the Peninsula's Midtown location in the middle of Fifth Avenue is a shopaholic's dream. The Beaux Arts building was completed in 1905 and has luxurious, bright guest-rooms with large windows and simple, contemporary furnishings that give nods to the chain's Asian roots with details like lacquered dressers and armoires. Tech-types get their due, too: Bedside controls mean you don't have to move to manage your music, temperature and lighting settings, and flat-screen TVs and speaker phones are within reach of the bathtubs. The hotel's library-like Gotham Lounge serves afternoon tea, which includes a selection of finger sandwiches such as smoked salmon and egg salad. For a spicier cocktail, head to the rooftop lounge Salon de Ning where 1930's Shanghai meets Midtown Manhattan in an exotic blend of pillow-strewn chaises, potent potables and Asian-influenced appetizers. The Peninsula Spa by ESPA continues the Far East theme with rich bamboo floors and orchid arrangements aplenty. Don't forget your swim suit; the glass-enclosed rooftop pool is ideal for an evening dip amidst the city skyline.
239 rooms. Restaurant, bar. Fitness center. Pool. Spa. Business center. $351 and up

★★★★★THE RITZ-CARLTON NEW YORK, CENTRAL PARK
50 Central Park South, Midtown, 212-308-9100; www.ritzcarlton.com

The Ritz is all about, well, being ritzy. This link in the exclusive hotel chain is no exception, epitomizing New York glamour and sophistication at every turn. Guests barely lift a finger from the time they arrive in the wood-paneled lobby and are escorted to rooms with 400 thread-count French sateen linens, feather duvets and a selection of seven pillow types. Oversized marble bathrooms have deep soaking tubs, Frédéric Fekkai toiletries and a choice of terry-waffle or sateen-cotton bathrobes. Visitors in the park-view rooms get telescopes for bird (or people) watching, and when they tire of that, it's a toss-up between having a jet-lag therapy, facial or other treatment at the second-floor La Prairie spa or taking one of the hotel's on-call Bentleys or limos for a leisurely drive around the park.
259 rooms. Restaurant, bar. Fitness center. Spa. Business center. Pets accepted. $351 and up

★★THE ROOSEVELT HOTEL
45 E. 45th St., Midtown, 212-661-9600; www.therooseverthotel.com

Named for President Theodore Roosevelt and opened in 1924, this Madison Avenue hotel is situated in the heart of Midtown, where shopping, theater and business converge. The sprawling Colonial American-style building, which is near historic Grand Central Terminal, takes up a full city block and is a tourist stop itself because of its design. Crystal chandeliers and a large clock hang from the soaring ceilings over the large multistory marble lobby; the smaller but equally refined Palm Room has a sky mural on its ceiling. Rooms are simple, and have ergonomic desks, sofas and wireless access. The rooftop lounge, mad46, is a favorite of Times Square office workers who like its 19th floor

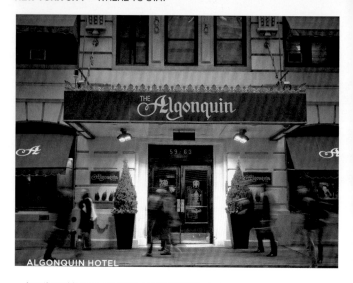

ALGONQUIN HOTEL

location with open-air views of Manhattan's skyscrapers.
1,015 rooms. Restaurant, bar. Fitness center. Business center. $251-350

★★★ROYALTON HOTEL
44 W. 44th St., Midtown, 212-869-4400; www.royaltonhotel.com
Many consider the Royalton to be the original boutique hotel. It's the one that set the standard for hipness with its famously spare Philippe Starck design and a fashion-magazine crowd that frequented the lobby bar in the '90s. A recent renovation upped the sophistication level in a quiet, clubby way. The dark lobby, with a mix of icy glass, varnished wood, steel and brass, is softened by a giant fireplace, warm leather-covered walls and furniture upholstered in suede and hide. The large guest rooms have also been updated, and use soft colors like light blues, grays and whites as a backdrop for the built-in banquettes that run from one end of the room to the other. Flowing curtains, down comforters and Philippe Starck-designed bathrooms with five-foot circular tubs and steel sinks continue the cozy-meets-mod aesthetic. Back downstairs, restaurateur John McDonald (Lure Fishbar, Lever House), has overhauled Bar 44 and the intimate 100-seat Brasserie 44 with honey-teak walls, rope arches and white-glass globe lighting.
168 rooms. Restaurant, bar. Fitness center. Business center. Pets accepted. $351 and up

★★★★★THE ST. REGIS NEW YORK
2 E. 55th St., Midtown East, 212-753-4500; www.starwoodhotels.com
No New York hotel may be better suited for shoppers than the St. Regis, with its prime location around the corner from Pucci and Japanese department store Takashimaya, and with the famed De Beers boutique right in the lobby. The opulent 1904 Beaux Arts landmark building (restored in a $100 million undertaking in 2006) is an impressive throw-back to old-school New York elegance. The lobby is dripping with gilded cornices and Italian marble, and if that isn't glitzy enough, a large glittering chandelier hangs over the reception

WHICH HOTEL HAS THE BEST BEDS?
The St. Regis New York *(page 110)* The mattress is thick, pillow-topped and comfortable, the Pratesi linens are soft as silk, and the overstuffed feather pillows are heaven. The bed's duvet, piled so high you feel like you're sleeping on a cloud, is what pushes this bed over the top. (Somehow, it manages to stay both warm and cool at the same time.)

WHICH HOTELS OFFER THE BEST VALUE?
Hotel Roger Williams *(page 106)* Rooms have fun touches such as colorful quilts, bright blue paint and bowls full of Oreos and other snacks rather than a mini-bar. Perhaps the best feature is the breakfast pantry in the morning, stocked with H+H bags and coffee.

Jane Hotel *(113 Jane St., West Village, 212-924-6700; www.thejanenyc. com)* You'll need to pack your sense of humor when you check into this value-oriented hotel—the former seaman's hotel has nautical themed "berths," shared bathrooms and great prices for solo travelers.

desk from the soaring Trompe l'oeil ceiling which resembles a bright-blue sky. A visit to the legendary King Cole Bar—with its famous 1906 Art Nouveau oil mural by Maxfield Parrish—is definitely in order. Ask for a Red Snapper (people call it a Bloody Mary everywhere else, but don't try that here—the bar claims to be its birthplace) and then head to Adour, chef Alain Ducasse's onsite restaurant and wine bar. Guest rooms have a lavish appeal with silk wall coverings and antique furniture. Beds come dressed in soft Egyptian-cotton sheets and feather-down comforters, and the Remède bath amenities are pure indulgence for the skin. If you have any last-minute needs before falling asleep, each floor has its own 24-hour butler.
256 rooms. Restaurant, bar. Fitness center. Spa. Business center. $351 and up

★★★SOFITEL NEW YORK
45 W. 44th St., Midtown, 212-354-8844; www.sofitel.com
You'll be greeted with a polite "bonjour" at this 30-story French export, a curved, modern limestone-and-glass building in the heart of Midtown. Paris- and New York-influenced Art Deco motifs are mixed throughout the hotel, including in photographs of the two cities in each room. Guest suites are compact and comfortable, with beautiful maple headboards affixed to the walls above the beds and marble baths. Top-floor rooms have private terraces and dazzling city views to boot.
398 rooms. Restaurant, bar. Fitness center. Business center. Pets accepted. $351 and up

★★★THE WALDORF ASTORIA
301 Park Ave., Midtown East, 212-355-3000; www.waldorf-astoria.com
Opened in 1893 by millionaire William Waldorf Astor, this grande dame of New York luxury hotels moved to its present location from a little further south on Fifth Avenue in 1931, and it still retains some of the original hotel's Art Deco interior. The lobby has the decadent feel of a ballroom with its sweeping marble staircases, and glamour seeps from every crevice of the hotel, which sits on a full city block. As you would suspect from such a historic hotel, every room located in the Waldorf Astoria and Waldorf Towers (which has a separate lobby, concierge, long-term leases and roomier suites) is adorned with thick draperies and ornately carved furniture, though some rooms are quite small. The hotel's

Bull and Bear Steakhouse & Bar, Inagiku Japanese restaurant, and cocktail terrace overlooking the Park Avenue lobby are always busy. A new Guerlain spa offers complimentary valet parking and relaxing foot baths upon arrival.
1415 rooms. Restaurant, bar. Fitness center. Spa. Business center. Pets accepted. $351 and up

THEATER DISTRICT/TIMES SQUARE
★★★RENAISSANCE NEW YORK HOTEL TIMES SQUARE
714 Seventh Ave., Theater District, 212-765-7676; www.marriott.com

An extensive makeover by famed designer Jordan Mozer transformed this Marriott-owned hotel from cookie-cutter to au courant. The lobby is modern without being steely, thanks to blue and red leather chairs and funky orb-shaped ceiling fixtures. Rooms have stylish, dark hard-wood furniture and blue and gold accents, plus modern necessities like technology panels where you can plug in all your electronics—iPod, cell phone, laptop—in one place. Bathrooms have robes and LATHER products. The restaurant Two Times Square on the second floor has sweet views of Times Square. (For just-as-cool views of the square, ask for an upper-floor room overlooking Seventh Avenue).
305 rooms. Restaurant, bar. Fitness center. Pets accepted. $251-350

★★★W NEW YORK TIMES SQUARE
1567 Broadway, Midtown, 212-930-7400; www.starwoodhotels.com

Located in Times Square, this hotel is just as colorful as its surroundings. The ultra-contemporary lobby, located on the seventh floor, has tile floors and leather benches, and it houses the hip Living Room bar. Guest rooms are minimalist and stylish, with contemporary furnishings in muted grays and dark-wood touches or, in the recently renovated rooms, lavender tones with glass desks and cube-shaped nightstands. It goes without saying that the views from the rooms can't be beat: Watch the action unfold below on Times Square as you relax on your pillow-top bed and goose-down pillow. And though this W doesn't have a Bliss Spa, it does have the homegrown spa's signature products sink-side. Once you're rested and primped, head down to the Blue Fin restaurant and start the night with a cocktail at Whiskey bar before heading out into the square, just outside the lobby doors.
507 rooms. Restaurant, bar. Fitness center. Business center. Pets accepted. $351 and up

★★★THE WESTIN NEW YORK AT TIMES SQUARE
270 W. 43rd St., Theater District, 212-201-2700; www.westinny.com

This 45-story hotel near Times Square is an oasis in a sea of nonstop action. Regular rooms are kitted out with the hotel's trademarked Heavenly Bed & Bath, and have views of Times Square and the Hudson River. The "Spa-Inspired" guest rooms take relaxation to the next level with aroma air diffusers, a Kinjoy Shiatsu massage chair that can be adjusted to "zero gravity" position and a variety of soothing CDs for your listening pleasure. Book a $2,000-a-night "Renewal suite" and your own personal "host" (in other words, butler) caters to your every wish so you can focus on rejuvenation. There may not be much more you'll need beyond the fresh white roses, orchids and lotus flowers supplied throughout the suite, a bamboo-floored exercise space which includes a spinning cycle and other exercise equipment, and spa bathroom with a Kohler Chromatherapy whirlpool bath, plus cashmere robes and slippers.
863 rooms. Restaurant, bar. Fitness center. Spa. Business center. $251-350

THE CARLYLE, A ROSEWOOD HOTEL

TRIBECA/MEATPACKING DISTRICT

★★★HOTEL GANSEVOORT

18 Ninth Ave., Meatpacking District, 212-206-6700;
www.hotelgansevoort.com

This hotel is just as stylish as its trendsetting neighbors in the Meatpacking
District, a neighborhood home to high-end-but-downtown-chic retailers like
Scoop and Stella McCartney. Room palettes consist of neutrals with blue-
purple splashes. Everything, including headboards, armoires and walls, are
awash in leather and fabrics, while 9-foot ceilings add airiness. The hotel is
famous for its rooftop destination Plunge, a restaurant, bar and lounge with
wraparound views of the city and a 45-foot-long outdoor, heated pool that's
surrounded by glass panels and open year-round.

*180 rooms. Restaurant, bar. Fitness center. Pool. Spa. Business center. Pets
accepted. $351 and up*

★★★THE GREENWICH HOTEL

377 Greenwich St., Tribeca, 212-941-8900; www.thegreenwichhotel.com

If individuality is your thing, The Greenwich Hotel should be your auberge of
choice. Each of the 88 guest rooms is unique, adorned with global influences
such as Parisian antiques, Moroccan tilework, Tibetan rugs and repurposed
Japanese lumber. The brainchild of actor/director Robert De Niro (his office is
across the street), this boutique property is yet another resplendent addition
to the ever-expanding Tribeca 'hood. The 1,700-square-foot Greenwich Suite
is a worthy splurge with 30-foot skylit windows, two master bedrooms and a
wood-burning stone fireplace. Don't forgo a trip to the sublevel Shibui Spa; it
may be your one opportunity to relax under a 250-year-old Japanese wooden
farmhouse and lantern-lit swimming pool. For a good gauge of the neighborhood, snag a sidewalk table at Locanda Verde and watch the locals sashay by.

*88 rooms. Restaurant, bar. Fitness center. Pool. Spa. Pets accepted.
$251-350*

WHAT ARE THE BEST PLACES TO STAY NEAR CENTRAL PARK?

Hôtel Plaza Athénée *(page 105)* The Hôtel Plaza Athénée sits on a tranquil, tree-lined street just a few blocks from Central Park.

Mandarin Oriental, New York *(page 118)* Pick up a picnic lunch next door at Whole Foods and then cross the street to the park.

The Plaza *(page 116)* One of the most storied hotels in the world occupies New York's most prestigious address at the intersection of Fifth Avenue and Central Park South.

The Ritz-Carlton New York, Central Park *(page 109)* Visitors in the park-view rooms get telescopes for bird (or people) watching. Guests can also call up to have the house Bentley take them for a drive around the park.

WHICH HOTELS HAVE THE MOST UNIQUE DÉCOR?

Chambers Hotel *(page 102)* More than 500 pieces of artwork make the Chambers feel like a chic downtown gallery. The rooms are also more upscale apartment than cookie-cutter hotel, with a soothing neutral palette and luxe furnishings.

Library Hotel *(page 107)* Flip through any one of the 6,000 books shelved throughout this cozy hotel located on "Library Way," where the rooms are identified by the Dewey Decimal System.

6 Columbus *(page 117)* Mid-Century Modern fans may feel as though they've landed at Idlewild (or JFK, as it's called today) when they step through the doors of this shag-carpeted 60s-era throwback. You can spy renditions of classic furnishings by mod stars Eames, Saarinen, Miller and more just about everywhere you look.

★★★TRIBECA GRAND HOTEL
2 Avenue of the Americas, Tribeca, 212-519-6600;
www.tribecagrand.com

This edgy-but-elegant hotel is a goldmine for those looking to party like rock stars, or just appear like they do. The soaring triangular atrium off the lobby is where an international roster of DJs spin in the sofa-filled Church Lounge, and the lower level has a 100-seat theater for private movie screenings. Rooms are smallish, but have phones and TVs in the bathrooms, gourmet mini-bars, and, if you request one, a live goldfish to keep you company. Some suites look out over the lounge, which can feel like opening the door into a round-the-clock party, but that's fine by most of the people who stay here. If you're into gadgets, book an "iStudio," tricked out with Apple's latest goods, including G5 computers with film-, photo- and sound-editing software.
203 rooms. Restaurant, bar. Fitness center. Business center. Pets accepted. $351 and up

UNION SQUARE/FLATIRON DISTRICT/GRAMERCY PARK/MURRAY HILL
★★★GRAMERCY PARK HOTEL
2 Lexington Ave., Gramercy Park, 212-920-3300;
www.gramercyparkhotel.com

Despite being a favorite haunt of the likes of Humphrey Bogart and Babe Ruth, who frequented the bar here, the Gramercy has been known as a low-key (and at times tired) spot since its opening in 1925. When hotelier Ian Schrager gave

THE NEW YORK PALACE

the place a major overhaul before reopening it in 2006, he managed to make improvements without turning it into yet another cookie-cutter Mid-Century mod property. The lobby now boasts impressive smoked-wood beams, a 10-foot-high fireplace and Moroccan checker-tiled floor. Rooms are decorated in rich reds, royal blues and other jewel tones instead of de rigueur minimalist neutrals, and velvets, leathers and tapestries adorn Julian Schnabel-designed furniture. The Rose Bar is lined with paintings by Andy Warhol, Jean-Michel Basquiat and Schnabel himself. The prettiest perk is something even lifelong New Yorkers never see: keys to the exclusive and elegantly landscaped Gramercy Park, an honor normally reserved for residents of the 39 buildings that surround the oldest private park in the country.

184 rooms. Restaurant, bar. Fitness center. Business center. $351 and up

★★★W NEW YORK-UNION SQUARE
201 Park Ave. South, Union Square, 212-253-9119;
www.starwoodhotels.com/whotels

This Union Square outpost of the contemporary hotel chain does a nice job blending an uptown atmosphere with some downtown coolness. Set on the open square with a leafy park in its center, this W (there are four others around Manhattan) located in the 1911 Beaux Arts Guardian Life building has the same clean modern lines and comfortable beds that guests swear by, and twice-daily maid service, as the other locales. There's also an in-hotel lounge and a branch of Todd English's Italian/Mediterranean restaurant Olives, but with the East Village, Tribeca and Soho so close, you're better off heading out on an adventure than staying in.

270 rooms. Restaurant, bar. Fitness center. Pets accepted. $351 and up

UPPER EAST SIDE
★★★★THE CARLYLE, A ROSEWOOD HOTEL
35 E. 76th St., Upper East Side, 212-744-1600; www.thecarlyle.com
Everyone from heads of state to celebs like Tom Cruise and Katie Holmes

favor this classic hotel when they're in New York City, but the attentive and discreet staff is famous for treating all guests like visiting A-listers. Opened in 1930, the classic Art Deco hotel (named for British essayist Thomas Carlyle) is all about understated, old-fashioned elegance. Uniformed elevator operators guide you to floors where rooms and suites are mixed with 60 residential apartments (lucky live-ins get the same perks as hotel guests). The rooms were originally designed by Dorothy Draper and later updated by Mark Hampton, Thierry Despont, Alexandra Champalimaud and other well-known designers. The furnishings range in style from classic British to modern décor, and some of the larger suites include powder rooms, foyers with full wet bars and even grand pianos. Luxurious touches include custom-made Limoges ashtrays, oversized umbrellas at the ready and a significant nod to modern technology with plasma televisions, DVD players and iPod docking stations. Step back in time outside your room by hitting the classic Café Carlyle, where acts include Eartha Kitt and, occasionally, a clarinet-playing Woody Allen.

187 rooms. Restaurants, bar. Fitness center. Spa. Business center. Pets accepted. $351 and up

★★★★THE LOWELL
28 E. 63rd St., Upper East Side, 212-838-1400; www.lowellhotel.com
Located in a landmark 1920s building on the Upper East Side, the Lowell captures the essence of an elegant country house with a blend of English prints, floral fabrics and Chinese porcelains that surprisingly works. Many suites boast wood-burning fireplaces, a rarity in Manhattan. All rooms are individually decorated, and the Lowell's specialty suites are a unique treat. The Hollywood Suite reflects the 1930s silver-screen era with photos of glamorous ingenues. The English influences extend to the Pembroke Room, where Anglophiles can throw their pinkies up at tea time (breakfast and brunch is also served). But for something uniquely American, check out the clubby Post House, a well-respected New York steakhouse that serves terrific chops.

72 rooms. Restaurant, bar. Fitness center. Business center. Pets accepted. $351 and up

★★★THE PLAZA
768 Fifth Ave., Upper East Side, 212-546-5499; www.theplaza.com
With a standard for luxury that dates back more than a century, it is no surprise that the renovated Plaza hotel reopened its doors in 2008 to universal pomp and pageantry. After three years and $400 million, The Plaza now bridges Old World enchantment and contemporary technology. Guest rooms are thoughtfully detailed in Beaux Arts-inspired décor with spacious closets, custom Italian Mascioni linens and bathrooms flaunting 24-karat gold-plated Sherle Wagner faucets, handcrafted solid marble vanities, inlaid mosaic tiles and Miller Harris bath products. If that's not enough pampering for you, make your way to the

---

WHICH HOTELS HAVE THE BEST CONCIERGES?

The St. Regis New York *(page 110)* The gracious and polite staff is skilled at anticipating your every need without being overwhelming.

The Peninsula New York *(page 109)* It seems as if the concierge staff at this hotel have a mental Rolodex; they're able to access, sort through and edit out only the pertinent information you need to quickly and effortlessly execute any whim.

WHICH HOTELS ARE UNIQUELY LOCATED?
W New York-Union Square *(page 115)* Located in the 1911 Beaux Arts Guardian Life building, this W is set on the open square with its leafy central park and lively outdoor greenmarket.

Gramercy Park Hotel *(page 114)* Only residents who live in the buildings surrounding the park and guests of this pretty hotel get keys to the exclusive Gramercy Park.

The Standard *(page 100)* This hotel literally rises above the newly built High Line, Manhattan's newest, and highest, park.

WHICH HOTELS ARE ICONIC NEW YORK?
The Carlyle, A Rosewood Hotel *(page 115)* Uniformed elevator operators still whisk you up to your room originally designed by Dorothy Draper at this New York classic that is as elegant and sophisticated as ever.

The Plaza *(page 116)* As much a part of New York as the Empire State building and the Statue of Liberty, The Plaza looks better than ever.

The Waldorf Astoria *(page 111)* One of New York's grand hotels, the Waldorf has been catering to the rich and famous since 1893.

Caudalié Vinotherapie Spa, the first of its kind in the United States, where face and body treatments can—and should—be followed up by a visit to the French Paradox Wine Lounge. Fitness legend Radu Teodorescu (known simply as Radu to his celeb clientele) is the force behind the new 8,300-square-foot fitness center, which includes an Olympic-sized lap pool and basketball court. Stop by the storied Palm Court for sumptuous afternoon tea, or enjoy a cocktail at the Rose Club or Champagne Bar.
282 rooms. Restaurant, bar. Fitness center. Business center. Spa. Pets accepted. $351 and up

UPPER WEST SIDE/COLUMBUS CIRCLE
★★★6 COLUMBUS
6 Columbus Circle, Columbus Circle, 212-204-3000;
www.sixcolumbus.com
There's an überchic aesthetic and too-cool-for-school vibe at this mod hotel, which replaced a dive that sat here long before it. The lobby's slender leather couch, white shag rug and powder-blue saucer chairs read *I Dream of Jeannie*, and that '60s feel carries through to the blue-toned Steven Sclaroff-designed rooms, decked out with teak walls, Saarinen-style side chairs and tables, and classic Guy Bourdin prints on the wall. The Euro crowd doesn't seem to mind unloading their Euros for current amenities such as maki from Blue Ribbon Sushi, or shelling out $4,500 a night for the privilege of staying in a two-story loft space with a terrace overlooking Central Park and Columbus Circle.
88 rooms. Restaurant, bar. $351 and up

★★HOTEL BEACON
2130 Broadway, Upper West Side, 212-787-1100; www.beaconhotel.com
This Upper West Side hotel was converted from a residential building, and many of its rooms are still leased as long-term apartments. All of the Beacon's spacious rooms are simply furnished and decorated in a floral motif, and one- and two-bedroom suites come with one king or two double beds in each

THE PLAZA

room as well as a pull-out couch, making this a good option for larger families who want to be near neighborhood institutions like the American Museum of Natural History and Lincoln Center. Fully equipped kitchenettes in all the rooms include microwaves and coffeemakers. Otherwise, the hotel restaurant is open 24-hours.

258 rooms. Restaurant. Business center. $151-250

★★★★★MANDARIN ORIENTAL, NEW YORK
80 Columbus Circle, Columbus Circle, 212-805-8800;
www.mandarinoriental.com

With all that the Mandarin Oriental offers, it's possible you may never want to leave. First, there are the views: The hotel, which occupies the 35th to 54th floors of the Time Warner Center, boasts impressive floor-to-ceiling windows that look out onto Columbus Circle, midtown Manhattan, the Hudson River and Central Park. Then there are the shops and restaurants: They include the buttoned-up shirtmaker Thomas Pink and famed $450-per-person sushi restaurant Masa. Finally, there's the décor: Standard rooms are dressed in black, red, gray or cream colors with Asian cherrywood furniture and fresh orchids, while superior rooms have lavish Spanish marble bathrooms with Italian granite vanities. The best amenity may be the view; each room serves up a panorama of either Central Park or the Hudson River. For the supreme pampering experience reserve the 2,640-square-foot Presidential suite on the 53rd floor, which includes a living and dining area, gourmet kitchen and study, all outfitted with oriental rugs, upholstered silk walls and other Asian artifacts. Dine at the Mandarin's wonderful Asiate restaurant, take a dip in the 75-foot lap pool (rumored to be the largest in Manhattan) or order room service and a movie—and put the high-tech entertainment system that's standard in every room to good use.

248 rooms. Restaurant, bar. Fitness center. Pool. Spa. Business center. Pets accepted. $351 and up

WHICH ARE NEW YORK'S NEWEST HOTELS?

The Greenwich Hotel *(page 113)* This new Tribeca hotel, the idea of Robert De Niro, whose office is across the street, feels more like you're staying in someone's home who has loads of style.

The Standard *(page 100)* The East Coast version of the L.A. hot spot opened last year in a unique location straddling the new High Line elevated parkway. Rooms are spare and modern, with little to distract from the great views of the city or Hudson River.

WHAT ARE THE CITY'S MOST HISTORIC HOTELS?

Algonquin Hotel *(page 101)* This hotel is the spot where legendary writers, including Dorothy Parker, Edna Ferber and George S. Kaufman, met daily after World War I.

The Waldorf Astoria *(page 111)* Opened in 1893 by millionaire William Waldorf Astor, this grande dame of New York luxury hotels still retains some of the original hotel's Art Deco interior.

★★★★★TRUMP INTERNATIONAL HOTEL & TOWER

1 Central Park West, Columbus Circle, 212-299-1000;
www.trumpintl.com

As with most things Trump, this 52-story building at the crossroads of Broadway, Columbus Circle and Central Park is anything but understated. Designed by architects Philip Johnson and Costas Kondylis, only a portion of Trump's black-glass tower—fronted by an unmistakable, massive silver globe sculpture—is taken up by the hotel's 167 rooms. The premises are also home to the lauded French-fusion restaurant Jean Georges *(page 90)* and the luxurious 6,000-square-foot Trump spa. Rooms have Trump-style basics: blond wood furnishings, marble bathrooms, European-style kitchens with china, crystal glassware and Christofle serving trays, and amazing park and city views through the floor-to-ceiling windows. Leave it to the Donald to add an extra-special touch by assigning each of the hotel guests their own personal attaché to assist with everything from personalized stationary to a custom-stocked fridge.

167 rooms. Restaurant. Fitness center. Pool. Spa. Business center. Pets accepted. $351 and up

2 FEET 6 INCHES

★SPAS

GREAT JONES SPA

URBAN RENEWAL

No other city in the U.S. has the nerve-rattling energy that New York does. Just the sheer act of walking down the street is an exercise in evading too-busy-to-mind locals and navigating traffic. Don't get us started on trying to catch a taxi or negotiating a multi-train transfer. That's why some of the best spas in the world call the Big Apple home: If it's good enough for frazzled New Yorkers, you bet it'll be good enough for you.

STAR-RATED SPAS

★★★★★THE PENINSULA SPA BY ESPA

The Peninsula New York, 700 Fifth Ave., Midtown, 212-903-3910; www.peninsula.com

When a superlative spa refuses to rest on its laurels by constantly adding improvements, you should plan on becoming a regular. This much-loved spa at the Peninsula has undergone a complete renovation in conjunction with spa consultants ESPA. It's part of a collaboration that began in 2006 with a super swanky re-do of the spa chain's flagship Hong Kong property. The sparkling new addition here is the only ESPA spa in the city, and the only place to try signature treatments like the Yin Uplifter ($465), designed to rid you of chills with a stone massage and application of clay mixed with cinnamon, licorice and ginger before you're placed in a linen wrap. Meanwhile, the Yang Soother ($465) addresses overheated or sensitive skin with a body treatment that mixes chrysanthemum, black lychee and marine mud or algae that leaves skin as smooth as silk. (Both treatments last for two hours.) The commanding space on the 21st and 22nd floors of the hotel, with skyline views, 12 treatment rooms, one couples' suite and private lounges is as relaxing as it gets. Locker rooms offer aromatherapy showers plus steam, sauna and thermal suites.

★★★★THE SPA AT FOUR SEASONS HOTEL NEW YORK

Four Seasons Hotel New York, 57 E. 57th St., Midtown East, 212-758-5700; www.fourseasons.com

This subterranean spa reflects the Four Seasons' signature style with an unobtrusive-yet-attentive staff and a penchant for luxurious details. The quiet space located beneath the hotel lobby provides services inspired by international practices, but eschews New Age notions. You can schedule acupressure combined with back-walking ($230) here, but you'll have to go elsewhere if you want your chakras balanced. The Four Seasons New York Signature Therapeutic Massage ($295), draws from four complementary traditions (shiatsu, Thai stretching, Swedish massage and reflexology) to ensure you're de-stressed and as loose-limbed as possible. Or go native with the Big Apple Antioxidant Body Treatment ($275), which uses two apple-based preparations—an apple/brown sugar scrub with Vichy shower followed by an apple body butter massage—and capitalizes on the natural enzymes in the fruit to leave your skin with a dewy glow.

★★★★★THE SPA AT MANDARIN ORIENTAL, NEW YORK

Mandarin Oriental, New York, 80 Columbus Circle, Columbus Circle, 212-805-8800; www.mandarinoriental.com

Sweeping views of Central Park and the Hudson River from floor-to-ceiling windows aren't the only thing that'll put this 35th-floor hotel spa at the top of your list of favorites. First, book a 90-minute block of time, then consult with

THE SPA AT MANDARIN ORIENTAL, NEW YORK

the top-notch staff to determine the best treatments to fill it. Asian-influenced services range from relaxing (the signature Thai Yoga Massage combines kneading with gentle yoga poses and assisted stretching; $315-$325) to rejuvenating (Ama Releasing Abhyanga loosens congestion and promises to free your body of toxins with a combination of exfoliation, cleansing and massage; $450-$470). While you're alleviating tension, take advantage of complimentary amenities, including an Oriental Tea Lounge, vitality pool and amethyst-crystal steam chamber, all awash in soothing beiges and golds.

OTHER SPAS

BLISS SOHO
Various locations; Flagship: 568 Broadway, Soho, 877-862-5477; www.blissworld.com
Cheeky, cheery and spotless—that's the formula that Bliss started out with in 1996 when its first spa opened in Soho, and it's worked like a charm ever since. Today, there are a stable of satellite locations, including two additional spots in Manhattan, plus spas in Atlanta, Dallas, Chicago, Scottsdale, L.A., San Francisco, London and Hong Kong. Book well in advance at this location to get your pick of popular treatments with a Bliss twist, like the slimming Thinny Thin Chin ($45) to tighten up skin on the neck and upper chest or a Quadruple Thighpass cellulite-busting process ($125). Combine two of your favorite things with the Double Choc Pedicure ($70), which comes with a mug of hot cocoa to sip while feet get scrubbed. Finish the fun by grabbing some take-home treats from the Bliss store. All locations offer similar services and bright, ultramodern décor.

CAUDALÍE VINOTHÉRAPIE SPA AT THE PLAZA
The Plaza, 1 W. 58th St., Upper East Side, 212-265-3182; www.caudalie-usa.com
Who would have thought that wine, massage and pampered relaxation go so well together? The powers behind Caudalíe Paris have brought the concept of vinotherapy stateside in the form of an immaculate new spa space at The Plaza.

The wine theme carries throughout, from the French Paradox wine lounge to the vines hanging effortlessly on the walls to bowls of crisp cold grapes in the relaxation rooms. Even the treatments incorporate the fruit of the vine. The Honey and Wine Wrap ($95) works to fortify and hydrate aging skin by applying a warm mixture of wine yeast and honey before wrapping the body in toasty blankets, while the signature Caudalíe Massage ($165) uses grapeseed oils to resculpt any problem areas in the body. A post-treatment stop in the wine lounge, which serves blends from the Caudalíe family vineyard, is an intoxicating way to keep the relaxation vibe going into the evening hours.

FÉLINE DAY SPA
235 W. 75th St., Upper West Side, 212-496-7415;
www.felinedayspa.com
The grand, iron-gated doors outside Féline may seem imposing—almost stuffy—but once inside, you'll find the warmth and welcome of a soothing monochrome décor with amber-wood floors, plus a gracious staff. Féline's services run the typical gamut, from Swedish massages to body wraps, and also include manicures and pedicures, plus hair and makeup. Reasonably priced packages allow you to get all your needs met in one stop. The Beauty Express ($176), for example, lasts 2 ½ hours and includes an aromatherapy pedicure, manicure, express facial and a half-hour massage. And that's just one of a plethora of options on Féline's superlengthy menu, where even a hot stone massage comes in four varieties: Energy ($125), Facial ($150), Back ($125) and Whole Body ($180).

GREAT JONES SPA
29 Great Jones St., East Village, 212-505-3185;
www.greatjonesspa.com
Stepping inside this 15,000-square-foot spa feels more like a walk through the great outdoors far beyond the concrete streets of Manhattan, thanks to exposed-rock walls, palm fronds and huge skylights overlooking a three-story waterfall. But instead of being greeted by mosquitoes or rogue grizzlies, you'll find a staff ready to cater to your every whim. Wash away stress at the popular Water Lounge, which includes a thermal hot tub, river rock sauna, cold plunge and chakra-light steam room, where a series of colored lights—one for each of the body's chakra points—gradually change, supposedly increasing the steam's benefits. (The $50 fee to use this area is waived if you spend $100 on treatments). Services range from classic massages and the fragrant compresses of the Aromatic Hot Towel Infusion Massage ($140) to gemstone-and-crystal healing therapy and ear candling. Finish your stay with a smoothie at the juice bar to give yourself a boost before heading back into the urban jungle.

WHAT ARE THE BEST HOTEL SPAS?
The Spa at Mandarin Oriental, New York *(page 121)* Overlooking Central Park, this spa has exquisite treatments, a pretty tea lounge and an amethyst-crystal steam chamber that's totally rejuvenating.

The Peninsula Spa by ESPA *(page 121)* The much-loved spa has undergone a complete renovation and is now even swankier.

The Spa at Four Seasons Hotel New York *(page 121)* The signature top-notch service, soothing treatments and luxurious details make this one of NYC's top spas.

HAVEN

150 Mercer St., Soho, 212-343-3515; www.havensoho.com

Haven has been pampering discerning Soho denizens since 1998, so rest assured that they are experts in the art of relaxation and results. The draws here are the peace-inducing space, a top-notch staff and expertly executed waxing services. Facials include aggressive treatments like the Boot Camp ($175), which uses Sonya Dakar botanicals and acid peels to battle facial foes ranging from fine lines to acne. Extend your stay to enjoy a straightforward-but-expertly executed massage of any session length: Squeeze in a quick half hour ($65) or luxuriate for 90 minutes ($140), depending on how much time you have until your dinner reservation.

LA PRAIRIE AT THE RITZ-CARLTON SPA

The Ritz-Carlton New York, Central Park, 50 Central Park South, Midtown, 212-308-9100; www.ritzcarlton.com

Services at this small hotel spa (with just six treatment rooms) use the La Prairie line of Swiss skincare products. Treatments include a long list of pleasures for the face, body and nails. The Stress Release Facial ($200) uses aromatherapy products and soothing music to refresh your skin and ease your mind. The Jet Lag Therapy ($415) combines a 30-minute aromatherapy massage, 30 minutes of foot/hand reflexology and a 30-minute facial—leaving you perfectly pampered for your big adventure in the city. There's plenty of details to remind you that you're at the Ritz, too: The women's changing area has a steam room and all the personal amenities you might need, plus lockers with their own jewelry boxes. The men's area has a supersized steam room, which is said to have hosted more than one business meeting.

OHM SPA

260 Fifth Ave., Midtown, 212-481-7892; www.ohmspa.com

This small spa is owned by a couple who keep the services no-nonsense and the aesthetic gender-neutral so they don't scare away male clientele. Japanese fighting fish are a testosterone-inspired influence in fishbowls throughout the spa, and Human Touch iJoy massage chairs and flat-screen TVs make even a Green Tea Antioxidant Mani-Pedi ($85) feel less frou-frou. Massages ($129) are customized to target trouble spots, and therapists use unscented gel (when requested) that leaves no oily residue. So relax—no one has to know you've treated yourself to a spa day unless you want to tell.

OKEANOS CLUB SPA

211 E. 51st St., Midtown, 212-223-6773; www.okeanosclubspa.com

If a tsar lived in Manhattan, he'd fit right in at Okeanos, a spa that oozes with Russian influence. Treatments are centered on the steamy Russian sauna called a banya (complimentary if you book $120 in services or with a $50 half-day club pass). Add-on treatments include Platza ($50), which gets you brushed with a bundle of birch leaves while you steam, and then doused with cold water. A little less brutal, the Invigorating Okeanos Massage ($120) uses Siberian ginseng as a secret weapon to revive you and reduce stress. The clubby furnishings and old-fashioned barber services remind you this spa was created with men in mind, though women are welcome. Finish your visit with a complimentary shot of vodka in the spa bar and you'll feel like you've taken a quick trip to Moscow—minus the jetlag.

THE PENINSULA SPA BY ESPA

SERENITY SPA

776 Sixth Ave., Chelsea, 212-481-7898; www.serenityspanewyork.com

A criminal defense lawyer and an architect aren't the typical pair you'd expect to open a spa together, but their combined knowledge of stress and environmental influences have helped these owners create a superlative experience. Traveling with kids? Drop them off at the Tutor Time childcare center upstairs—and start relaxing. If you're pressed for time, try a 50-minute body treatment like a seaweed wrap, mud wrap or body polish ($110 each). Most massages are offered in 50- or 80-minute sessions ($100-$170), but you can get a half-hour Swedish or Shiatsu quick-pick-me-up ($60) if the clock's really ticking. Look for specials listed on the spa's Web site such as 10 percent off massages on Monday. Go on Tuesday for the mani/pedi combo for $34.99. Serenity Spa does a great job at both nail and spa treatments.

SILK DAY SPA

47 W. 13th St., Greenwich Village, 212-255-6457; www.silkdayspa.com

As smooth and luxurious as its namesake fabric, Silk Day Spa has been winning accolades since its debut in 2003 for its signature blend of Eastern and Western approaches to pampering in an elegant underground hideaway. Enter through the ground-level boutique, then descend a bamboo staircase to reach this Asian-inspired oasis. Sleek furniture and lush plants fill a soothing, warmly lit setting dotted with treasures that look as though they've been plucked from a Singapore museum. Let loose to the strokes of a Silk Supreme Massage ($215), a full-body rub with Darphin oils that incorporates Swedish and other massage styles to relax muscle tension and shiatsu to realign your internal energy (perfect after a frenetic day of shopping and gallery-hopping in nearby Soho). Detox your skin from all those urban pollutants with a Silk Supreme Facial ($225) that aims to balance and protect by using products selected for your skin's specific needs.

THE SPA AT FOUR SEASONS HOTEL NEW YORK

SOHO SANCTUARY

119 Mercer St., Soho, 212-334-5550; www.sohosanctuary.com

Let the men do their own thing while you duck into this women-only downtown favorite for eco-conscious spa services, skincare and beauty treatments, plus fitness classes ranging from yoga to gyrotonic training. An all-female staff works in the converted loft space, and there's more of a nurturing feel here than at some other spas. You'll start your visit in the "Quiet Area," where you can sip herbal tea and flip through a magazine, kicking back to rest your weary feet from all that shopping and sightseeing. Though the ambiance—whitewashed brick walls, wood floors and the clean simplicity of the décor—will have you so relaxed you'll wonder if you need much else, hold out, because the massages in particular here are a true treat. The Sanctuary Signature Massage ($125) includes an aromatherapy thermal neck wrap and a blend of Swedish, deep-tissue and acupressure techniques. (There's a 30-minute option for $75 if you only have time for a quick rub.) And if you have an extra half-hour to spare, get the citrus back facial ($75), a deep pore cleansing which uses a salt scrub, steam, extractions, a mask and moisturizer to beautify your habitually

WHICH SPAS HAVE THE BEST MASSAGES?

The Spa at Four Seasons Hotel New York *(page 121)* The skilled therapists will customize your massage; you also can't go wrong with the signature treatment, which incorporates four types of massage, including shiatsu, Thai, Swedish and reflexology.

The Spa at Mandarin Oriental, New York *(page 121)* All of the massages here are highly effective; the Thai Yoga massage is great when you are feeling especially tense.

neglected back. The Sanctuary is a favorite of in-the-know moms and moms-to-be, who claim the pre- and post-natal massages ($170) here are the best in town.

THE SPA AT CHELSEA PIERS
Pier 60, West Side Highway near 23rd Street, Chelsea, 212-336-6780; www.chelseapiers.com

This sun-drenched sports-and-fitness facility sits on four piers that jut out into the Hudson River. With $75 worth of spa services, you get a day pass to the whole Sports Center—where you can swim, take a yoga class, climb a rock wall, run on the track or engage in almost any other kind of workout you can imagine before or after your treatments. Many spa services are designed to relieve the sore muscles of fitness fiends, including seven types of massages ranging from sports to Swedish ($80-$160). If you've been engaging in major doses of the Big Apple's favorite form of locomotion—pounding the pavement—opt for the Tibetan Foot Revival ($75), which includes a soak, lower leg reflexology massage and optional buffing or color for your toes.

SPHATIKA
1841 Broadway, Columbus Circle, 212-265-5885; www.sphatika.com

The emphasis here is on achieving a deep state of rest to ultimately boost healing and rejuvenation. Treatments are designed to help you sleep, literally. Fans say they snooze better the night of their treatment and for days afterward. Your treatment will begin in an infrared sauna where the spa's own sleep-inducing piano and flute music is piped in. The Royal Sphatika Signature Experience ($375) follows the sauna with skin brushing, an Orchid Body Mask, steam canopy (yes, it lowers right over you), Hemp Oil massage and lymphatic drainage facial. The express version is $250 and covers the same territory in two hours instead of three. Or opt for the Crystal & Cashmere Castor Oil variation ($250), which includes an abdominal massage and hand/foot massage, or the Warm Precious Jade Stone variety ($250), which taps the rebalancing power of the green gems. Services incorporate use of Sphatika's signature skincare line containing an elixir of quartz crystal, said to enhance the healing powers of the other ingredients. Post-treatment, you're brought to a relaxation room, where you can take your time easing out of your serene state—or dose off for a bit longer.

TOWNHOUSE SPA

TAKASHIMAYA
693 Fifth Ave., Midtown, 212-350-0118; www.takashimaya-ny.com
There are just a handful facial treatments offered in a single room tucked at the back of this outpost of the Japanese department store's first floor. But Irina, the store's sole aesthetician, makes it well worth a visit here. The velvet touch of her fingertips will lull you into a deep relaxation as she strokes Babor products over your face, shoulders and hands in the Takashimaya Babor European Facial ($130). So stroll past the shelves of gorgeous products to the window-less private space and give yourself over while ethereal music helps drown out the sounds of shoppers outside your door. Then make time to visit the renowned Tea Box Restaurant for a snack while showing off your fresh face.

TRACIE MARTYN SALON
59 Fifth Ave., Greenwich Village, 212-206-9333; www.traciemartyn.com
Whether you're heading to the Tony Awards or box seats at Carnegie Hall, or simply strutting across the red carpet in your bedroom, Tracie Martyn will have you glowing like a superstar both inside and out. A celeb in her own right, British import Martyn has rubbed elbows with (and the cheekbones of) Susan Sarandon, Madonna and Kate Winslet, to name a few. What's her secret? Three words: The Resculpting Facial. This signature service combines microdermabrasion, low-level electric current and calming creams to plump up, smooth out and redefine every inch of your face. With high-end clients comes a high-end atmosphere. Thanks in part to feng shui mastermind David Raney, the salon exudes harmony and style with bright antique-laden treatment rooms, elaborate floral displays and ginger tea-scented candles.

TOWNHOUSE SPA
39 W. 56th St., Midtown, 212-245-8006; www.townhousespa.com
This three-floor spa catering to both sexes may be in an elegantly restored townhouse complete with leather seating and mahogany accents, but there's nothing old-fashioned about the services here. A high-tech facial called Super

Sonic Skin Polishing ($245) uses a supersonic frequency to give you a soft glow, plus vibrations to stimulate blood supply. The men's spa area has a steam room with individual cooling showers, while ladies can dip into futuristic hydropod capsules—hot tubs with radiant heat, light therapy, aromatic steam and 30 massaging jets ($45 with a massage; $65 solo). The lounge area has tech accoutrements including a projection-screen TV and wireless Internet.

TRIBECA MEDSPA
114 Hudson St., Tribeca, 212-925-9500; www.tribecamedspa.com

If you're serious about your skin but don't love the dermatologist's clinical office, head to Tribeca MedSpa. Plastic surgery for the face or body is under the direction of top doctor Gerald D. Ginsberg, M.D., F.A.C.S. But if you're not in town to go under the knife, you'll still find plenty of pampering along with skin science. Dermatological offerings include laser treatments and injectables like Botox. Freshen your face with a peel such as glycolic acid or Retinol, or go for the City Grime Detox Skin Therapy ($225), a cleansing facial massage using fruit enzymes, dermaplaning and blue-light therapy to prevent breakouts. You'll be guaranteed to go home with better skin, making your friends green with envy over your New York secret.

MOSS

IT'S IN THE BAG

There is perhaps no better place than New York City for serious shopping. You could spend days walking up and down Fifth Avenue, starting at Bergdorf's and ending up at Saks. Then you'll want to head downtown, where many of the stores are show-stoppers themselves (Prada, Dolce & Gabbana). Here, a list of other great stores to visit—in between the ones you already know and love.

CHELSEA

LINGO

257 W. 19th St., Chelsea, 212-929-4676; www.lingonyc.com

The who-wore-it-better debate is a popular topic for *Us Weekly* and celebu-tants across Manhattan who commonly lose sleep over whether someone else will be wearing the same outfit as them at a party. No such fear for Lingo patrons, as each piece is custom made by a local designer and stocked solely at this hidden Chelsea gem. The owner (and her well-behaved shepherd mix) provides an atmosphere that is more akin to a friend's fabulous closet than a chic department store dressing room. Lines like Fresh Meat and Sirius lead the charge when it comes to casual to evening wear, and accessories from purses to jewels are plentiful. Pricetags won't blow your bank account, and the sleep you'll get from knowing you're wearing an original? Priceless.

Tuesday-Saturday 1-8 p.m., Sunday 1-6 p.m.

MICHAEL ARAM

136 W. 18th St., Chelsea, 212-461-6903; www.michaelaram.com

Inspired by India's rich tradition of metalworking, this American home furnish-ings designer's first boutique offers a darkly handsome space for his elegant, handcrafted tableware and furniture. Black brick walls and gold displays let the shimmering stainless steel pitchers, gold-dipped bowls and silverplated tea kettles take center stage. Earthy types will gravitate toward the intricate leaf-shaped trays, vases cast to resemble the bark of white birch trees and twig-like serving spoons.

Monday-Saturday 10 a.m.-7 p.m., Sunday noon-6 p.m.

CHINATOWN/LITTLE ITALY/NOLITA

DUNCAN QUINN

8 Spring St., Nolita, 212-226-7030; www.duncanquinn.com

For dapper gents, this minuscule yet swank haberdashery jams in plenty of Savile Row style within its stripe-wallpapered walls. Known for its slim fit and rock 'n' roll sensibility, Quinn's signature suiting is cut from exceptional Scottish and British fabrics, and there's a smart bespoke collection when ready-made won't do. Elegant shirts, Italian ties, pocket squares, enamel cuff links and sterling-silver collar stays should please detail-oriented dandies.

Monday-Saturday noon-8 p.m., Sunday noon-6 p.m.

GROUPE 16SUR20

267 Elizabeth St., Nolita, 212-343-0007; www.16sur20.com

What do vintage cars and Oxfords have in common? We're not quite sure of the link either, but the rotating lineup of pristine autos (you might find an '87 Lotus Turbo Esprit and an '83 Aston Martin parked inside the front window with price tags on them) provides a handsome counterpoint to the tony men's apparel in this cement-floored store. Cut in a slim silhouette from finely spun

GROUPE 16SUR20

Italian fabric, the shirts draw devotees to this more relaxed spin-off of nearby men's boutique Seize sur Vingt.
Monday-Saturday 11 a.m.-7 p.m., Sunday noon-6 p.m.

RESURRECTION
217 Mott St., Nolita, 212-625-1374; www.resurrectionvintage.com
Nicolas Ghesquière, Marc Jacobs and Anna Sui have all rummaged through the racks of pristine pre-loved garb at this legendary vintage dealer. Perhaps it's because these designers know that fashion works in cycles; the latest trend can trace its design roots to some of the 20th-century finery neatly organized by item here. Though the stock in this crimson-hued store contains a preponderance of mod '60s styles including Courrèges dresses, there are also slinky Halston gowns from the disco era and '80s punk-rock trousers. Look, too, for enduring classics such as Chanel quilted purses and Hermès leather cuffs.
Monday-Saturday 11 a.m.-7 p.m., Sunday 1 p.m.-6 p.m.

SEIZE SUR VINGT
243 Elizabeth St., Nolita, 212-343-0476; The Plaza Retail Collection, 1 West 58th St., 212-832-1620; www.16sur20.com
Prepare for a shirt storm at the natty, older sibling to nearby Groupe 16sur20. Made from silky Egyptian cotton or crisp broadcloth, the traditional, well-tailored button-downs here are painstakingly custom-made from European fabrics, earning them raves from investment bankers and fashion editors alike. Browse through the bulky binders bursting with swatches of checks, stripes

---

WHICH SHOP HAS THE MOST UNIQUE ITEMS?
Opening Ceremony *(page 135)* Sort of a United Nations of fashion, this ultra-creative boutique/gallery/showroom showcases designers from around the world, as well as American talents like Chloë Sevigny.

WHERE ARE THE BEST BARGAINS IN NEW YORK?

New Yorkers are always looking for a deal, and there are many to be found, even in this expensive city. Everyone's favorite **Century 21** *(22 Cortlandt St., 212-227-9092; www.c21stores.com)* is beloved for its deep discounts on designer pieces. Another bargain treasure trove for designer labels on the cheap is the Chelsea flagship of **Loehmann's** *(101 Seventh Ave., 212-352-0856; www.loehmanns.com)*. Its "Back Room" is renowned for gems from the likes of D&G, Prada and Marc Jacobs. **Clothingline** *(261 W. 36th St., 212-947-8748; www.clothingline.com)* is only open when there's a sale—usually for 40 weeks out of the year, when you can score knocked-down prices on direct-from-the-showroom Tocca, Kate Spade, Helmut Lang and more. Eco-chic shoppers can save the earth and some green at the sustainably minded **Samples for eco(mpassion)** *(2 Great Jones St., 917-226-9765; www.greenfinds.com)*. Snap up pieces like 7 for All Mankind jeans at a steal, and five percent of your purchase will be donated to such charities as Trees for the Future. A 10-minute walk south, Soho's doubleheader, **Topshop** *(478 Broadway, 212-966-9555; www.topshopnyc.com)*—a longtime British favorite, and **Mango** *(561 Broadway, 212-343-7012; www.mngmango.com)* is a savvy stylista's home run, thanks to ultra-trendy pieces that may just last a season, but that's the point.

New Yorkers go to **Pearl River Mart** *(477 Broadway, 212-431-4770; www.pearlriver.com)* for ceramics, pretty Chinese slippers, stationary and lots more. And no trip to New York is complete without a visit to the epicenter for thrifty finds—**Chinatown**. Here, open-air stalls packed with designer knockoff bags, jewelry, scarves, hats and clothing line Canal Street from Broadway to the Bowery. Though the police have been cracking down on creators of Gucci, Dolce & Gabbana and other knock-offs—not to mention bootleg DVDs (save yourself a headache at the airport and skip buying these poorly filmed, pirated blockbusters)—there are still plenty of vendors to be found on the bustling strip. Most salespeople are open to some haggling, so don't be afraid to talk down a price. To help seal the deal, tell them you saw the same item for less down the street.

and plaids to create a made-to-order Oxford wardrobe for either gender, as well as men's suits and cashmere sweaters. Fellas in need of quick gratification can grab off-the-rack shirts with quirky names like The Back of Love and Genuine Risk in this soothing, spare shop.
Monday-Saturday 11 a.m.-7 p.m., Sunday noon-6 p.m.

GREENWICH VILLAGE/SOHO/WEST VILLAGE
3.1 PHILLIP LIM
115 Mercer St., 212-334-1160; www.31philliplim.com
Beloved by fashionistas and celebrities for his clean-cut, casual aesthetic, designer Phillip Lim has claimed a piece of coveted Soho turf for his burgeoning empire's first flagship. Unlike other frenzied neighborhood stores pumping with loud soundtracks, this more serene spot draws on Lim's elegant but approachable style with a wall constructed of oak flooring and a chandelier fashioned from glass bocce balls. The fact that Lim's pared-down womenswear, menswear and accessories are all gathered under one roof should come

---

WHAT IS THE BEST BOUTIQUE FOR ONE-OF-A-KIND PIECES?
Lingo *(page 131)* Each piece is custom made by a local designer and stocked solely at this hidden Chelsea gem.

WHAT ARE THE BEST HOME GOODS BOUTIQUES?
Michael Aram *(page 131)* Inspired by India's rich tradition of metalworking, this American home furnishings designer's first boutique offers beautiful handcrafted tableware and furniture.

Moss *(page 134)* Moss' temple of high-end housewares sells reproductions of Wiener Werkstätte champagne coupes and 18th-century Meissen porcelain, among other noteworthy pieces.

---

as a relief to those used to running all over town to snap up his pieces.
Monday-Saturday 11 a.m.-7 p.m., Sunday noon-6 p.m.

AEDES DE VENUSTAS
9 Christopher St., West Village, 212-206-8674; www.aedes.com
Scent connoisseurs make a beeline to Aedes de Venustas for its passel of niche perfumes, skin-care lines and bathtime indulgences. Kitted out with a crystal chandelier and crimson carpet, the shop carries everything you need to surround yourself in a cloud of gardenia, white pepper or saffron, thanks to fragrances from Creed, Annick Goutal and obscure brands like Escentric Molecules. Its array of Diptyque candles, Santa Maria Novella organic potpourri and Duchess Marden Damascena rose water also make luxe presents.
Monday-Saturday noon-8 p.m., Sunday 1-7 p.m.

MOSS
150 Greene St., Soho, 212-204-7100; www.mossonline.com
Don't be fooled by the striking museum-quality pieces behind the glass here: Murray Moss' temple of high-end housewares may feel like MoMA for the domestic set, but virtually everything is for sale. With reproductions of Wiener Werkstätte champagne coupes and 18th-century Meissen porcelain, the stock offers a brief history of tableware. This is Moss, remember—not Macy's or Martha Stewart—so you'll find contemporary, noteworthy pieces such as Fernando and Humberto Campana's whimsical chairs amassed from stuffed animals, Maarten Baas's neon-green clay side tables, and Tom Dixon's polished metal orb-shaped pendant lights.
Monday-Saturday 11 a.m.-7 p.m., Sunday noon-6 p.m.

MUJI
455 Broadway, Soho, 212-334-2002; 620 Eighth Ave., Midtown,
212-382-2300; 16 W. 19th St., 212-414-9024, Chelsea; www.muji.us
Its name is shortened from the Japanese phrase for "no-brand goods," and the Tokyo-based chain churns out everything from stationery and furniture to clothing and umbrellas—all with a no-frills charm that has made Muji a favorite of design purists. Basics here are affordable and thoughtfully designed, like popular portable speakers that arrive flat and easily fold out to pop into action. You won't see any logos or flashy patterns splashed on the cereal bowls, notebooks, or bedroom slippers; instead, you'll find neutral-hued staples with a minimalist aesthetic.
Monday-Saturday 11 a.m.-9 p.m., Sunday 11 a.m.-8 p.m. Chelsea: Monday-Saturday 11 a.m.- 8 p.m., Sunday 11 a.m.-6:30 p.m.

MZ WALLACE

93 Crosby St., Soho, 212-431-8252; 102 Christopher St., West Village, 212-206-1192; www.mzwallace.com

It's no surprise that mixing a chic fashion stylist and an experienced acces-sories editor and designer is a recipe for success. The true feat of MZ Wallace has been its staying power in the fierce handbag-eat-handbag world of Soho fashion. Since opening its doors nearly a decade ago, this small white-washed boutique is all about functionality and classic style. You're unlikely to find any in-today-out-tomorrow designs. Instead, owners Monica Zwirner and Lucy Wallace Eustice employ lightweight, durable materials and versatile sizes and colors to give women a tote they can actually tote everywhere, from an afternoon play date to an evening at Carnegie. The store also stocks a fun variety of accessories including wallets and cosmetic bags, in case there's no more room in your luggage for yet another handbag.

Monday-Saturday 11 a.m.-7 p.m., Sunday noon-6 p.m.

ODIN

199 Lafayette St., Soho, 212-966-0026; 328 E. 11th St., East Village, 212-475-0666; www.odinnewyork.com

This slick men's chain might be named after a Norse god, but its well-curated casual threads are assuredly for mere mortals. Nautically themed t-shirts by Rogues Gallery, Engineered Garments plaid shirts and Stetson fedoras exude an everyman vibe, albeit a smartly dressed one. Culty accoutrements like Comme des Garçons wallets and Shane bejeweled belt buckles round out the mix. Check out the new sister boutique, Den, located next to the East Village store, which features one designer at a time offering one-of-a-kind pieces and lines unavailable in the U.S.

Soho store: Monday-Saturday 11 a.m.-8 p.m., Sunday noon-7 p.m. East Village store: Monday-Saturday noon-9 p.m., Sunday noon-8 p.m.

OLIVER SPENCER

750 Greenwich St., West Village, 212-337-3095; www.oliverspencer.co.uk

With fans like the Rolling Stones and Scissor Sisters, you'd think this London-based designer would be known for skin-tight leather leggings, not well-tailored trench coats and other menswear. Opened in partnership with the owners of men's chain Odin, Spencer's first stateside boutique provides a clubby nook for his designs. Bell jars enclose silk ties, Bill Amberg carryalls rest on an antique apothecary, and a small selection of Sharps shaving creams keep metrosexuals on the razor's edge.

Monday-Saturday noon-8 p.m., Sunday noon-7 p.m.

OPENING CEREMONY

35 Howard St., Soho, 212-219-2688; www.openingceremony.us

Known as the United Nations of fashion, the premise behind this ultra-creative boutique/gallery/showroom is to shine the spotlight on a single country for one year, gathering together the designs from established and upcoming designers, vintage items and select pieces from open-air markets. Since its opening, the store has focused on Hong Kong, Brazil, Germany, England, Sweden and Japan, each time entering into exclusive agreements with top retailers in those countries—for example, when they were highlighting the UK back in 2005, Opening Cermony was the only place to buy pieces from Topshop. World travelers and owners Humberto Leon and Carol Lim have also

WHERE IS THE BEST SHOPPING IN MIDTOWN?

Home to Broadway theaters, media powerhouses and much of the city's commerce, Midtown is quite literally the center of New York City and boasts some of its toniest emporiums. Time-pressed office workers jostle for elbow room with gaggles of tourists on the well-trodden sidewalks of Fifth and Madison avenues.

❶ Start your spree three avenues east at **Bloomingdale's** sprawling flagship, which takes up an entire city block (*1000 Third Ave., 212-705-2000; www.bloomingdales.com*). Bloomies offers more democratically priced items than the next few department stores on your list. It also has a huge selection of jeans on the second floor, great men's formalwear and loads of shoes for brides.

❷ Your next stop is hip department store **Barneys New York** (*660 Madison Ave., 212-826-8900; www.barneys.com*), where creative director Simon Doonan's over-the-top, often humorous windows have featured a live actor playing Sigmund Freud and a mannequin of Margaret Thatcher in dominatrix garb. Inside, the loot is less risqué but equally attention-grabbing, ranging from Stella McCartney to Manolo Blahnik. Don't even think about skipping the shoe department; locals love to lunch at Fred's, up on the ninth floor, where the chicken soup will keep you fortified.

❸ Get ready to drop a bundle at luxe **Bergdorf Goodman** (*754 Fifth Ave. at East 58th Street, 212-753-7300; www.bergdorfgoodman.com*). Ladies can peruse Valentino gowns and Prada clutches or the pieces inside specialty designer boutiques within the store for Chanel, Armani and other high-end labels. Gents get their due just across the street at **Bergdorf Goodman Men's** (*745 Fifth Ave.*), three entire floors devoted to Y chromes with John Varvatos jackets and William Rast jeans.

❹ Nearby lies a trinity of goodies for accessory fiends at leather-good icon **Louis Vuitton** (*1 E. 57th St., 212-758-8877; www.louisvuitton.com*), bastion of the iconic little blue box **Tiffany & Co.** (*727 Fifth Ave., 212-755-8000; www.tiffany.com*) and diamond king **Harry Winston** (*718 Fifth Ave., 212-245-2000; www.harrywinston.com*). Label hounds can then hit the Trump Tower for **Gucci** (*725 Fifth Ave., 212-826-2600; www.gucci.com*) before heading down to trendy **Henri Bendel** (*712 Fifth Ave., 212-247-1100; www.henribendel.com*), which draws in young ladies craving makeup, gorgeous lingerie and designs by the next big things in fashion.

❺ Continue south past 55th Street to pop into upscale Japanese chain **Takashimaya** (*693 Fifth Ave., 212-350-0100; www.ny-takashimaya.com*). Its serene digs and in-house flower shop should provide you with a Zen spell, and you can refuel on Asian nibbles at its soothing Tea Box Restaurant before sprinting three blocks south to glamorous **Versace** (*647 Fifth Ave., 212-317-0224; www.versace.com*).

❻ Start praying to the retail gods for heavy markdowns as you head a block-and-a-half farther south, to the name-sake flagship of **Saks Fifth**

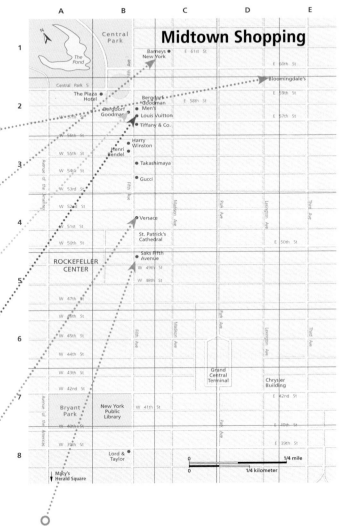

Midtown Shopping

Central Park

The Pond

Central Park S

The Plaza Hotel

Bergdorf Goodman

Barneys New York

Bergdorf Goodman Men's

Louis Vuitton

Tiffany & Co.

Harry Winston

Henri Bendel

Takashimaya

Gucci

Versace

St. Patrick's Cathedral

ROCKEFELLER CENTER

Saks Fifth Avenue

Bloomingdale's

Bryant Park

New York Public Library

Grand Central Terminal

Chrysler Building

Lord & Taylor

Macy's Herald Square

E 61st St
E 60th St
E 59th St
E 58th St
W 57th St
E 57th St
W 56th St
W 55th St
W 54th St
W 53rd St
W 52nd St
W 51st St
W 50th St
E 50th St
W 49th St
W 48th St
W 47th St
W 46th St
W 45th St
W 44th St
W 43rd St
E 42nd St
W 42nd St
W 41st St
E 40th St
W 40th St
E 39th St
W 39th St

Avenue of the Americas
Fifth Ave
Madison Ave
Park Ave
Lexington Ave
Third Ave

0   1/4 mile
0   1/4 kilometer

Avenue (611 Fifth Ave., 212-753-4000; www.saksfifthavenue.com), whose shoe department nearly boasts its own zip code. Then, walk the 11 blocks from Saks to mainstay **Lord & Taylor** (424 Fifth Ave., 212-391-3344; www. lordandtaylor.com).

❼ End your day by heading five blocks further south and an avenue west to behemoth **Macy's** (151 W. 34th St., Herald Square, 212-695-4400; www. macys.com), the world's largest department store.

expanded the minimally embellished store's focus to also include a colloberation with Chloë Sevigny, and periodically offer special lines from retailers such as Tretorn created exclusively for the shop.

Monday-Saturday 11 a.m.-8 p.m., Sunday noon-7 p.m.

UNIQLO

546 Broadway, Soho, 917-237-8811; www.uniqlo.com

Japan's version of Gap has landed stateside, and its Soho outpost is Uniqlo's largest anywhere, brimming from floor to ceiling with casual sportswear—some sold only at this location. A wall near the entrance showcases artful tees, while cashmere sweaters get their due with a Crayola-box-like array of hues near the back. Everything from button-down shirts and blazers to socks and gym shorts are stocked in the tri-level space. One-off capsule lines by designers like Alexander Wang and Alice Roi up the fashion quotient.

Monday-Saturday 10 a.m.-9 p.m., Sunday 11 a.m.-8 p.m.

TRIBECA/MEATPACKING DISTRICT

AUTO

805 Washington St., Meatpacking District, 212-229-2292; www.thisisauto.com

Good design gets the green light at Auto. Husband-and-wife team Renata Bokalo and Roman Luba have an impeccable eye for gorgeous housewares, fashion accessories, baby goods and gifts. The boutique's white walls, shelves and tables offer a clean backdrop for the bright, juicy colors of Missoni floor cushions, John Robshaw India-inspired printed bedding and Poem Crown environment-friendly canvas totes. Next door at 803 Washington is Auto's sister shop, which sells jewelry and accessories.

Monday-Friday noon-7 p.m., Saturday 11 a.m.-7 p.m., Sunday 11 a.m.-6 p.m.

DIANE VON FURSTENBERG

874 Washington St., Meatpacking District, 646-486-4800; www.dvf.com

Sure, von Furstenberg might be the president of the Council of Fashion Designers of America, but first and foremost, she'll always be queen of the wrap dress. Located on a prime corner in the Meatpacking District, her glittering flagship exudes a girly, futuristic vibe via fuchsia couches, white walls and a sprinkling of circular mirrors on the ceilings. DVF's ultrafemme pieces abound, including signature curve-skimming frocks along with chunky bracelets and jawbreaker-sized cocktail rings, the result of a collaboration with H. Stern jewelry. A slightly hidden set of stairs leads to a VIP dressing room, where you just might meet the diva herself (her studio is above the shop).

Monday-Wednesday, Friday-Saturday 11 a.m.-7 p.m., Thursday 11 a.m.-8 p.m., Sunday noon-6 p.m.

EARNEST SEWN

821 Washington St., Meatpacking District, 212-242-3414; 90 Orchard St., Lower East Side, 212-979-5120; www.earnestsewn.com

Urban cowboys and city slickers alike are devoted to this local denim company's rustic emporium. Modeled after an old-fashioned general store with copper ceilings and roughed-up floorboards, the selvage haven proffers stacks of ready-made, pre-distressed jeans that look as if they were smuggled out of Clint Eastwood's wardrobe from *The Good, the Bad and the Ugly*. Folks afraid of style doppelgängers can choose from a range of pocket silhouettes

WHAT IS THE BEST STORE FOR VINTAGE CLOTHING?
Resurrection *(page 132)* Rummage through the racks of pristine preloved garb at this legendary vintage dealer and you might just score a slinky Halston gown, classic Chanel quilted purse or Hermès leather cuff.

WHAT IS THE BEST STORE FOR GIFTS?
Shanghai Tang *(page 140)* Colorful Asian treasures, including bright lacquer boxes, cool cufflinks and adorable baby items, make this swank Chinese department store the perfect place to pick up unique gifts.

WHAT IS THE BEST STORE FOR CASUAL SPORTSWEAR?
Uniqlo *(page 138)* Japan's version of Gap is brimming with casual sportswear—some sold only at the Soho location.

and upscale fabrics to whip up a custom pair. A new line, Lit'l Earnie, features adorable jeans, jackets and skirts for kids. The back room houses an ever-changing array of pop up shops, which carry limited edition goods like sunglasses from Moscot and rugged outerwear from Filson.
Meatpacking District: Monday-Friday, Sunday 11 a.m.-7 p.m., Saturday 11 a.m.-8 p.m. Lower East Side: Monday-Friday noon-8 p.m., Saturday 11 a.m.-8 p.m., Sunday noon-7 p.m.

JEFFREY NEW YORK
449 W. 14th St., Meatpacking District, 212-206-1272; www.jeffreynewyork.com
A former footwear buyer for Barneys, Jeffrey Kalinsky established his department store in 1999 as a low-key yet high-end alternative to uptown bastions like Bergdorf Goodman, Saks and his previous employer. Today, the rehabbed warehouse space contains a finely tuned assortment of runway-fresh clothing by Prada, Chloé, Gucci, Missoni and Dsquared sold by a sweet, low pressure sales staff that won't spritz you to death in the perfume section (a rare find in NYC). Don't miss the store's treasure trove of on-trend shoes and accessories, including hard-to-find VBH (V. Bruce Hoeksema) leather clutches.
Monday-Wednesday, Friday 10 a.m.-8 p.m., Thursday 10 a.m.-9 p.m., Saturday 10 a.m.-7 p.m., Sunday 12:30 p.m.-6 p.m.

STEVEN ALAN
103 Franklin St., Tribeca, 212-343-0692; 229 Elizabeth St., Nolita, 212-226-7482; 69 Eighth Ave., West Village, 212-242-2677; Outlet, 465 Amsterdam Ave., Upper West Side, 212-595-8451; 349 Atlantic Ave., Brooklyn, 718-852-3257; www.stevenalan.com
If Brooks Brothers had a love child with Barneys, it might resemble this stronghold of classic style. Alan's eponymous line of artfully rumpled button-down shirts subtly tweaks the basics for both genders, and his well-edited picks from a slew of other up-and-coming labels such as Engineered Garments, Mayle and Lyell follow suit. The well-worn, airy shops are just small enough to be manageable, and the payoff for your closet can be immense, especially if your visit coincides with Alan's legendary biannual sample sales in mid-May and the first week of November. If you can't make the markdown fest, the Upper West Side outlet brims year-round with discounted blasts from past seasons.
Monday-Saturday 11:30 a.m.-7 p.m., Thursday 11:30 a.m.-8 p.m., Sunday noon-6 p.m. Nolita: Monday-Saturday 11:30 a.m.-7 p.m., Sunday noon-6 p.m.

Upper West Side: Monday-Saturday 11 a.m.-7 p.m., Sunday 11 a.m.-6 p.m.
Brooklyn: Monday-Saturday 11:30 a.m.- 7 p.m., Sunday noon-6 p.m.

THOM BROWNE
100 Hudson St., Tribeca, 212-633-1197; www.thombrowne.com

The New York designer has earned both snickers and cheers for his snug, shrunken men's suits that dare to bare ankles. His first eponymous showroom feels like the set of *Mad Men* and veers from his more adventurous runway looks (think feather-trimmed trousers and plaid skirts for men). Call ahead to make an appointment to try on tailored basics like gray three-button jackets, preppy cashmere sweaters and snappy dress shoes or to get measured for a bespoke pair of those trademark short pants.
Monday-Saturday 11 a.m.-7 p.m. or by appointment.

YOHJI YAMAMOTO/Y-3
1 Gansevoort St., Meatpacking District, 212-966-3615;
www.yohjiyamamoto.co.jp

The Japanese designer's minimalist, deconstructed designs might just be as artful as his unusually shaped pair of boutiques. A handful of gorgeously constructed, asymmetric garments in a mostly black palette are exhibited like sartorial sculpture in the light-flooded, triangular storefront. (Don't worry about the sparse stock on hand; a storage room lies across the courtyard.) Across the street at Y-3 *(317 W. 13th St., Meatpacking District, 917-546-8677; www.adidas.com/y-3)*, you'll find scads of sleek sneakers, polos, track pants and the like from Yamamoto's sporty collaboration with athletics giant Adidas.
Monday-Wednesday 11 a.m.-7 p.m., Thursday-Saturday 11 a.m.-8 p.m., Sunday noon-6 p.m.

UPPER EAST SIDE
SHANGHAI TANG
600 Madison Ave., Upper East Side, 212-888-0111;
www.shanghaitang.com

Putting the East in East Coast, this small Chinese department store specializes

---

WHICH SHOPS ARE THE BEST LIFESTYLE BOUTIQUES?
Auto *(page 138)* The boutique's white walls, shelves and tables offer a clean backdrop for the bright and colorful housewares and accessories.

Muji *(page 134)* This Tokyo-based chain churns out everything from stationery and furniture to clothing and umbrellas—all with a no-frills charm that has made Muji a favorite of design purists.

WHAT ARE THE BEST DESIGNER BOUTIQUES?
3.1 Phillip Lim *(page 133)* Designer Phillip Lim has claimed a piece of coveted Soho turf for his burgeoning empire's first flagship.

Diane von Furstenberg *(page 138)* What more could you ask for besides an incredible selection of the designer's ultra-femme dresses? Her collection of jewelry with H. Stern.

WHAT IS THE BEST PLACE TO BUY JEANS?
Earnest Sewn *(page 138)* Get custom jeans at this cult local denim company or take home a few pairs of the ready-made, pre-distressed ones.

BIRD

in eye-popping Asian treasures. Roaring dragons perch on wine stoppers, silver-plated chopsticks nestle into lime-fabric-lined cases, and Chinese characters adorn jacquard-covered photo albums. Vivid colors punch up Shanghai Tang's traditionally inspired clothing, which runs the gamut from relaxed-fit silk pajamas and curvy cheongsam dresses to modern mandarin-collar men's jackets and beaded cocktail frocks that wouldn't seem out of place on the red carpet. New parents can snag baby slippers that come in a cute, coordinating drawstring purse, and cuddly pandas dressed in Tang suits.

Monday-Wednesday, Friday-Saturday 10:30 a.m.-7 p.m., Thursday 10:30 a.m.-8 p.m., Sunday noon-6 p.m.

BROOKLYN

BIRD

220 Smith St., Cobble Hill, Brooklyn, 718-797-3774; 316 Fifth Ave., Park Slope, Brooklyn, 718-768-4940; www.shopbird.com

Brooklyn's retail scene has taken flight, and this breezy womenswear emporium is one of the borough's style pioneers. Known for its carefully honed range of on-the-cusp designers, Bird sells charming dresses, edgy ankle boots and slouchy leather hobo bags from local talents such as Lily Raskind of Sunshine & Shadow and Caitlin Mociun. Adorned with vintage-looking floral-print wallpaper and a tin ceiling, the Smith Street outpost also offers a comfy spot to sort through an international array of labels like Sonia by Sonia Rykiel, Tsumori Chisato and Nicole Farhi.

Monday-Friday noon-8 p.m., Saturday noon-7 pm., Sunday noon-6 p.m.

ZOË

68 Washington St., Dumbo, Brooklyn, 718-237-4002; www.shopzoeonline.com

Though Brooklyn has made a name for itself as a haven for indie brands, this 3,500-square-foot temple to big-ticket European fashion houses means you can still get your Jimmy Choos on this side of the East River. The white-walled,

WHERE ARE NEW YORK'S SAMPLE SALES?

Every season agencies and designers descend on New York City's retail market with samples of what's to come. Once those retailers make their picks and place their orders, the samples are put on the seller's block to make room for next season's look books. The result: A sea of designer clothing at a fraction of their retail price.

Before learning how to get the most out of a sample sale, let's clear up some misconceptions. First things first. You don't have to be a celebrity with dark glasses and a paparazzi tail to get in. And every piece of clothing is not a teensy size two. The more digging you're willing to do, the more treasures you're apt to find.

The best way to ensure admittance is to call ahead and make an appointment if you can. Know where you're going. These sales often are in random loft spaces or office buildings, and don't come with two-story signs and neon arrows pointing you in the right direction. Something else they don't come with: dressing rooms.

Sample sales are much like liquidation events: Everything must go, and it will, eventually. If you want the best selection, show up early. If you want the best price, sneak in toward the end. Whatever you do, just don't show up at lunchtime unless you're more inclined to crowd-surf than shop. And bring cash, as many sample sales don't accept credit or debit cards, or personal checks.

Before your trip, scout out which sample sales are taking place by checking out magazines like *New York* and *Time Out New York* or online at *www.dailycandy.com* or *www.topbutton.com*. There's always a good sample sale going on somewhere.

industrial-looking spot dishes up clothes and accessories for both genders from the likes of Lanvin, Marni, Burberry and James Perse. You can also stock up on down-to-earth staples like Splendid tees, J Brand jeans and cozy and cool Rag & Bone cardigans.
Monday 11 a.m.-7 p.m., Tuesday-Thursday, Saturday 11 a.m.-8 p.m., Friday 11 a.m.-9 p.m., Sunday 11 a.m.-6 p.m.

THE FUTURE PERFECT

115 N. Sixth St., Williamsburg, Brooklyn, 718-599-6278;
www.thefutureperfect.com

Forward-thinking David Alhadeff fills his design stronghold with quirky home décor for the *Surface*-reading set. Irony is a strong theme here with mainstays like Jason Miller's ceramic antler chandeliers, Sarah Cihat's recycled and rehabilitated tea sets and unique candelabras from various artists. You'll also find tongue-in-cheek toile du Jouy wallpaper with urban embellishments, and gifts such as Kelly Lamb's geometric birdhouse and Kristin Victoria Barron's sterling silver Taxicab Receipt Necklace. A free gallery space downstairs hosts a rotating roster of art.
Daily noon-7 p.m.

WHAT IS THE BEST SHIRT SHOP?

Steven Alan *(page 139)* Alan's eponymous line of artfully rumpled button-down shirts subtly tweaks the basics for both genders.

WHICH STORE HAS THE MOST CUTTING-EDGE CLOTHING?

Yohji Yamamoto/Y-3 *(page 140)* Hugely popular in Tokyo, the Japanese designer's minimalist, deconstructed designs can now be found at his flagship stores in New York.

PDT

MANHATTAN, STRAIGHT UP

In New York, the first question of the night is usually: Are you going Uptown or are you going Downtown? Upscale cocktail parlors, gritty dive bars, base-thumping clubs, elegant lounges—the neighborhoods comprising lower Manhattan have them all. Times Square and Rockefeller Center, just blocks apart in the heart of Midtown, are the tourist hubs in this part of Manhattan. Locals and out-of towners converge and take advantage of upscale hotel bars, theater-district entertainment and the surrealism of Times Square's eternal electric glow. Further north along both sides of Central Park, pleasant watering holes fill up with thirsty park strollers and young professionals winding down from a day's work. But whether you choose to end up in super-cool Downtown or laid-back Uptown, one thing's for sure: you're bound to have a night to remember.

CHELSEA/HELL'S KITCHEN/GARMENT DISTRICT

THE IMPERIAL

17 W. 19th St., Chelsea, 212-352-2001; www.theimperialnyc.com

At 5,000-square-feet, it's difficult to imagine getting in the door could be such a feat. Unfortunately it is, thanks to a recent surge of bridge and tunnel traffic and local ravers seven nights a week here. The upside is that once you're in, you're nearly guaranteed a night of sensory overload, and that's a good thing. The sound system is top-notch—a necessity for the number of celebrity DJs who show up to spin—the décor is a neon medley of graffiti art, disco balls and eerie mannequins. VIPs are treated to secluded lounges with bottle service and a private dance floor. If you can muster enough patience for the inevitable line out front, come on a Friday or Saturday night.

Nightly 10 p.m.-4 a.m.

SLATE

54 W. 21st St., Chelsea, 212-989-0096; www.slate-ny.com

If you need more than just a highball to keep you entertained, head to this grown-up game room, where you can go a-buck-a-ball at billiards or test your skills in the ping-pong lounge between sips. This Chelsea pool hall is more upscale than most—the felt is clean, the tables are wellspaced and the attached lounges and dining room are comfortable. It's the perfect spot to focus on your bank shot in peace.

Monday-Thursday noon-2 a.m., Friday noon-midnight, Saturday 4 p.m.-4 a.m., Sunday 4 p.m.-midnight.

CHINATOWN/LITTLE ITALY/NOLITA

BEAST

171 E. Broadway, Chinatown, 212-228-3100; www.broadwayeast.com

Your first mission is to locate this Chinatown speakeasy. Hidden below the vegan-friendly Broadway East restaurant (and down a dimly lit hallway, through an unmarked door, etcetera, etcetera), sits Beast, a rare combination of classy date-spot and low-key club lounge. Exposed brick walls, slate floors and a state-of-the-art sound system set the mood, while an emphasis on eco-friendly fare and potables tempts the tastebuds. Cocktails fall in harmony with the organic aims of Beast's upstairs neighbor, showcasing wines and liquors from sustainable proprietors and green production lines. Whether you're looking for a relaxing post-meal nightcap or a dependable spot to absorb the local scenery, this is it—if you can find it.

Daily 10 p.m.-4 a.m.

ONIEAL'S
174 Grand St., Little Italy, 212-941-9119; www.onieals.com

This Little Italy corner spot is part sultry cocktail lounge, part tourist attraction, and it was made famous by its cameo as the bar "Scout" on *Sex and the City*. But prior to its 15 minutes in the pop culture limelight, Onieal's was a Prohibition-era speakeasy and brothel connected by underground tunnel to—get this—the NYPD police headquarters that used to be across the street. The elegant, era-styled wood ceiling, comfortable sofas and chic lounge atmosphere make this the kind of place where you can spend an hour or a whole evening. If camera wielding tourists aren't your thing, call ahead to make sure the SATC bus tour won't be coming through while you're there. And go ahead, try the cosmo. You won't be the only one.

Monday-Thursday 11:30 a.m.-2 a.m., Friday-Sunday 11 a.m.-4 a.m.

EAST VILLAGE/LOWER EAST SIDE

THE BOWERY HOTEL BAR
335 Bowery, Lower East Side, 212-505-9100; www.theboweryhotel.com

You might be on the Lower East Side but you'd swear you were in Paris. All of the bar areas here are some of the the most opulent in the city, replete with Persian rugs, velvet settees and handpainted murals. Grap a seat in front of the sandstone fireplace and order a martini or a healthy glass of whiskey. Or, belly up to the zinc-covered bar on one of the velvet bar stools. There's also a lovely patio out back. As you soak up the rich atmosphere, don't be suprised if you see a rockstar or two, or at the very least, chic-looking creative types who clearly let you know that you're in New York.

Sunday-Thursday 5 p.m.-2 a.m., Friday-Saturday 5 p.m.-4 a.m.

BURP CASTLE
41 E. Seventh St., East Village, 212-982-4576;
www.burpcastlenyc.wordpress.com

Down the street from the ever-popular McSorley's ale house, this dark and quiet (the "monks" behind the bar shush you when speaking above a whisper) spot is not your average Belgian beer mecca. It's much better. It usually has a rotating selection of twelve drafts and over forty bottles of beers from all over the world that should surprise even the most experienced beer drinkers. On Sunday, Monday or Wednesday evenings, you get free pommes frites (around 5-6:30 p.m.), which come with tasty sauces like the Vietnamese pineapple mayo or the curry ketchup especial. The aforementioned "monks" are obviously not really monks at all, so don't go confessing to anyone after a few too many of

---

WHAT ARE THE CITY'S BEST HOTEL BARS?

The Bowery Hotel Bar *(page 145)* Dripping with a Parisian opulence that is somehow right at home on the Bowery, this chic hotel is the place to grab a cocktail when you're downtown.

King Cole Bar *(page 150)* King Cole is warm in that dark-and-woodsy kind of way that makes you think about all the people who might have had a drink here before.

The Living Room *(page 152)* Young singles, romancing couples and the occasional pre- and post-theater groups all make themselves at home in this übermodern space with chic leather furniture.

the strong Belgian offerings.

Monday-Tuesday 5 p.m.-midnight, Wednesday-Thursday 5 p.m.-1 a.m., Friday 5 p.m.-3 a.m., Saturday 4 p.m.-3 a.m., Sunday 4 p.m.-midnight.

PDT (PLEASE DON'T TELL)
113 St. Mark's Place, East Village, 212-614-0386; www.pdtnyc.com
The super-secret, lodge-chic (stuffed otters, raccoons and deer heads adorn the walls) spot is hidden in the back of a hot dog joint. Enter the phone booth at CRIF Dogs, pick up the receiver and you'll be whisked away, *Get Smart* style, through a hidden door into the cozy PDT, where you can enjoy unique twists on old favorites, like a bacon-infused bourbon cocktail, along with food from next door Crifs *(www.crifdogs.com)*, which specializes in deep-fried Jersey style hot dogs. (Oddly enough, it's a pairing that works.) Same-day reservations are required for all parties, and are taken by phone after 3 p.m.
Sunday-Thursday 6 p.m.-2 a.m., Friday-Saturday 6 p.m.-4 a.m.

SALT BAR
29A Clinton St., Lower East Side, 212-979-8471; www.saltnyc.com
Warmly lit and cozily hemmed in by exposed brick, this intimate Lower East Side spot that serves dinner as well as drinks is a favorite of neighborhood residents who have no lack of hip, trend-pushing places nearby to spend their money (Wylie Dufresne's avant-garde WD-50 is a block down the street). But Salt Bar serves up an earthy, rustic aura seasoned with exposed wood beams, soft candle lighting and antique accents alongside reasonably priced wine and a delectable selection of American small plates. Just a dash of low-key goes a long way in these parts. Come prepared, Salt Bar only takes American Express or cash.
Tuesday-Thursday 5 p.m.-1 a.m., Friday-Saturday 5 p.m.-3 a.m., Sunday 5 p.m.-1 a.m.

SPITZER'S CORNER
101 Rivington St., at Ludlow, Lower East Side, 212-228-0027; www.spitzerscorner.com
Located on a sprawling Lower East Side corner, this neighborhood gastropub has hipsters from all over the city clamoring for its chef-driven pub grub. The large community tables and reclaimed wood walls combined with steel light fixtures and glass shelving create a sleek and modern pub atmosphere that allows chef Sung Park's excellent food to shine. Add to this the well-edited selection of more than 40 beers on tap and you're done for the night. How about Coney Island's aptly named Mermaid Pilsner with a bowl of the pork fat-laced popcorn and a short rib burger with Guss' famous pickles? That's just one yummy combo at this supremely satisfying gastropub.
Monday-Tuesday noon-3 a.m., Wednesday-Friday noon-4 a.m., Saturday 10 a.m.-4 a.m., Sunday 10 a.m.-3 a.m.

TERROIR
413 E. 12th St., between First Avenue and Avenue A, East Village, 646-602-1300; www.wineisterroir.com
From the owners of local favorite Hearth comes this tiny food and esoteric wine-focused watering hole. Marco Canora and crew make the nibbles (think paninis, cheese, fried salty snacks) down the street at Hearth and Paul Grieco picks the extensive wine list choosing wines that best represent the land (or terroir). With thirty-six wines by the glass changing often and a recession

KETTLE OF FISH

special of six small plates for $25, each visit offers something new. There are different types of bruschetta, hand-cut charcuterie, cripsy paninis and other great "bar" food (try the sage-wrapped lamb sausage) to savor with your wine. Be sure to also try one of the popular wine- and beer-based cocktails, such as the unique Abbey Flip, which mixes Ommegang Abbey Ale, pomegranate molasses, coriander syrup, nutmeg and egg yolk.

Monday-Saturday 5 p.m.-2 a.m., Sunday 5 p.m.-midnight.

GREENWICH VILLAGE/SOHO/WEST VILLAGE

BLIND TIGER ALE HOUSE
281 Bleecker St., West Village, 212-462-4682;
www.blindtigeralehouse.com
Recently relocated, the rustic new home of this long-standing popular beer house is still drawing a crowd. Those looking for a common place and pedestrian offerings such as Bud Light best look elsewhere, as the selection here leads more toward lesser-known but fuller flavored beers from the rotating selection of 28 drafts and occasional cask beers and smaller batch vintage ales. Although the beer is the initial draw, the food is also very good, allowing you to go ahead and order another round.

Daily 11:30 a.m.-4 a.m.

BROOME STREET BAR
363 W. Broadway, Soho, 212-925-2086
It calls itself an American bistro, but from the lion's heads carved into the bar to the aging Victorian-looking glass cabinetry, this eatery and pub has an Anglophile vibe as well. A multicultural crowd settles in during the evening to nosh on real pub-style grub (blue cheese and pear salad, quality burgers, a sardine platter) and sample a quality selection of beer like Chimay Tripel, Schneider Weisse and local brews from Brooklyn and Ithaca. Good food, good drink and subtle background music from an online jukebox is a commodity worth taking advantage of in trendy Soho.

Sunday-Thursday 11 a.m.-1:30 a.m., Friday-Saturday 11 a.m.-2 a.m.

WHICH PLACES ARE BEST FOR CLASSIC COCKTAILS?

The Campbell Apartment *(page 150)* Go uppercrust with a glass of "Prohibition" Punch or other drinks of bygone eras like the Delmonico or Banker's Julep at this beautifully restored apartment within Grand Central.

Little Branch *(page 149)* This unmarked subterranean lounge is a classic-cocktail-lover's house of worship. Order the bartender's choice; you won't be disappointed.

Smith & Mills *(page 153)* Every detail of this exclusive lounge is intended to bring you back to a simpler time, from the sultry lighting and carefully curated feel to the nicely-prepared drinks.

WHAT ARE THE BEST WINE BARS?

Black Duck *(page 153)* At this elegant wine bar, you'll find a good $5 pinot during happy hour, live jazz on Friday and Saturday, and not a whiff of snobbery.

Morrell Wine Bar and Café *(page 151)* The bar and café is situated next to Morrell & Company's wine shop, allowing it to tap into an inventory of more than 2,000 bottles from vineyards around the world.

Wine and Roses *(page 156)* This celebrity-studded neighborhood wine bar has a knowledgeable staff eager to make recommendations from its list of 188 by-the-bottle and 38 by-the-glass offerings.

EAR INN
326 Spring St., Soho, 212-226-9060; www.earinn.com
This bar certainly has a funny name since it is not an actual inn, nor does it have anything to do with ears (a neon sign that hangs above the entrance reads "Ear" instead of "Bar"). But this historic—and some say haunted—west side bar is housed in a landmark building that dates back to 1817, and needless to say, has a lot of history. This building has changed over the years, as it was once the home of James Brown (an aide to George Washington), a restaurant, and a speakeasy during the prohibition. The upstairs portion has also been a boarding house and a brothel (and where ghost-sightings were reported). Come in to relax and enjoy a beer, some home cooking and the Earegulars jazz quartet who play every Sunday. Don't go expecting bells and whistles here, as this is the definition of a bare-bones, old-time bar—and the reason why customers keep coming back after all these years.
Sunday-Thursday noon-3 a.m., Friday-Saturday noon-4 a.m.

KETTLE OF FISH
59 Christopher St., West Village, 212-414-2278; www.kettleoffishnyc.com
The Kettle has offered a comfortable, warmly lit respite for West Village bohemians (it's one of Jack Kerouac's old haunts) and barstool academics alike for nearly six decades. But the diverse patronage—graying, tweedy intellectuals, expat Green Bay Packer diehards (game days are for the green-and-gold-clad only) and twenty-somethings tossing darts—gets along famously over pints of Yuengling and turns at the classic Ms. Pac-Man machine.
Monday-Friday 3 p.m.-4 a.m., Saturday-Sunday 2 p.m.-4 a.m.

THE CAMPBELL APARTMENT

LITTLE BRANCH
22 Seventh Ave. South, West Village, 212-929-4360; www.littlebranch.net
This unmarked subterranean lounge is a classic-cocktail-lover's house of
worship. From the same team as super-exclusive Milk & Honey (the London/
New York members-only mystery joint run by acclaimed mixologist Sasha
Petraske and co-owner Joseph Schwartz), the intimate Little Branch is
comfortable, conversational and less presumptuous than its nearby sister site.
High-backed booths are occupied by the young and old, who listen to live
piano jazz, punctuated only by the sound of ice rattling in cocktail strainers as
the proficient bartenders create Gatsby-era drinks. (The staff is said to arrive
two hours before opening to chill glasses, squeeze fresh juices and hand-cut
blocks of ice—which supposedly keep the drinks from diluting too quickly).
We like the Rye Daisy (a sweet and lemony whiskey-rocks) and the Floridita
(a better, re-imagined take on the tired daiquiris of your college days), but if
you simply tell the bartenders what you like, they'll conjure up something just
to suit your taste.
Daily 7 p.m.-3 a.m.

PEGU CLUB
77 W. Houston St., Soho, 212-473-7348; www.peguclub.com
From one of the original cocktail mavens (before there really were cocktail
mavens in this town), Audrey Saunders, comes this upscale second floor den
above Houston Street. Fresh juices, housemade syrups and ginger beer, and
meticulous bartenders come together in this gorgeous and fairly spacious
lounge. Cocktails are not the only draw here, though, as the decadent Asian-
inspired small plates pair perfectly with the civilized environs and reflect on the
inspiration of the club's name—the original Pegu Club was a British Officer's
club in Burma.
Sunday-Wednesday 5 p.m.-2 a.m., Thursday-Saturday 5 p.m.-4 a.m.

THE SPOTTED PIG

314 W. 11th St., West Village, 212-620-0393; www.thespottedpig.com

This quintessential gastropub also happens to be New York's first. Chef April Bloomfield, a London transplant, co-owner Ken Friedman and their cache of celebrity backers (including chef Mario Batali) keep this tiny west side bi-level pub and eatery packed to the gills day-in and day-out. The sheep's ricotta-filled gnudi (a cheese-gnocchi type thing that's out of this world) are nearly famous but all the British-inspired grub is worthy of the sometimes two-hour wait. Take our advice and go after lunch, when it's less crowded, and dig in to the rightfully legendary Roquefort burger with an endless pile of ultra crispy shoestring potatoes all washed down by a hand-pulled cask draft ale.

Monday-Friday noon-2 a.m., Saturday-Sunday 11 a.m.-2 a.m.

VOL DE NUIT

148 W. Fourth St., West Village, 212-982-3388; www.voldenuitbar.com

The open-air atrium alone is enough of a selling point for us, but you might also want to check out this Belgian beer house for its extensive drink selections, which range from $5 draws to $20-plus bottles (from Duvel to traditional Gueuze, they're exclusively Belgian) and a food menu of Belgian classics, like Moules Frites (steamed mussels and French fries). A hopping singles scene emerges around the atrium's patio tables and in the upstairs bar at night, but this is more of a fine-beer-lover's establishment. NYU is down the street, and weekend crowds can be especially student-heavy.

Sunday-Thursday 4 p.m-1 a.m., Friday-Saturday 4 p.m.-3 a.m.

MIDTOWN/MIDTOWN EAST/MIDTOWN WEST

THE CAMPBELL APARTMENT

15 Vanderbilt Ave., Midtown, 212-953-0409; www.hospitalityholdings.com

Railroad tycoon John Campbell purchased this cavernous space in the southwest corner of Grand Central Station during the 1920s for use as a grand office—complete with leaded windows and hand-painted timber ceilings—that was convenient for his clients and an easy commute from his Westchester home. Campbell died in 1957, and the space underwent various transformations until a massive $1.5 million renovation/restoration in 1999 turned it into this bar. The ceiling was returned to its original grandeur and a steel safe that was once hidden behind a wall now sits in a huge fireplace. Pretend you're uppercrust like Campbell and toast the old man with a glass of "Prohibition" Punch or other drinks of bygone eras like the Delmonico or Banker's Julep. Because the apartment caters largely to a commuting crowd (and well-dressed; the dress code here doesn't allow shorts, t-shirts, sneakers and the like). It's not a late-night locale, but with drinks this strong, you won't need to stick around all night.

Monday-Thursday noon-1 a.m., Friday noon-2 a.m., Saturday 3 p.m.-2 a.m., Sunday 3 p.m.-11 p.m.

KING COLE BAR

The St. Regis New York, 2 E. 55th St., Midtown, 212-753-4500; www.stregis.com

King Cole's is legendary for a handful of reasons. Artist Maxfield Parrish's famous mural of the Merry Old Soul looms large behind the bar, and the entire space is warm in that dark-and-woodsy kind of way that's good for impressing important people, many of whom are already seated at the favored banquette.

Often subdued, King Cole's has been known to get a bit boisterous from time to time.

Monday-Thursday 11:30 a.m.-1 a.m., Friday-Saturday 11:30 a.m.-2 a.m., Sunday noon-midnight.

MORRELL WINE BAR AND CAFÉ

1 Rockefeller Plaza, Midtown, 212-262-7700; www.morrellwinebar.com
Directly across the street from NBC Studios in Rockefeller Plaza, Morrell is a mainstay in the New York wine business. The bar and café is situated next to Morrell & Company's wine shop, allowing it to tap into an inventory of more than 2,000 bottles from vineyards around the world. The impressive mirrored bar is tiered with carefully perched bottles upon bottles of delicious wine. If it's a nice evening, the only place to be is on the street-side patio, enjoying your vintage of choice in a prime spot for Midtown people-watching.

Monday-Saturday 11:30 a.m.-midnight, Sunday noon-6 p.m.

P.J. CLARKE'S

915 Third Ave., Midtown, 212-317-1616; www.pjclarkes.com
Amid a bar scene that changes rapidly, P.J. Clarke's is a rare institution. It's lasted for more than 125 years in Midtown and remains a modest-but-popular red-brick, two-story building surrounded by modern towers. You'll fit in no matter what era you come from: Graying higher-ups slurp raw oysters next to young high-finance types, while bow-tied barkeeps pour reasonably priced cocktails for a thirsty after-work crowd that stays well into the evening. A juxta-position of old and new exists even in the décor, with portraits of Kennedy and Lincoln yellowing beneath a new flat screen television hinged on the wall. The kitchen is open until 3 a.m., making this stalwart acceptable as a place to start an evening or end it.

Daily 11:30 a.m.-4 a.m.

RINK BAR

Rockefeller Center, Fifth Avenue at 50th Street, Midtown, 212-332-7620; www.rapatina.com
Rockefeller Center's ice rink is a Christmas-in-New York must, but when the summer sun comes out, so do the frozen cocktails. That's when the rink is trans-formed into an urban oasis where you'll find umbrella-shaded tables dotting the

---

WHAT ARE NEW YORK'S BEST PUBS?

Broome Street Bar *(page 147)* A multicultural crowd settles in during the evening to nosh on real pub-style grub and sample a quality selection of beer.

The Ginger Man *(page 154)* If you're looking for a good old Irish pub, you're looking for the Ginger Man. This beer-lover's delight has plenty to offer in terms of selection, seating and price.

WHAT ARE THE BEST PLACES FOR BEER?

Burp Castle *(page 145)* A great selection of beers from around the world, plus free pommes frites on certain days in the early evening make this a must on your list of brew houses.

Vol de Nuit *(page 150)* Head to this Belgian beer house for a bottle of Gueuze and a yummy plate of steamed mussels and French fries.

RINK BAR

substreet-level plaza—a welcome escape from the searing pavement above. Daiquiris, mojitos and other tropical concoctions are the gimmicks here; you'll find work-weary Manhattanites mixing with parched tourists cooling off. (In winter months, opt for a hot toddy on the other side of the glass at the Rock Center Café, and be glad you're inside instead of showing off your ice skating skills in front of hundreds of onlookers.)

Monday-Thursday 11:30 a.m.-10 p.m., Friday 11:30 a.m.-11 p.m., Saturday 11 a.m.-11 p.m., Sunday 10 a.m.-10 p.m.

SALON DE NING
The Peninsula New York, 700 Fifth Ave., at 55th Street, Midtown, 212-903-3097; www.peninsula.com
Located on a terrace atop the recently refurbished and always luxurious Peninsula Hotel, Salon de Ning's views of Manhattan and Fifth Avenue below is the first draw for guests. But the enclosed portion of the bar, which recalls Shanghai in the 30's, is as equally appealing as the dazzling outside terrace. Gaze at the unusally-hung paintings while lounging on a day bed or take a seat at the sleek bar. Order a dirty martini or one of the bar's signature cocktails, such as the Ning Sling, made with Absolut Mandarin, Soho Lychee liqueur, fresh mint and lychee and passion fruit juices, while taking in the city's lights from this exotic spot.

Daily 4 p.m.-1 a.m.

THEATER DISTRICT/TIMES SQUARE
THE LIVING ROOM
W New York-Times Square, 1567 Broadway, Times Square, 212-930-7447; www.whotels.com
The W hotel chain has branded itself a hip, modern option in a sea of stodgy traditional hotels, and the lobby bar on the seventh floor of the W New York-Times Square fits right into that mold. Filled in the evening with young singles, romancing couples and the occasional pre- and post-theater groups, the

übermodern space features chic leather furniture in small seating arrangements amid a crisp-edged design scheme of glass and marble. The bar is standard and fancy signature cocktails are better found elsewhere in the neighborhood, but for bourbon on the rocks or a glass of champagne, the Living Room is a fine place to settle in and make yourself at home. If you suddenly feel like dancing, head to the Whiskey downstairs, where a colored-square dance floor complements modern electro-lounge tunes.

Sunday-Wednesday 11 a.m.-2 a.m., Thursday-Saturday 11 a.m.-3 a.m.

TRIBECA/MEATPACKING DISTRICT

APT
419 W. 13th St., Meatpacking District, 212-414-4245; www.aptnyc.com
Resembling a sleek, modern bachelor pad, APT is a club that feels more like a bar that charges a small cover ($10) after 11 p.m. most nights. Upstairs, fresh beats are served up alongside $10-15 cocktails in the comfy "kitchen/living room," where a long dining table and a smattering of couches invite guests to make themselves at home. If a dance party is more your thing, head to the basement, where contemporary furnishings and throbbing house music create a completely different atmosphere. Long a neighborhood gem, this is not a hot new place to see and be seen, which is arguably APT's greatest merit. If bottle service and a who's-who crowd from New York's high-fashion scene are more what you're after, try Kiss and Fly *(409 W. 13th St., 212-255-1933; www.kissandflyclub.com)* a few doors down.
Monday-Saturday 7 p.m.-4 a.m.

SMITH & MILLS
71 N. Moore St., Tribeca; www.smithandmills.com
You'll need luck finding this tiny unmarked watering hole in a former carriage house in Tribeca. Go for the delicious drinks and pristine oysters and exclusive feel, but stay and wonder about the details that went into creating this old-time cocktail wonderland. Everyone seems to love the Dark and Stormy with their fresh ginger beer and dark rum. Every detail is intended to bring you back to a simpler time with the sultry lighting and carefully curated feel. This one is not to be missed, that is if you didn't miss it.
Daily 5:30 p.m.-3 a.m.

UNION SQUARE/FLATIRON DISTRICT/GRAMERCY PARK/MURRAY HILL

230 FIFTH
230 Fifth Ave., Flatiron, 212-725-4300; www.230-fifth.com
What may be New York's best rooftop terrace is also one of its best bars, no matter what level it's on. The cozy inside with ultra seductive lighting is as inviting as the terrace, so this is one rooftop you can save for a rainy day as well as summer's finest. Water fountains and lush palm trees create a tropical feel while the exotic small plates such as the famous spiced sliders pair perfectly with the well-shaken cocktails. It's one of the largest rooftops in New York so there is no excuse for you not to stop on by.
Daily 4 p.m.-4 a.m.

BLACK DUCK
Park South Hotel, 122 E. 28th St., Murray Hill, 212-204-5240; www.blackduckny.com
At wine bars, there's often a price to pay in pretense before you get to the wine

---

WHAT ARE THE BEST GASTRO PUBS?

Spitzer's Corner *(page 146)* This neighborhood gastropub has hipsters from all over the city clamoring for its chef-driven pub grub—the pork fat-laced popcorn is addicting, and there's a vast beer menu.

The Spotted Pig *(page 150)* This quintessential gastropub is packed to the gills day-in and day-out with people drinking and eating the delicious bites such as the sheep's ricotta-filled gnudi or the mouthwatering Roquefort burger.

---

drinking. Thankfully, that's not how it is at the Black Duck. This is a wine bar where you'll find a good $5 pinot during happy hour (5-8 p.m., every day), live jazz on Friday and Saturday (at 9 p.m.), and not a whiff of snobbery. Named for a legendary rum-running vessel, this beautiful extension of the Park South Hotel is elegant (claw-foot cocktail tables and an alabaster bar) and oh-so-comfy without resorting to haughtiness. We like to duck in after dinner for a glass of dessert wine and an order of the bar's banana and berries foster.
Daily 5 p.m.-1 a.m.

CIBAR
56 Irving Place, Union Square, 212-460-5656; www.cibarlounge.com
Cibar's got the recipe for a classically comfortable cocktail lounge: Combine equal parts modern, neo-Victorian furniture and sophisticated martini dressings (think Godiva chocolate or pear purée). Shake with a handful of small-plate appetizers, splash with gooey-eyed lovers and crisply dressed professionals. Serve in a rosy-hued, candlelit space that's never too crowded and seems miles away from nearby Union Square. Garnish seasonally with a cozy back patio.
Monday-Wednesday 5 p.m.-1 a.m., Thursday-Friday 5 p.m.-2 a.m., Saturday 6 p.m.-2 a.m.

FLATIRON LOUNGE
37 W. 19th St., Flatiron District, 212-727-7741;
www.flatironlounge.com
A cavernous lounge framed in accents of blue glass and red leather, this spot serves a list of signature martinis, plus favorites poured by guest mixologists from around the city. Order something interesting from the rotating drink menu or try a martini flight, consisting of three mini-martinis that span a common theme such as the Flight to Hawaii (tropical and fruity) or the Flight Back in Time (classic Sinatra-era favorites). Hushed jazz plays upstairs, where the bar is a mahogany masterpiece brought over from long-ago celeb haunt The Ballroom and restored to its original 1927 condition. Downstairs, a younger set imbibes and gets down to modern club music, but the Rat Pack motif remains. If you're arriving post-dinner, post your party at one of the corner wraparound booths upstairs and let the good times keep rolling.
Sunday-Wednesday 5 p.m.-2 a.m., Thursday-Saturday 5 p.m.-4 a.m.

THE GINGER MAN
11 E. 36th St., Murray Hill, 212-532-3740; www.gingerman-ny.com
If you're looking for a good old Irish pub, you're looking for the Ginger Man. This beer-lover's delight has plenty to offer in terms of selection, seating and price. A pan-European wall of 70 taps hosting everything from crisp German

wheats to frothy Irish stouts pours $6 pints, while a laundry list of more than 100 worldly bottled beer options ensure you'll find something that tickles your cultured palate (Belgian? Check. Japanese? Check. Czech? Check.) The bar can accommodate a large crowd, but the lounge in the back—furnished with armchairs and leather sofas—is by far the best place to quietly contemplate why you don't spend more time drinking beer in armchairs and leather sofas.
Monday-Thursday 11:30 a.m.-2 a.m., Friday 11:30 a.m.-4 a.m., Saturday 12:30 p.m.-4 a.m., Sunday 3 p.m.-midnight.

RARE VIEW
Affinia Shelburne Hotel, 303 Lexington Ave., Murray Hill, 212-481-8439; www.rarebarandgrill.com
Atop the Affinia Shelburne hotel sits Rare View, the sister bar to Rare Bar and Grill 16 floors below. As its name implies, the bar offers jaw-dropping vistas of the Empire State and Chrysler buildings, making it especially breathtaking to be here when both are aglow come sunset. When you're lit up on boozy, fruity concoctions (mango margaritas, anyone?), it's even better. Should the roof be full or the rain clouds gather, fear not; though the street-level bar lacks the grandeur of the rooftop views, it serves magnificent burgers in front of large windows where you can imbibe while watching the city go by.
May-October, Monday-Wednesday noon-11 p.m., Thursday-Friday noon-midnight, Saturday 4 p.m.-midnight, Sunday 4 p.m.-midnight.

ROSE BAR
Gramercy Park Hotel, 2 Lexington Ave., Gramercy Park, 212-920-3300; www.gramercyparkhotel.com
Inside the neo-boho Gramercy Park Hotel, Rose Bar hits on nearly all the senses. Bathed in shades of rose (surprise) and dark wood, the space is a modern vision of a baroque parlor, accented by original artwork from 20th century masters such as Andy Warhol, Jean-Michel Basquiat and Julian Schnabel (who helped design the hotel). The diverse background music is commissioned from DJs from around the globe, the furniture is custom-designed by Schnabel himself and the sophisticated cocktails (think pineapple and ginger margaritas and pisco-champagne flutes) are mixed from ingredients that line a massive oak leaf-shaped bank of shelves behind the bar. This is a great place to grab a pre-dinner drink or spend an evening sipping cocktails and mingling with moneyed Manhattanites and the occasional celebrity. Reservations are required after 9 p.m.
Monday-Saturday 4 p.m.-4 a.m., Sunday 4 p.m.-8 p.m.

UPPER WEST SIDE/COLUMBUS CIRCLE
WEST 79TH STREET BOAT BASIN CAFE
West 79th Street, Upper West Side, 212-496-5542; www.boatbasincafe.com
Whether you have a baby, a boat or a basset hound in tow, you will be in good company at this seasonal Riverside Park hangout. The view is the main sell, especially around sunset—though some argue the burgers run a close second. Limestone archways, a covered rotunda and open air patios packed with cafe tables impart a casual vibe for neighborhood locals and preppy twentysomethings schmoozing over alumni connections and recent trips to the Cape. The see-and-be-seen crowd usually dwindles after dark, but who cares? With a frozen cocktail like the Electric Lemonade with Absolut Citron in one hand

WHERE ARE THE BEST ROOFTOP BARS?

230 Fifth *(page 153)* Water fountains and lush palm trees create a tropical feel, while the exotic small plates pair perfectly with the well-shaken cocktails.

Rare View *(page 155)* As its name implies, the bar offers jaw-dropping vistas of the Empire State and Chrysler buildings, making it especially breathtaking to be here with a mango margarita in hand when both are aglow.

Salon de Ning *(page 152)* This stunner at The Peninsula New York overlooks Fith Avenue and looks like it belongs in 1930s Shanghai.

WHAT ARE THE BEST OUTDOOR SPOTS FOR A DRINK?

Rink Bar *(page 151)* When the summer sun comes out, so do the frozen cocktails. That's when the rink is transformed into an urban oasis where you'll find umbrella-shaded tables dotting the sub-street-level plaza.

West 79th Street Boat Basin Café *(page 155)* Limestone archways, a covered rotunda and open air patios impart a casual vibe for neighborhood locals and preppy twenty-somethings schmoozing over alumni connections and recent trips to the Cape at this Riverside Park hangout.

and an unencumbered view of the New Jersey Palisades, you'll have all you need to see right in front of you.

April-October, Monday-Wednesday noon-11 p.m., Thursday-Friday noon-11:30 p.m., Saturday 11 a.m.-11:30 p.m., Sunday 11 a.m.-10 p.m.

WINE AND ROSES
286 Columbus Ave., Upper West Side, 212-579-9463;
www.wineandrosesbar.com
This *West Elm* catalog clone with a Mediterranean twist has a knowledgeable staff eager to make recommendations from its list of 188 by-the-bottle (bottles start at around $30) and 38 by-the-glass offerings. Wine and Roses sits in one of New York's most charming residential neighborhoods, far removed from Midtown's bustle. If the weather cooperates, you can while away some time on the pretty patio out front after a stroll along Central Park West, just one block away.

Monday-Friday 4 p.m.-2 a.m., Saturday noon-3 a.m., Sunday noon-1 a.m.

ARTS & CULTURE

ON WITH THE SHOW

As the culture capital of the world, there is no place like New York City for a big dose of art, theater, music and more. Every year, people arrive in the city hoping to make it here on account of their ceaseless creativity and limitless drive. See what's happening in the city's galleries, music halls, theaters and sports stadiums. If it's happening here, you can bet it will be good, or at the very least, interesting, thought-provoking and inspiring.

WHAT ARE SOME OF THE CITY'S BEST ART GALLERIES?

DAVID ZWIRNER GALLERIES

525 W. 19th St. (between 10th Avenue and West Street), Chelsea, 212-727-2070; www.davidzwirner.com

David Zwirner Gallery has been in the business of beautiful things for more than 15 years. But in just the past few, it has become one of the largest and best known in New York for pieces by emerging contemporary artists from here and abroad. Zwirner moved from his original locale in Soho to West 19th in Chelsea in 2002; then, in 2006 he expanded that space from 10,000 square feet to 30,000 square feet, stretching it down the block to accommodate up to three simultaneous exhibitions by artists like Tomma Abts, R. Crumb and Raymond Pettibon. With so much space, a visit here can seem more like a museum trip than a gallery stroll, though if you'd like to purchase something off the wall, we're sure Mr. Zwirner would oblige.
Tuesday-Saturday 10 a.m.-6 p.m.

GAGOSIAN GALLERIES

522 W. 21st St., Chelsea, 212-741-1717; 555 W. 24th St., Chelsea, 212-741-1111; www.gagosian.com

Larry Gagosian is considered among the world's biggest players in contemporary art, and because he's got seven galleries scattered around the globe—including two within blocks of each other in Chelsea (a third is located at 980 Madison Avenue, Upper East Side; others are in Beverly Hills, Rome and London)—we're not arguing otherwise. Thanks to rotating exhibitions of post-war American and European mixed media, sculpture, painting and photography, the Gagosian galleries are as much exhibition spaces as they are dealerships. The amount of star power on the walls—the 21st Street location recently exhibited Pablo Picasso, Andy Warhol, Hiroshi Sugimoto, Roy Lichtenstein and Marcel Duchamp in the same show—these galleries can challenge many museum collections.
Tuesday-Saturday 10 a.m.-6 p.m.

POSTMASTERS

459 W. 19th St., Chelsea, 212-727-3323; www.postmastersart.com

New technology and new media are the stars of the show at Postmasters, and in the last 23 years this has been the go-to gallery to check out avant-garde rule-benders. So it's perfectly normal that their signature small, outré shows take place in a former garage in Chelsea. A recent 2009 show included In G.O.D. We Trust (the G.O.D. stands for Global Obama Domination) by Kenneth Tin-Kin Hung, featuring a digital video created with media images that hold political satire using Obama in place of different cultural deities from Jesus Christ to Mohammad to Krishna and Buddha.
Tuesday-Saturday 11 a.m.-6 p.m.

WHERE ARE THE BEST COMEDY SHOWS?

CAROLINE'S ON BROADWAY

1626 Broadway (between 49th and 50th streets), Times Square, 212-757-4100; www.carolines.com

When Caroline Hirsch opened her eponymous club in Chelsea in 1981, it was a cabaret, and no one knew then that some of the performers—including Jay Leno and Jerry Seinfeld—would go on to shape America's comedic landscape. Soon she was booking nothing but comedians, and the club became synonymous with groundbreaking stand-up. It later moved to South Street Seaport, where A&E network's *Caroline's Comedy Hour* television series was filmed, and then to its current 300-seat space in Times Square. The new club, a sleek space that won the American Institute of Architecture Award for Best Interior Club Design (no joke), is still cracking up audiences with performances by luminaries like Chris Rock, Sara Silverman, Norm MacDonald, and Gilbert Gottfried.

Shows: Daily, generally at 8 p.m. and 10:30 p.m.; check Web site for specific show times and ticket prices.

UPRIGHT CITIZENS BRIGADE THEATER

307 W. 26th St. (at Eighth Avenue), Chelsea, 212-366-9176;
www.ucbtheatre.com

Created by the comedy troupe of the same name (current members are Matt Besser, Amy Poehler, Ian Roberts and Matt Walsh), UCB made its way to New York from Chicago more than 10 years ago and is now a New York comedic mainstay. The theater showcases a mix of high-profile and up-and-coming talent, and tickets rarely go for more than $10 (Tina Fey, Conan O'Brien and others have performed for $8 or less). UCB often puts on three or four whip-smart improv shows per night, arranging more than 25 shows per week, a feat that's no laughing matter.

Daily. Check Web site for times and ticket prices.

WHERE CAN YOU SEE GREAT DANCE?

THE JOYCE THEATER

175 Eighth Ave., Chelsea, 212-691-9740; www.joyce.org

The Joyce has supplied a blank canvas in the form of a stage to more than 270 dance companies over its near-30-year existence. Both local and international acts, modern and classical styles have solidified this Chelsea venue as a major player in the avant gard dance community. Well-established companies such as Pilobolus, who's body-bending comedic antics leave audiences grinning for days, return year after year to sell-out crowds. Good seats are a given thanks to the intimate 472-seat design of this renovated old-school movie house. If that's still too big a crowd for you, try the theater's sister property, Joyce SoHo *(155 Mercer St., Soho, 212-431-9233)*, which offers a tiny 74-seat performance space along with two rehearsal studios.

Check Web site for specific company dates.

DAVID H. KOCH THEATER

20 Lincoln Center, Upper West Side, 212-870-5570;
www.nycballet.com

The New York City Ballet makes their home inside this theater at Lincoln Center when they're not summering at their other headquarters in Saratoga Springs). There is no doubt that the New York City Ballet is one of the

ROSELAND BALLROOM

world's premiere dance companies. Conceived by Lincoln Kirstein—an early acolyte of modern American film, dance, literature, architecture and all things cerebral—the company was created with the idea that New York was too great a city to import its talent from abroad. He landed the Russian-educated George Balanchine in 1933, and together the two shaped the history of 20th century dance. Today, under the direction of Peter Martins, the company is responsible for training its own artists and creating original works, pushing modern ballet into the future. It still keeps one graceful, slippered foot in its past (*The Nutcracker* remains a Christmas tradition) as it performs around the city, the state and the world.

Check Web site for specific dates and locations of shows.

WHAT ARE THE BEST VENUES FOR LIVE MUSIC?

ARLENE'S GROCERY
95 Stanton St. (between Orchard and Ludlow streets), Lower East Side, 212-995-1652; www.arlenesgrocery.net

It used to be a bodega, but since the mid-1990s Arlene's Grocery and the adjoining former butcher shop have been the go-to spots to catch rising stars on the music scene, not for buying cartons of milk. There are live performances of everything from country-western to hard rock, and if you're lucky you'll catch a band like the Strokes (before anyone's heard of them) for a measly $8 or $10 cover. The front Butcher Bar is always free—something the hipster crowd that keeps the place packed enjoys—and every Monday night you can join in rock 'n' roll karaoke (no cover).

Check Web site for performance calendar.

B.B. KING BLUES CLUB & GRILL
237 W. 42nd St. (between Seventh and Eighth avenues), Times Square, 212-997-4144; www.bbkingblues.com

This supper club is probably your best bet to catch a blues legend coming through town—everyone from Taj Mahal to Buddy Guy plays here. But plenty of quirkier acts take the stage, too—from The Misfits, Ghostface Killah and

KC and the Sunshine Band to a host of tribute bands playing homage to the likes of George Harrison, the Eagles and Bruce Springsteen. There's a Beatles tribute brunch on Saturday and a gospel brunch on Sunday, and a bit of a touristy vibe thanks to the gift shop and saxophone-shaped beer taps. Don't let that sway you from hitting one of the best spots in the city to catch a host of different kinds of music.

Check Web site for calendar of events.

BOWERY BALLROOM
6 Delancey St. (at the Bowery), Lower East Side, 212-533-2111; www.boweryballroom.com

Bowery and Ballroom are two words paired together that longtime New Yorkers might have once considered an oxymoron. But this long down-and-out neighborhood has seen massive gentrification in the past decade and is now home to what many consider the best music venue in the city. You won't find anyone doing the waltz or the cha-cha here, but the sound is great, the bar is a happening spot in its own right and the space plays host to indie acts ranging from country-rock and folksy to the alternative Breeders. The cash-only box office is located at Mercury Lounge *(217 E. Houston St.).*

Check Web site for calendar of events.

CITY WINERY
155 Varick St. (between Spring and Vandam streets), Soho, 212-608-0555; www.citywinery.com

Big name musical guests, delicious food and a wine selection more than 500 bottles deep puts City Winery at the top of the charts for unique entertainment venues in Manhattan. The 21,000-square-foot space epitomizes industrial chic with exposed brick walls and splintery wood columns. The functioning winery is sequestered to a back room as grapes ferment in enormous steel tanks and barrels. Instead of waiters, City Winery has wine stewards to help select that perfect bottle of cabernet or pinot. Plates of imported salumi and fromage act as tasty accoutrements to the wine—and keep you from getting too tipsy. Then there's the music. A full stage and state-of-the-art sound system transform the soaring space into an intimate concert hall where acts like Richie Havens and Matthew Sweet make you feel less citified and more wine-country cool.

Check Web site for calendar of events.

IRIDIUM JAZZ CLUB
1650 Broadway, Theater District, 212-582-2121; www.iridiumjazzclub.com

Unlike many of New York's most beloved music venues, the Iridium's history only goes back fifteen years. But the history lesson at this subterranean Theater District supper club is on the stage. Greats from bygone eras including drummer Louis Hayes and Thelonious Monk Jr. sometimes stop in to jam for an entire weekend. Ticket prices vary, and make sure to read the fine print as weekend shows often entail a food and drink minimum (usually $10 or $15 per person).

Check Web site for specific shows and times.

ROSELAND BALLROOM
239 W. 52nd St. (between Broadway and Eighth Avenue), Times Square, 212-247-0200; www.roselandballroom.com

The Roseland has been around since 1919, and has pretty much seen it all. It started out a block away on East 51st Street as a dance club where big band-era groups played. Quirkiness was a large part of its original appeal, too: Everything from marathon dancing and staged female prize fights were held here before more formal dancing took center stage. In 1956, Roseland Ballroom moved to its current location, a former ice skating rink. Today, the 3,500-person standing-room-only venue is mostly popular with indie rockers and as a site for special events—when the hall gets a custom makeover for the occasion, whether it's a Thai boxing match, premiere party for shows like *Entourage* or a tattoo convention.

Check Web site for calendar of events.

VILLAGE VANGUARD
178 Seventh Ave. South, Greenwich Village, 212-255-4037; www.villagevanguard.com

John Coltrane and Wynton Marsalis recorded in the basement of the Village Vanguard, and "Live at the Vanguard" albums have become synonymous with "making it" among jazz artists. It opened in 1935, first showcasing bohemian performers like Pete Seeger before switching strictly to jazz. Today, the walls of the Vanguard are adorned with a fading black-and-white mosaic of the greats who've performed here, and jazz connoisseurs gather around small cocktail tables to hear the new vanguard emerging in the wedge-shaped room renowned for its acoustics. Call ahead to make a reservation—just leave the relevant information on the answering machine, and you'll be set.

Daily 8 p.m.

WEBSTER HALL
125 E. 11th St., East Village, 212-353-1600; www.websterhall.com

In 2008 the New York Preservation Society voted to name Webster Hall a landmark, and with good reason: The venue's been around since 1886, and many consider it the country's first nightclub. Frequented by everyone from Marcel DuChamp to Nine Inch Nails, it sure would be something if the walls of Webster Hall could talk. Its incarnations have included a bacchanal parlor, recording studio and home to the Ritz nightclub in the 1980s, when it was considered one of the best places to see live music in New York City (Tina Turner, Eric Clapton and Prince have all played here). Nowadays, it's both a live music venue and dance club. The club is open on Thursday, Friday and/or Saturday nights—beware, though, the crowd is heavy on college students who can dance.

Check Web site for calendar of events.

WHAT IS THE BEST OPERA?
THE METROPOLITAN OPERA
Lincoln Center (10th Avenue between W. 62nd and 66th streets), Upper West Side, 212-362-6000; www.metoperafamily.org

This is arguably the most well-known opera company on the planet, historically showcasing orchestral and vocal talent with an international following. Maria Callas, Leontyne Price and the Met's most notable diva, Beverly Sills, have graced the stage. Offstage, conductors such as Andre Previn and

THE METROPOLITAN OPERA

directors like Julie Taymor have added their dash of star power. Even artists like Marc Chagall and David Hockney have showcased their talents here, creating high-concept set designs. The Met focuses on opera's canon but it doesn't shy away from premieres or new technology. (Supertitle translations have appeared on the back of every seat here since 1995.) Recent initiatives to further expand the Met's presence—perhaps as an effort to draw younger fans—include the broadcast of live Met shows in high-definition movie theaters around the world, public dress rehearsals (free) and reduced ticket prices (the cheapest go for as low as $15). Tickets go on sale a few months before shows open, so bookmark the site, visit religiously, and find something that works with your schedule and budget.

Check Web site for performance information.

WHAT ARE NEW YORK'S BEST PLACES TO CATCH A GAME?

CITI FIELD

12601 Roosevelt Ave. (next to Shea Stadium), Queens, 718-507-8499; www.mets.com

The New York Mets started the 2009 season in their new home, and just like the the new Yankee Stadium, this one was built right next door to the old one (Shea Stadium). This is the Mets' third home (they played their first two seasons at the Polo Grounds in Manhattan), and by far their swankiest to date. Original plans were to make the venue part of the city's bid for the 2012 Summer Olympics, but when that fell through, they were scaled back a bit. Still, this ballpark includes 12,000 square feet of integrated scoring and video boards throughout the stadium, expanded family and entertainment areas, and an interactive Mets museum. You can also expect wider seats, more legroom, fancier restaurants and—thank goodness—more bathrooms. The main entrance will be modeled after the rotunda at Brooklyn's old Ebbets Field and named for Major League Baseball's first African-American player, Jackie Robinson, who played there for the Brooklyn Dodgers. The entire

METS OR YANKEES?

When it comes to Major League Baseball in New York, you're either a die-hard Yankees fan or a die-hard Mets fan. There's just no wiggle room in this city of sports fans known for their confrontational nature: Loving one ball team means hating the other. Yankee loyalists are on the smug side—and rightfully so, with a long, gilded history of winning behind them. Mets fans, on the other hand, have endured a shorter, rockier and far less glamorous heritage—their team is the scrappy underdog playing in the vast shadow of baseball's most storied franchise.

The Yankees—founded in 1901 as the original Baltimore Orioles, one of the eight charter franchises of the American League—have earned their place as baseball's most-hated team, with a record 26 World Series championships and 39 American League pennants, plus a reputation for "buying" seasons with their perpetually oversized purse by luring attitude-heavy top talent. Babe Ruth had a legendary career with the Bronx Bombers, including hitting a record 60 home runs for the team in 1927. Roger Maris donned Yankee pinstripes when he broke the Bambino's record, hitting 61 homers in '61, and Joe DiMaggio and Mickey Mantle both played stellar ball here during the sunlight hours between their infamous nights on the town.

When billionaire businessman George Steinbrenner bought the franchise in 1973, following the team felt more like watching a soap opera. He developed a reputation for micromanagement, hiring and firing manager Billy Martin five times between 1975 and 1988. The Yanks of this era—which included players Reggie Jackson, Thurmon Munson and Catfish Hunter—were a feast for the tabloids, but successful nonetheless, with two series wins and four league pennants between 1976 and 1981. There was a long drought for the team until a new Yankee dynasty took hold during manager and native New Yorker Joe Torre's reign from 1996-2007. Fresh faces including Derek Jeter, Alex Rodriguez, Paul O'Neill, Mariano Rivera and Alfonso Soriano helped usher in six American League titles and four World Series wins—including their last in a 2000 "Subway Series" versus—the Mets.

Unlike their cross-town rivals, the Mets' (short for "Metropolitans") fortunes haven't been as good. An expansion team created to replace the much-missed Giants and Dodgers after their respective moves to California, the team was a laughing stock from the start, hiring aging relics and plucking 72-year-old former Yanks coach Casey Stengel to manage them. They finished their inaugural 1962 season with a dismal 40 wins and 120 losses, but their ineptitude proved endearing to fans. Endearment turned to passion when the '69 "Miracle Mets"—now with stars like Tom Seaver and Tug McGraw in the line-up—bested Baltimore for a surprise World Series victory. The team wouldn't see a title again until 1986, when Boston Red Sox first baseman Bill Buckner's infamous flub of an easy ground out breathed new life into a Mets team facing elimination in game six. They went on to win game seven and the series, reigniting fans' fervor in what many sports fans consider one of the most exciting World Series ever played.

Conversely, after close calls but not much luck since, the Mets experienced what is thought to be one of the greatest collapses in baseball history in September 2007. After dominating both leagues with the best team record for most of the season, the team lost 12 of their last 17 games and didn't even make it to the playoffs.

Both team's homes, Yankee Stadium in the Bronx and the Mets' Shea Stadium in Queens, met the wrecking ball after the 2008 season to make way for more modern facilities adjacent to them. The Yanks started the 2009 season in New Yankee Stadium; the Mets in Citi Field. Fans of each hope these fresh starts mean plenty of wins for their team, and nothing but losses for the other.

project cost roughly $600 million, with the bulk of the tab picked up by the Mets organization, and the rest funded by New York City and state taxes as well as Citigroup, which purchased the naming rights to the park for $20 million a year for the next 20 years.

MADISON SQUARE GARDEN
4 Penn Plaza, Eighth Avenue between 32nd and 33rd streets (next to Penn Station), Garment District; www.thegarden.com
The Garden is the home to two basketball teams (the NBA's Knicks and the WNBA's Liberty) and New York's NHL club (the Rangers), plus a slew of touring music and entertainment acts on nongame days. The current Garden has been standing since 1968, but it's seen three other incarnations dating back to 1879: Two were at Madison Avenue at 26th Street (Madison Square) and a third, known for hosting boxing bouts during sport's heyday (as depicted in the movie *Cinderella Man*), was at 50th Street and Eighth Avenue, not far from Times Square. The Garden almost met the wrecking ball again in early 2008, but the plan was scrapped and a renovation of existing facilities was approved instead. The arena accommodates more than four million fans a year for its events, hosting celebrities on stage and in the stands. (A Knicks game alone is a who's who of Hollywood-types and rappers, most notable among them hyper-fan/filmmaker Spike Lee.) Note: Renovations will continue through 2012, but the arena will remain open and fully operational, leaving the Knicks' and Rangers' schedules unaffected.

NEW YANKEE STADIUM
161st Street and River Avenue, Bronx, 718-293-4300; www.yankees.com
After 85 years playing in historic Yankee Stadium, the Bronx Bombers opened their 2009 season in a new pasture, in the form of a $1.3 billion, 4,000-seat-smaller bowl shaped stadium. New Yankee Stadium is located next to the site of the old ballpark, so it offers the same easy access to public transit (via the B, D and 4 trains) and a field of identical dimensions to the old one. So in theory, the Yanks should have no trouble winning another 26 titles in their new home. Though "The House that Ruth Built" (nicknamed for Babe Ruth's fan-drawing power) is missed by players and fans alike, the new stadium—perhaps "The House that A-Rod Built"—isn't having any trouble drawing crowds. If you're in town when the pinstripes are playing, try for tickets during the week, as the weekends can grow crowded. And if Boston is in town, be prepared to pay up for the privilege of watching one of the most heated rivalries in Major League Baseball.

WHAT ARE SOME OF THE BEST THEATERS?
NEW AMSTERDAM THEATER
214 W. 42nd St., Times Square, 212-282-2900; www.newyorkcitytheatre.com
Smack in the heart of Times Square, this theater has a history as tumultuous as the city's, weathering the cultural and economic ups and downs of fickle New York. But the circle of life here saw an upturn when Disney took over and began to rehab the New Amsterdam in 1993 for its eventual launch of *The Lion King* in 1998 (the show ran until 2006). Now it's home to Disney's *Mary Poppins*. Balcony dwellers, mind the flying umbrellas.
Check Web site for show times.

WINTER GARDEN THEATER
1634 Broadway, Theater District, 212-239-6200;
www.wintergarden-theater.com

Of all the theaters that line the Theater District, the Winter Garden is one of the most storied venues: It catapulted the likes of Barbra Streisand (*Funny Girl*) to stardom and gathered stars like Bob Hope, Eve Arden and Josephine Baker on the same stage in a 1936 version of the Ziegfeld Follies. Starpower aside, the Winter Garden is perhaps most famous as the home to *Cats*, one of the longest running shows in Broadway history. It was performed here 7,485 times between 1982 and 2000 (Just think: That's 7,485 beltouts of "Memory.") *Mamma Mia*!, the feel-good musical based on the Swedish pop group ABBA's songs (also released as a movie in 2008), has been playing here since 2001, with no end to the crooning of "Dancing Queen" and "Fernando" in sight.

Wednesday-Saturday 8 p.m., Sunday 7 p.m. Matinees: Wednesday, Saturday, Sunday 2 p.m.

WHAT ARE THE TOP SHOWS ON BROADWAY?

There's no business like show business—and in New York, there is no show business quite like theater. From megawatt Broadway musicals to off-Broadway theater, you'll never lack for stage productions, thanks to a steady stream of actors, playwrights and dramatists who flock to the city to hit it big or starve trying. It wouldn't be a real trip to Manhattan without squeezing in a show, so make time to check out one of our favorites.

BILLY ELLIOT
Imperial Theatre, 249 W. 45th St. (between Broadway and Eighth Avenue), 212-239-6200; www.billyelliotbroadway.com

It's hard to forget the endearing 2000 movie about a small-town, blue-collar boy with big dreams of being a ballet dancer and now, the musical, based on the movie, is exploding with ten 2009 Tony Award wins, including Best New Musical. With director Stephen Daldry (*The Reader*), who also directed Jamie Bell in the movie; choreographer Peter Darling and a score from none other than Sir Elton John, you'll see why this musical is earning raves.

Admission: $41.50-$136.50. Tuesday 7 p.m., Wednesday and Saturday 2 p.m. and 8 p.m., Thursday and Friday 8 p.m., Sunday 3 p.m.,

CHICAGO: THE MUSICAL
Ambassador Theater, 219 W. 49th St., Theater District, 212-239-6200; www.chicagothemusical.com

The Second City takes center stage in this raucous production set during the prohibition era. Based on a real 1924 murder trial, *Chicago* tells the tale of hoosegow hottie Velma Kelly and new girl on the (cell) block, Roxie Hart, following their jailhouse hijinks and kooky attempts to retain their ill-gotten fame. Full of "all that jazz" and hot dance numbers, this six-time Tony Award winner is even more of a hoot than the Richard Gere/Renée Zellweger film adaptation, and is perfect for first-time theatergoers.

Admission: $64-$131.50. Tuesday, Thursday and Friday 8 p.m., Wednesday and Saturday 2:30 p.m. and 8 p.m., Sunday 7 p.m.

WHERE ARE DISCOUNT THEATER TICKETS SOLD?

If you're looking for discount theater tickets—or you didn't make up your mind to see a show until the bright lights of Times Square beckoned—then your first stop should be TKTS. People line up down the block at the Times Square fixture *(Duffy Square, 47th Street and Broadway, 212-221-0013; www.tdf.org)* to get reduced-priced, day-of tickets—some for as cheap as 50 percent off the original price. You'll need to be flexible about what to see, but who cares—you're Broadway bound. Get in line at 5:30 p.m. if you want the shortest wait and the best selection (producers often send tickets over later in the day that they haven't sold). Besides selling more tickets, TKTS was created to get people talking about the theater. The fun of standing in line is getting the opportunity to chat with your fellow theater-goers about what you're going to see. Two other locations also sell matinee tickets the day before (these also usually have shorter lines).

Box office: Monday-Saturday 3-8 p.m., Sunday 3 p.m. until latest curtain time being sold. Matinees: Wednes-day, Saturday 10 a.m.-2 p.m., Sunday 11 a.m.-3 p.m. There's a $4 ticket handling surcharge. Other locations: South Street Seaport, corner of Front and John streets; Brooklyn, 1 MetroTech Center.

FUERZA BRUTA: LOOK UP
Daryl Roth Theatre, 101 E. 15th St., Union Square, 212-375-1110; www.fuerzabrutanyc.com

Forget the heels, pack the comfy sneaks, and prepare to stand for a while (because there aren't any seats). But prepare to be dazzled as well. Fuerzabruta means "brute force" in Spanish, and the off-Broadway show doesn't really have a plot—it's more performance art in the vein of *Cirque du Soleil* or the *Blue Man Group*. The troupe's charismatic performers swim atop Mylar sheaths, swing from colorful tapestries and run atop long treadmills while boxes hurtle their way. Pounding beats, flashing Technicolor lights—even a barrage of rainfall—are all a titillating treat for the senses.

Admission: $75. Wednesday-Friday 8 p.m., Saturday 7 p.m. and 10 p.m., Sunday 7 p.m.

MAMMA MIA!
Winter Garden Theatre, 1634 Broadway, Theater District, 212-239-6200, 800-432-7250; www.mamma-mia.com

One girl. Three possible fathers. A whole lot of ABBA. On the eve of 20 year-old Sophie's wedding, the young bride-to-be vows to have her father walk her down the aisle. The only problem? She doesn't know who he is. But after discovering her mother's diary revealing three former flames, she invites the men to her wedding to discover the truth. Set to the music of the '70s Swedish quartet (including their biggest hits like "Dancing Queen" and "Take a Chance on Me"), you might be tempted to dance in the aisles, just like the show's premiere audience did a decade ago.

Admission: $62.75-$251.50. Tuesday-Friday 8 p.m., Saturday 2 p.m. and 8 p.m., Sunday 2 p.m. and 7 p.m.

NEXT TO NORMAL
Booth Theatre, 222 West 45th St., Theater District, 212-239-6200; www.nexttonormal.com

From the director of *Rent* comes this original musical which takes the audience on an emotional journey of how one family lives with the challenges that come from mental illness. Alice Ripley won the 2009 Tony award for Best Leading Actress in her role as Diana, a bipolar suburban housewife who struggles with her unpredictable moods and worse, taking pills that make her numb to life. Although the core of the musical is how mental illness affects those who suffer from it, as well as those they love, you'll leave feeling hopeful and happy to be alive, not an easy task given the heavy content. Adding to the emotional performance is a can't-get-it-out-of-your-head score by composer Tom Kitt and lyricist Brian Yorkey (they also won the 2009 Tony award for Best Score).

Admission: $36.50-$200. Monday 8 p.m., Tuesday 7 p.m., Thursday-Friday 8 p.m., Saturday 2 p.m. and 8 p.m., Sunday 3 p.m. and 7:30 p.m.

THE PHANTOM OF THE OPERA
The Majestic Theatre, 247 W. 44th St., Theater District, 212-239-6200, 800-432-7250; www.thephantomoftheopera.com

Perhaps it's the haunting melodies penned by famed composer Sir Andrew Lloyd Webber. Or maybe it's the intriguing story of a masked man, his soprano protégé and their unrequited love. It could also just be the slew of talented performers the production's bolstered throughout the years, such as powerhouses Sarah Brightman and Michael Crawford. Whatever the reason, this monumental musical is one of the most iconic and longest-running shows on Broadway.

Admission: $26.50-$201.50. Monday 8 p.m., Tuesday 7 p.m., Wednesday and Saturday 2 p.m. and 8 p.m., Thursday and Friday 8 p.m.

WICKED
Gershwin Theatre, 222 W. 51st St., Theater District, 212-586-6510; www.wickedthemusical.com

Toto, I don't think we're in New York anymore. Long before Dorothy donned her ruby reds, a green gal named Elphaba and an ethereal beauty named Glinda met and became pals while studying at Oz's Shiz University. How one became the Wicked Witch of the West and the other Glinda the Good Witch is the tale at the heart of this popular Great White Way production. Based on the novel by Gregory Maguire (itself a take off from L. Frank Baum's endearing childhood fantasy), the show has garnered three Tony wins and will keep the family dreaming about somewhere over the rainbow all night long.

Admission: $50-$300. Tuesday 7 p.m., Wednesday and Saturday 2 p.m. and 8 p.m., Thursday and Friday 8 p.m., Sunday 3 p.m.

★ BEYOND NYC

THE BROOKLYN BRIDGE

ESCAPES FROM NEW YORK

One thing New Yorkers love about their city is that a great getaway is never far away. There are many interesting and beautiful places to visit within a short drive of congested Manhattan. Penn Station and Grand Central Terminal also host multiple bus and rail routes headed out of town daily, with the Metro-North and the Long Island Rail Road (LIRR) being the two main commuter lines.

WHAT ARE THE BEST DAY TRIPS OUTSIDE OF NEW YORK?

DIA:BEACON

Sure, you can get a taste of minimalism at one of Manhattan's many contemporary museums or galleries. But less than an hour and a half outside the city limits sits **Dia:Beacon** *(3 Beekman St., Beacon, New York, 845-440-0100; www.diabeacon.org; admission: adults $10, students and seniors $7, children under 12 free)*, one of the largest modern art museums in the world—and arguably one of the best. The 300,000-square-foot museum, opened in May 2003, is actually housed in three brick buildings originally built in 1929 as a box printing factory for the snack giant Nabisco. The extensive galleries and gardens, designed by Robert Irwin in collaboration with OpenOffice, a Manhattan architectural firm, are more intimate than imposing, with the enormous space feeling more like the halls of a private home (no small feat, considering the epic proportions of some of the masterpieces on display). Dia founders (then husband-and-wife team) Heiner Friedrich and Philippa de Menil collected much of their art during the 1960s and 1970s, though the collection now runs through the present. Much of it is conceptual and some of it is positively monumental in both size and scope. Among the pieces hang 72 canvases from Andy Warhol's Shadows, several large-scale sheet metal sculptures by Richard Serra, the graphite wall drawings of Sol LeWitt, and the abstract paintings of Agnes Martin. The museum is perched on the eastern bank of the Hudson River, and with its rolling green hills and soaring blue skies, it's the perfect setting for a picnic lunch and an easy place to forget that you're just a short train ride from the bustle of New York City.

How to get there: Dia:Beacon can be reached by Metro-North's Hudson Line from Grand Central train station.

THE GLASS HOUSE

Standing inside the Glass House (built by architect Philip Johnson in 1949 but only open to the public since 2007), the building almost vanishes—and that's the point. Built on all four sides with floor-to-ceiling glass supported by charcoal-colored steel beams on a brick platform, the walls give way to a verdant glade beyond, making it seem like the landscape itself makes up the true "walls" of the building. Declared a National Trust Historic site in 1997, the Glass House is an influential and intriguing example of modern architecture; it was built at a time when not even skyscrapers were sheathed in glass. For architecture and modernism buffs visiting the Big Apple, a trip here is essential. Located in picturesque New Canaan, Connecticut, Johnson's 47-acre estate includes 14 beautiful buildings in total, 11 of which were designed by the architect. The Glass House, though,

THE GLASS HOUSE

is his tour de force. The minimal structure, exquisite in proportion, symmetry and transparency, overlooks a pond that is largely hidden from view behind a low stone wall. Tour the impeccably preserved estate and the open interior of the Glass House (including the brick cylindrical bathroom, Johnson's only concession to privacy within the space). Tours run from April through October and fill up well in advance, so plan ahead by contacting the visitor center *(199 Elm St., New Canaan, Connecticut, 866-811-4111; www.philip-johnsonglasshouse.org)*. The town itself, one of the most affluent communities in the United States, is dotted with an eclectic mix of dining options, particularly along Main and Elm streets. For something quick and tasty, pop into **Vicolo's Pizza & Trattoria** *(62 Main St., New Canaan, Connecticut, 203-966-4966)*, but for a bit of indulgence, head to **Harvest Supper** *(15 Elm St., New Canaan, Connecticut, 203-966-5595)*. The intimate 38-seat restaurant opened by Jack and Grace Lamb (known for Jewel Bako, Jack's Luxury Oyster Bar and Degustation in the East Village), features small plates such as seared Hudson Valley foie gras with marinated blackberries, brioche croutons, vanilla yogurt and toasted almonds, and entrées including honey and citrus-basted Long Island duck breast with braised field greens, garnet yams, cherries and pistachios. If you're killing time before your train back to the city, swing by the **Silk Purse** *(118 Main St., New Canaan, Connecticut, 203-972-0898; www.thesilkpurse.com)* to browse antiques like vintage, stone-studded jewelry, gold goblets and 1930s serving trays.

How to get there: New Canaan's downtown is easily accessible by the Metro North stop on the New Haven line from Grand Central Terminal to New Canaan. If you're driving, take Merritt Parkway Connecticut 15 North toward New Haven and take exit 37 (New Canaan, Darien, Route 124). Make a left onto South Avenue (Route 124). Keep going for about two miles to the end of the town center, and turn left onto Elm Street to the visitor center.

WHAT'S A GOOD BEACH OUTSIDE THE CITY?

Another escape accessible via subway, **Rockaway Beach** is located at the end of the A subway line. Rockaway Peninsula, known to locals simply as "the Rockaways," is a slim strip of land that's part of the borough of Queens. It abuts New York Harbor (and the Atlantic Ocean) on one side and Jamaica Bay lagoon on the other. Since the 19th century, New Yorkers who aren't the Hamptons- or Jersey Shore-types have been treating Rockaway Beach as a summer resort, and though year-round communities have since sprung up in the area, the sandy shores remain fair game for more than 4 million people who come here each summer seeking fun in the sun. Rockaway Beach, also nicknamed the Irish Riviera (more than a quarter of the residents here are of Irish descent), provides more than enough seaside entertainment. It's the city's longest and most diverse beach, so expect everything from family barbecues to pockets of nude sunbathers to fishermen perched on the many rocky outcrops. Numerous handball courts, beach volleyball nets and hiking trails are available, while the lengthy boardwalk just begs for a sun-kissed stroll or the simple pleasure of a melting ice cream cone. Look for Whalemena, a whale sculpture that used to reside at the Central Park Zoo, at the beach's 95th Street entrance for a great photo-op. Fresh crab legs can be feasted on at the Rockaway Lobster House *(375 Beach 92nd St., Rockaway Beach, 718-634-2500; www.rockawaylobsterhouse.com)*. Decorated with surfboards and tiki torches, this laid-back shack also boasts a waterside deck where live bands (ranging from steel drums to acoustic guitar) fill the evening air.

How to get there: Take the MTA to the Rockaway Park Beach 116th Street stop, at the end of the A subway line.

HOW FAR IS ATLANTIC CITY FROM NEW YORK CITY?

Atlantic City is about 130 miles from NYC. It will take you about 2 ½ hours to get there, which makes it a little hard to swing as a day trip, but with all that is changing in this city (and a new express train that makes nine round trips over the weekend from Penn Station), you might want to consider staying at least a night or two. The **Borgata Hotel Casino & Spa** *(1 Borgata Way, Atlantic City, New Jersey, 609-317-1000; www.theborgata.com)* currently reigns as the hotel-of-the-moment and is setting out to chart a sophisticated new direction for the city. The 161,000-square-foot casino, 12 restaurants (including three from celebrity chefs Bobby Flay, Michael Mina and Wolfgang Puck), four nightclubs, swank spa, and surround-sound event center definitely up the luxury factor in Atlantic City. For a more private affair, check out The Water Club, Borgata's chic boutique hotel within a hotel. Of course, Trump also has a few star-worthy properties here including **Trump Plaza** *(Boardwalk at Mississippi Ave., Atlantic City, New Jersey, 609-441-6000; www.trumpplaza.com)*, **Trump Marina** *(Huron and Brigantine Blvd., Atlantic City, New Jersey, 609-441-2000; www.trumpmarina.com)* and **Trump Taj Mahal** *(1000 Boardwalk at Virginia Ave., Atlantic City, New Jersey, 609-449-1000; www.trumptaj.com)*.

The famed Atlantic City Boardwalk dates back to 1870—built to appease hoteliers who complained of beach sand in their hotel lobbies—and once stretched more than seven miles. Today it totals only four but has become more upscale in recent years, with high-end shops and restaurants replacing kitschy stores and fast-food joints. **The Pier Shops at Caesars** *(One Atlantic Ocean, at Arkansas, Atlantic City, New Jersey, 609-345-3100;*

www.thepiershopsatcaesars.com) has more than 70 retail stores, including Gucci, Louis Vuitton, and Burberry, and several restaurants, namely Stephen Starr's Buddakan and The Continental.

Upscale restaurants aside, no trip to Atlantic City is complete without a bag of sticky saltwater taffy. You can find this Atlantic City original at numerous shops lining the boardwalk. Other famous Atlantic CIty eats include the city's best raw bar and fresh seafood samplers at **Dock's Oyster House** (2405 Atlantic Ave., Atlantic City, New Jersey, 609-345-0092; www.docksoysterhouse.com). Around since 1897, there is rarely less than eight oyster varieties to choose from, and Dock's pan-sautéed crab cakes are as good (and far cheaper) than any you'll find in Manhattan. **White House Sub Shop** (2301 Arctic Ave., Atlantic City, New Jersey, 609-345-1564) is another solid option and a valuable reminder that New York isn't the only proximate metropolis. Philadelphia hoagies (that's "subs" to Garden Staters) have found their way down the shore. The sandwiches are enormous, piled high with meats, cheeses and loads of toppings. Celebrities like Frank Sinatra and the Beatles chowed at this low-key haunt back in the day, and some say that Bill Cosby has had White House's subs flown to him in California on occasion.

For other daytime fun, **Steel Pier** is packed with amusement rides including a giant slide, bumper cars and double-decker carousel. Or swing by the **Absecon Lighthouse** (31 S. Rhode Island Ave., Atlantic City, New Jersey, 609-449-1360). The 228 steps to the top may leave you winded, but the views of the Jersey Shoreline are worth the burn, along with bragging rights to having climbed the tallest lighthouse in the Garden State.

Once the lights go down on the Boardwalk, it is all about the roll of the die. Nearly every major hotel in Atlantic City has a casino onsite, so feel free to jump around until you find your own personal hot seat. If putting it all on the line sounds more like a nightmare than an adrenaline rush, check out one of the city's many entertainment venues instead. The Borgata and Trump resorts draw big-name comedians, musical acts and theater performances.

How to get there: The new Atlantic City Express Service (877-326-7428; www.acestrain.com) runs trains direct between New York City's Penn Station and Atlantic City every Friday, Saturday and Sunday. The trip takes 2 1/2 hours. The Garden State Parkway toll road also runs from NYC to the Jersey Shore.

WHAT IS THERE TO SEE AND DO IN BROOKLYN?

All you need is a MetroCard to hop a quick subway ride across the bridge to Brooklyn, which nearly 2.6 million people call home. This borough, located to the southeast of Manhattan, officially became part of New York City in 1898 and is home to many cultural attractions, entertainment options and historical draws. For an all-day trip that mixes the old with the ever-changing, pair a jaunt to Red Hook with an afternoon shopping in bustling, burgeoning Park Slope and strolling through Prospect Park. If it's a nice day, the best way to enter Brooklyn is on foot by crossing the Brooklyn Bridge, a National Historic Landmark since 1964. Start your two-mile walk in Manhattan at the Brooklyn Bridge-City Hall subway stop near City Hall Park, where you'll find the pedestrian overpass. Stop along the wood-planked walkway of the 6,016-foot bridge (the main span is 1,595 feet) to read plaques chronicling the construction of the steel structure—the longest suspension bridge in the

BAKED

world at the time it was built in 1883. Next, it's on to the Old World vibe of Red Hook. From the Brooklyn Bridge, make your way over to Red Hook by taxi, a train and bus combo, or water taxis

Walking through Red Hook, an industrial neighborhood that feels relatively removed from Manhattan, can feel like strolling through a slice of 1950s New York, with dilapidated trolley cars still on tracks of the Beard Street Pier and retro diners dotting the main drag. Today it's a mishmash of bars and bake shops, artist studios and antiques stores, and the whole place has a hip-and-gritty atmosphere. Start with a walk down **Van Brunt Street**, the main drag, to get a feel for the area and do a bit of window-shopping. Stop for a bite at **Hope & Anchor** *(347 Van Brunt St., Brooklyn, 718-237-0276)*, a scrumptious spot that kick-started the foodie focus in this neighborhood (try comfort dishes like flaky chicken pot pie and juicy burgers), before hopping onto one of the bright orange stools at retro sweet shop **Baked** *(359 Van Brunt St., Brooklyn, 718-222-0345; www.bakednyc. com)* and digging into old-school treats such as pillowy homemade marshmallows, sprinkle-topped cupcakes or Aunt Sassy's Pistachio Surprise—a thick slice of pistachio-infused white cake topped with vanilla honey buttercream frosting. Next, walk over to the offbeat **Red Hook Bait & Tackle** *(320 Van Brunt St., Brooklyn, 718-797-4892; www.redhookbaitandtackle.com)* to wash it all down with a beer or sample the impressive collection of local whiskeys and bourbons. Opened by four neighborhood friends, it's tucked into an actual old taxidermy-filled bait-and-tackle shop. For a real local treat, swing by **Steve's Authentic** *(204 Van Dyke St., Brooklyn, 718-858-5333; www.stevesauthentic.com)*, where Steve Tarpin has been handing out Swingles for more than 25 years. The frozen novelty is a wonderful sliver of frozen key lime pie (made with only freshly squeezed juice) that's dipped in chocolate. Antiques seekers should check out **Atlantis** *(351 Van Brunt St., Brooklyn, 718-858-8816; www.atlantisredhook.com)*, where they can score treasures like hand-painted glassware from the 1970s, midcentury lamps and kitschy, colorful 1960s dining sets. **The Louis Valentino, Jr. Park and Pier** (at Coffey and Ferris streets) affords some of the best land views of the Statue of Liberty, while **Red Hook Park** *(155 Bay St.)* is given over on weekends from April to September to makeshift bazaars of pan-Latin food and music.

From quirky, laidback Red Hook, a short subway ride will land you in Park Slope for some of the best shopping and cultural attractions in Brooklyn. This neighborhood, known for its Victorian brownstones and boutique-packed streets, has undergone a seemingly never-ending, massive gentrification over the last 20 years or so. Fifth Avenue is the main drag for restaurants, including popular exports from Manhattan like **Blue Ribbon** *(280 Fifth Ave., 718-840-0404; www.blueribbonrestaurants.com)*, while Seventh Avenue is positively crammed with specialty shops and high-end stores where you can buy everything from heart-rate-sensing sports bras to handmade stationery and lamb's-wool throw blankets.

Prospect Park *(718-965-8999; www.prospectpark.org)*, a 585-acre, lush urban oasis that lies between the Park Slope and Prospect Heights neighborhoods, offers everything from waterfalls and bird-watching opportunities to a 400-animal zoo *(at Flatbush and Ocean avenues; 718-399-7339)*, plus an antique carousel. Designed by Calvert Vaux and Frederick Law Olmsted (the same duo behind Central Park), this rolling green haven is also ideal for horseback riding *(check out Kensington Stables, 51 Caton Place, 718-972-4588; www.kensingtonstables.com)*, roller-blading, biking or just wandering the many trails. At the northern edge of the park, you'll find the **Brooklyn Botanic Garden** *(1000 Washington Ave., 718-623-7200; www.bbg.org)*, best known for the Cherry Blossom Festival that fills the verdant space with a riot of fragrant blooms each April. But the 52-acre space, which includes beautiful formal Italian and Japanese gardens, is worth a visit any time of year. Finally, no trip to Brooklyn is complete without a stop at the **Brooklyn Museum** *(200 Eastern Parkway, 718-638-5000; www.brooklynmuseum.org)*. Though delightfully less crowded than its Manhattan brethren, the museum is home to approximately one million art objects and is considered one of the premier art museums in the world. Highlights include one of the most important Egyptian collections in the world, the African galleries (one of the first of its kind in the U.S.), and a dizzying number of European classics by masters like Claude Monet, Edgar Degas, Camille Pissarro, Paul Cézanne and Berthe Morisot. And whatever you do, don't leave the borough without stopping at any one of myriad pizza places for a requisite slice. You wouldn't really be going native without it.

How to get there: Take the MTA to the Brooklyn Bridge-City Hall subway stop by City Hall Park. To get to Red Hook from the base of the Brooklyn Bridge, you can either grab a taxi; take the F or G trains to Smith-9th Street, then hop on the B77 bus; or on weekends take the New York Water Taxi (www.nywatertaxi.com, $15-$25) from Pier 11 at South Street to the Red Hook Beard Street Pier. To get to Park Slope from Red Hook, take the F train from Smith-Ninth streets to Seventh Avenue.

KNOW BEFORE YOU GO

TIMES SQUARE

WHAT'S THE BEST WAY TO GET TO MANHATTAN FROM THE AIRPORTS?

The quickest option to get to Manhattan or other points from either LaGuardia, JFK or Newport airports is to take a city-licensed yellow taxi for a zoned fee. (Avoid the car-service drivers and unlicensed drivers who often lurk near the baggage area, and head to a designated taxi stand instead). Not including tolls—which are the passengers' responsibility—or tip, the ride to Midtown Manhattan from JFK is around $45, from LaGuardia between $25 and $30, and from Newark about $60-75. Public transportation from the airports can be time-consuming, but it's definitely the cheapest option. From JFK, take the **AirTrain** ($5) to the Z, E, J or A subway line ($2.25) *(visit www.airtrainjfk.com for more info)*. From LaGuardia, the **M60 bus** ($2.25) runs from the airport through Harlem and to the Upper West Side in Manhattan. From Newark, take a **New Jersey Transit train** ($15) from the airport to Penn Station in Manhattan. A good alternative is a shuttle service, which generally costs $12-$25 depending on your starting and ending points. **SuperShuttle** *(800-258-3826; www.supershuttle.com),* which services all three major airports, and **New York Airport Service** *(212-875-8200; www.nyairportservice.com),* which services JFK and LaGuardia, are two popular options.

WHAT ARE NEW YORK'S BOROUGHS?

New York City is made up of five boroughs: Manhattan (the smallest borough landwise and also the most dense; this is what most people have in mind when they think "New York City"), Brooklyn, Queens, the Bronx and Staten Island. Each borough is operated by a separate administrative division of the municipal government and has its own distinct character (Staten Island, accessible only by ferry or the Verrazano-Narrows Bridge from other points in the city, has a remote, suburban feel). Within each are dozens of neighborhoods boasting unique identities of their own, mostly because of their demographic makeup. For example, Williamsburg in Brooklyn is home to both artsy hipsters and one of the largest Orthodox Hasidic Jewish communities in the world—an only-in-New-York-style mix.

WHAT MAJOR EVENTS TAKE PLACE THROUGHOUT THE YEAR?

Though there are bound to be festivals, concerts and community events planned on nearly every single day somewhere in the city, the following is a taste of notable events that draw national crowds each year.

Fall the New York Film Festival and Halloween Parade in Greenwich Village (October); New York City Marathon (November); the Macy's Thanksgiving Day Parade, as well as the pre-parade balloon inflating the night before (November).

Winter The Radio City Christmas Spectacular (December); Christmas Tree-Lighting Ceremony in Rockefeller Center (late November/early December); Times Square New Year's Eve Ball Drop (December); Chinese New Year Parade (February).

Spring The Tribeca Film Festival (April); Cherry Blossom Festival (May); Bike New York (May); Lower East Side Festival of the Arts (May).

Summer The Mermaid Parade (June); Gay & Lesbian Pride March (June); Nathan's Famous Fourth of July Hot Dog Eating Contest (July); Shakespeare in the Park (July); the Metropolitan Opera in the Park (July/August); and U.S. Tennis Open (August/September).

WHERE CAN YOU GET MEDICAL TREATMENT IN NEW YORK?

In an emergency, dial **911** (free from any payphone). If possible, make sure you have comprehensive health insurance before you head to the Big Apple; an uninsured trip to the hospital here can be prohibitively expensive. Emergency rooms are open 24 hours a day at **Mount Sinai Medical Center** *(Madison Avenue at 100th Street, 212-241-7171),* **New York-Presbyterian Hospital** *(525 E. 68th St., 212-746-5454; www.nyp.org),* **St. Luke's Hospital** *(1111 Amsterdam Ave., 212-523-4000; www.slred.org)*, **Roosevelt Hospital** *(1000 10th Ave., 212-523-4000; www.slred.org)* and **St. Vincent's Hospital** *(170 W. 12th St., 212-604-7000; www.svcmc.org).*

All buildings constructed after 1987 are required by city law to be fully accessible to the disabled, including entrances, exits and restrooms. Many older buildings and most major sightseeing destinations have also made efforts to be accessible. Still, it's always best to phone ahead. **Access for All,** an online guide created by Hospital Audiences Inc. *(212-575-7676; www.hospaud.org)*, offers great details on how accessible New York's cultural attractions are.

WHICH NEWSPAPERS AND MAGAZINES SERVE NEW YORK?

The Big Apple is a media town like no other. In addition to the usual spots (bodegas, bookstores, convenience stores), you can also find newspapers and magazines—sometimes a global array of them—at tiny, curb-side stands throughout the city. New York City has three daily newspapers: Broadsheet *The New York Times (www.nytimes.com)*, and tabloids the *New York Post (www.nypost.com)*, the nation's oldest continuously published daily, and the *New York Daily News (www.nydailynews.com)*, both of which are known for their hilarious headlines. Rival alt-weeklies include newspapers the *Village Voice (www.villagevoice.com)*, a liberal, arts-oriented alternative, and *New York Press (www.nypress.com)*, a conservative alt weekly that gives the Village Voice a run for its money. Weekly magazines *Time Out New York (www.timeout.com)*, *New York (www.nymag.com)* and *The New Yorker (www.newyorker.com)* offer extensive listings of what's going on in the city every week—from concerts to art openings to shopping deals.

HOW SAFE IS NEW YORK CITY?

Though New York has somewhat shaken its reputation for seedy neighborhoods and rampant crime, this is still a major city, so bring along your street smarts. Leave valuables in your hotel safe, and only carry necessities—cash, I.D. and credit cards. Stay alert for pickpock-ets in crowded, touristy areas like Times Square and Penn Station, and avoid deserted or poorly lit streets. Muggers tend to hang out in shadowy doorways, so walk closer to the street if alone. Try to avoid the subway late at night if possible, especially if you're traveling to more remote stations. Of course, if you are accosted, hand over your valuables without a fight, then dial 911 as soon as you can (it's a free call from any payphone if your cell has been taken).

WHAT'S THE BEST WAY TO NAVIGATE THE SUBWAY?

What may seem daunting at first glance is actually a very quick, inexpensive (and some think fun), round-the-clock way to move around the city. Generally, the subway is faster and easier to navigate than city buses. Each subway route is marked by either a number or a letter and is color-coded according to the line on which it runs *(see page 183 for a map)*. The names of subway stops correspond to the nearest street or landmark. For example, the 2 train stops at **Penn Station** *(34th Street)*, as well as **Times Square** *(42nd Street)*. Local trains make every stop along their routes, while express trains make only the major station stops (generally marked by a white dot on subway maps). Be sure to check—express trains might go past 50 blocks before stopping.

Many stations have separate entrances for uptown and downtown trains, and some entrances are open 24 hours (marked by a green globe), while others have limited hours (and red globes). Likewise, train schedules can change, especially late at night and on weekends, so read posted signs carefully. On each train platform, overhead signs will indicate which trains stop on those tracks and during what hours, if any, the trains are express. The **Metropolitan Transportation Authority** *(www.mta.info)* operates both the subway and buses; a MetroCard will work on both systems. You can buy one at subway station vending machines (they accept cash, credit and debit cards), from the station booth, at many hotels and at the **NY Convention & Visitors Bureau** *(www.nycvisit.com)*. You can either load a card with money (from $4 to $80) and it will deduct $2.25 each time you ride a train or bus, or you can pay once for unlimited rides during a set number of days. With a pay-per-use card, up to four people can use the same card, and putting $20 on the card will actually credit you with 10 trips for the price of 9. If you'll be traveling often, an unlimited rides card is a smart choice. A one day Fun Pass costs $8.25, a 7-day pass costs $27, a 14-day pass costs $51.50 and a 30-day pass costs $89. You can't share a MetroCard that has unlimited rides on it with anyone else. Reduced fares are available for people 65 years or older and those with a disability. Children 44 inches and shorter can ride the subway (and bus) for free with an adult.

IS IT NECESSARY TO RENT A CAR?

If you'll be spending most of your time in Manhattan and nearby parts of the outer boroughs, there is little reason to rent a car in the city. Traffic is often heavy, drivers are fearless (especially cabbies) and parking options are either a pricey garage or a hassle on the street (almost all streets are off-limits for at least a few hours each day, so you'll need to move your parked car—read posted signs carefully). If need be, rental cars are available through car-sharing services like **Zipcar** *(212-691-2884; www.zipcar.com)* or rental companies including **Alamo** *(888-826-6893; www.alamo.com)*, **Avis** *(800-352-7900; www.avis.com)*, **Enterprise** *(800-261-7331; www.enterprise.com)* and **Hertz** *(800-654-3131; www.hertz.com)*.

HOW DO TAXIS WORK IN NEW YORK CITY?

Taxis are pretty abundant in Manhattan, particularly downtown (there are more than 13,000 of them operating throughout the city). If you're trying to hail a taxi (by moving to the curb and raising one arm—just like in the movies) and you don't see any, try walking to one of the busier avenues (north/south streets) for better luck. Use only licensed, yellow medallion taxis. Unregulated "gypsy" cabs and off-duty car service drivers may approach, but these vehicles may be uninsured and are unmetered—increasing the chance the driver might take your wallet for a ride. Look like a local by trying to hail only available taxis—you can tell it's unoccupied and on duty if the center lights on its roof are lit. If you're traveling with luggage or bulky packages, you can ask the driver to open the trunk. Once inside, simply tell the driver where you're going. Most drivers know the addresses of major sightseeing destinations, but if you're giving a lesser-known address, knowing the cross street is helpful. Some drivers may give you guff about driving to the outer boroughs, but legally they're required to drive you anywhere within the city limits. Up to four people can ride in a taxi for the same price: $2.50 is the initial fee, plus 40 cents per every fifth of a mile or 40 cents per minute when the taxi is idling. Late-nights and rush hours may incur a small surcharge, and tipping (15-20 percent) is expected. Some taxis have an integrated machine on the back seat that allows you to pay by credit card, though if you plan to do that, its always best to check if it's possible before you get in. Taxi receipts have medallion numbers printed on them, so if you lose something, you can call **New York City Taxi & Limousine Commission** *(212-227-0700; www.nyc.gov/taxi)* to try and retrieve it.

IS NEW YORK A WALKABLE CITY?

Manhattan is a walker's paradise—every block is densely packed with noteworthy sites and interesting people—and even the most geographically challenged will be able to navigate with ease. The island is 13.4 miles long by 2.3 miles at its widest point. While the older streets of Lower Manhattan can be a confusing tangle, most of the streets are on a simple grid, with streets running east-west and avenues running north-south. (The other four boroughs don't have such simple layouts.) To figure out how close a destination is, know that twenty city blocks equals one mile. When talking about locations, New Yorkers often refer to cross streets rather than exact addresses. So art lovers are more likely to say the Museum of Modern Art (MoMA) is on 53rd between Fifth and Sixth, rather than at its actual address, 11 W. 53rd Street.

WHAT IS THE BEST TIME TO VISIT NEW YORK?

Visitors fill New York City in pretty equal measure year-round, and while locals grouse about the winter (which can be very cold, though not usually too snowy) and summer (very humid), the weather is generally mild and the four seasons distinct. Autumn has the clearest skies and both it and spring are lovely. September and October have the most full-sun days, while July and August regularly have the highest temps (around 85 degrees) and the most humid weather. You'll find the streets a little quieter on summer weekends, when locals do their best to escape to the beaches and mountains.

MAPS

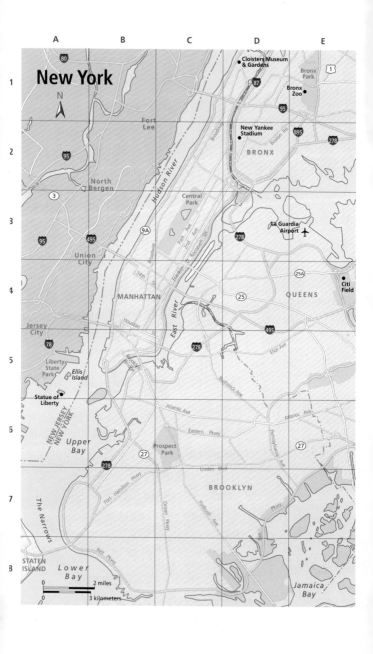

New York

N

	A	B	C	D	E

80

Cloisters Museum & Gardens

Bronx Park

1

Bronx Zoo

87

Fort Lee

95

New Yankee Stadium

895

278

BRONX

95

North Bergen

3

Hudson River

Central Park

La Guardia Airport

9A

278

Union City

95

495

25A

Citi Field

MANHATTAN

East River

25

QUEENS

Jersey City

78

Houston St

Liberty State Park

Ellis Island

278

Eliot Ave

Bushwick Ave

Statue of Liberty

Atlantic Ave

NEW JERSEY
NEW YORK

Eastern Pkwy

Atlantic Ave

Upper Bay

Prospect Park

27

278

27

Linden Blvd

BROOKLYN

The Narrows

Port Hamilton Pkwy

Ocean Pkwy

Flatbush Ave

Belt Pkwy

STATEN ISLAND

Lower Bay

Jamaica Bay

0 — 2 miles
0 — 3 kilometers

182

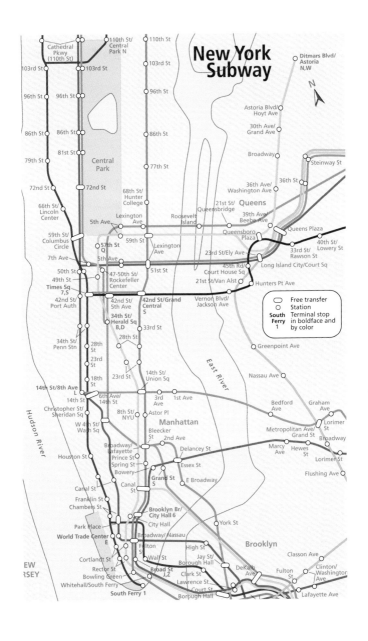

New York Subway

Free transfer
Station
South Ferry 1 Terminal stop in boldface and by color

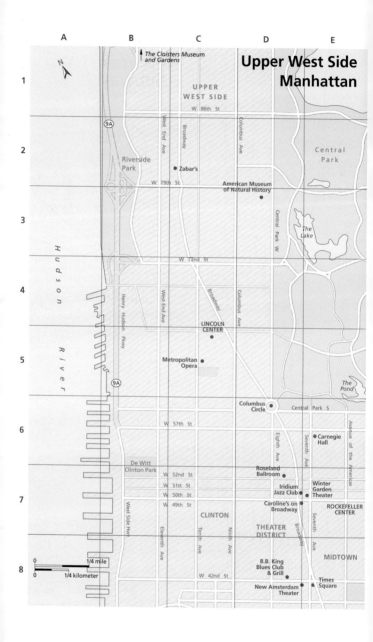

Upper West Side Manhattan

The Cloisters Museum and Gardens

UPPER WEST SIDE

W 86th St

West End Ave

Broadway

Columbus Ave

Central Park

Riverside Park

Zabar's

W 79th St

American Museum of Natural History

Central Park W

Hudson River

The Lake

W 72nd St

Henry Hudson Pkwy

West End Ave

Broadway

Columbus Ave

LINCOLN CENTER

Metropolitan Opera

The Pond

Columbus Circle

Central Park S

W 57th St

Eighth Ave

Seventh Ave

Carnegie Hall

Avenue of the Americas

De Witt Clinton Park

W 52nd St

Roseland Ballroom

W 51st St

W 50th St

Iridium Jazz Club

Winter Garden Theater

West Side Hwy

W 49th St

CLINTON

Caroline's on Broadway

Broadway

Seventh Ave

ROCKEFELLER CENTER

Eleventh Ave

Tenth Ave

Ninth Ave

THEATER DISTRICT

MIDTOWN

0   1/4 mile

B.B. King Blues Club & Grill

W 42nd St

Times Square

0   1/4 kilometer

New Amsterdam Theater

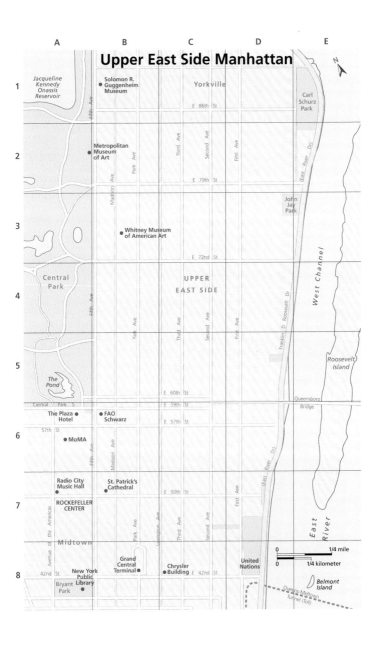

Upper East Side Manhattan

A   B   C   D   E

1

Jacqueline
Kennedy
Onassis
Reservoir

Solomon R.
Guggenheim
Museum

Yorkville

E 86th St

Carl
Schurz
Park

2

Metropolitan
Museum
of Art

Fifth Ave

Madison Ave

Park Ave

Third Ave

Second Ave

First Ave

East River (East River Dr)

E 79th St

John
Jay
Park

3

Whitney Museum
of American Art

E 72nd St

West Channel

Central
Park

4

UPPER

EAST SIDE

Fifth Ave

Park Ave

Third Ave

Second Ave

First Ave

Franklin D. Roosevelt Dr

5

The
Pond

E 60th St

Roosevelt
Island

Central Park S

E 59th St

Queensboro
Bridge

The Plaza
Hotel

FAO
Schwarz

E 57th St

6

57th St

MoMA

Fifth Ave

Madison Ave

East River Dr

Radio City
Music Hall

St. Patrick's
Cathedral

E 50th St

First Ave

7

ROCKEFELLER
CENTER

Avenue of the Americas

Park Ave

Lexington Ave

Third Ave

Second Ave

East
River

Midtown

8

42nd St

New York
Public
Library

Grand
Central
Terminal

Chrysler
Building   E 42nd St

United
Nations

0   1/4 mile
0   1/4 kilometer

Belmont
Island

Bryant
Park

Queens-Midtown
Tunnel (Toll)

185

Lower Manhattan

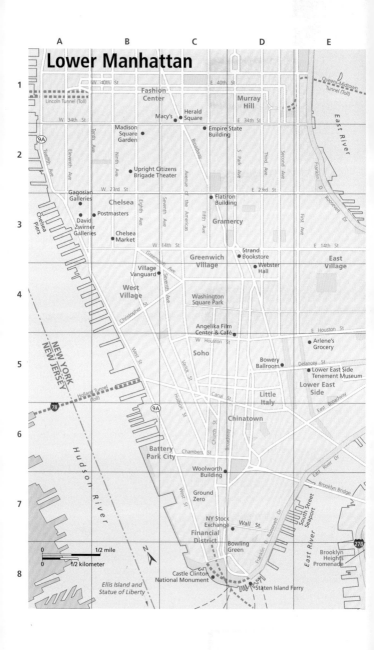

A · B · C · D · E

1

Lincoln Tunnel (Toll)
W. 40th St.
E. 40th St.
Queens–Midtown Tunnel (Toll)

Fashion
Center

Murray
Hill

W. 34th St.
Macy's
Herald
Square
E. 34th St.

9A

Madison
Square
Garden

Empire State
Building

East
River

2

Tenth Ave.
Eleventh Ave.
Twelfth Ave.
Ninth Ave.

Upright Citizens
Brigade Theater

S. Park Ave.
Third Ave.
Second Ave.
Franklin D. Roosevelt Dr.

W. 23rd St.
E. 23rd St.

Gagosian
Galleries

Chelsea

Eighth Ave.
Seventh Ave.
Avenue of the Americas
Fifth Ave.

Flatiron
Building

3

Chelsea
Piers

Postmasters
David
Zwirner
Galleries

Gramercy

First Ave.

Chelsea
Market
W. 14th St.
E. 14th St.

Greenwich
Village

Strand
Bookstore

East
Village

Village
Vanguard

Greenwich Ave.
Seventh Ave.

Webster
Hall

4

NEW YORK
NEW JERSEY

West
Village

Washington
Square Park

Christopher St.

Angelika Film
Center & Café
W. Houston St.
E. Houston St.

Arlene's
Grocery

5

West St.
Varick St.
Hudson St.

Soho

Bowery
Ballroom
Delancey St.
Lower East Side
Tenement Museum

Lower East
Side

Holland Tunnel
(Toll)

78

9A

Canal St.

Little
Italy

East Broadway

6

Church St.

Chinatown

Hudson River

Battery
Park City

Chambers St.

7

West St.

Woolworth
Building

Ground
Zero

Franklin D. Roosevelt Dr.
South Street Seaport Dr.

Brooklyn Bridge

East River Dr.

NY Stock
Exchange
Wall St.
Financial
District

Bowling
Green

East River

Brooklyn
Heights
Promenade

278

0 ___ 1/2 mile
0 ___ 1/2 kilometer

N

8

Ellis Island and
Statue of Liberty

Castle Clinton
National Monument

Staten Island Ferry

INDEX

THE METROPOLITAN MUSEUM OF ART

ART CREDITS

Tenement Museum, Guggenheim Museum, Ellis Island, Grand Central, New York, Botanical Garden, Prospect Park, Roseland Ballroom, Brooklyn Bridge at Night, Brownstones in Brooklyn Heights: all courtesy of Jeff Greenberg/NYC & Company

The Metropolitan Museum of Art. Photograph Courtesy The Metropolitan Museum of Art:

Rockefeller Center Viewing Platform: Bart Barlow/©RCPI Landmark Properties LLC Lincoln Center: David Lamb Facade, New York Public Library ©Peter Aaron Esto

American Museum of Natural History:

Fredrick Phinease & Sandra Priest Rose Center for Earth and Space ©AMNH/D. Finnin

Jean Georges Restaurant: Jean Georges Restaurant
Per Se: Per Se
L'Atellier de Joel Robuchon: Four Seasons Hotels and Resorts
Daniel: Daniel
Gramercy Tavern: Gramercy Tavern
Eleven Madison Park Restaurant: Eleven Madison Park Restaurant
Gotham Bar and Grill: Gotham Bar & Grill
Adour Alain Ducasse: Adour
Del Posto: Del Posto
Corton: Corton
'21' Club: '21' Club
Gordan Ramsey at the London: Gordan Ramsey at the London
The Grocery: The Grocery
Cru: Cru

St Regis New York Guestroom: St Regis New York
Mandarin Oriental Columbus Circle: Mandarin Oriental Hotel Group
Trump: Trump NYC
The Peninsula New York: The Peninsula Hotels
Algonquin: The Algonquin Hotel
The Carlyle: The Carlyle Hotel
The New York Palace: The New York Palace
The Plaza: Fairmont Hotels and Resorts

Great Jones Spa: Great Jones Spa
The Spa at Mandarin Oriental: Mandarin Oriental Hotel Group
The Peninsula Spa by ESPA: The Peninsula Hotels
The Spa at the Four Seasons: The Four Seasons
Townhouse Spa: Ken Jones/Townhouse Spa

Moss Display: Moss
16sur20: 16sur 20
Bird: courtesy of Bird

PDT (Please Don't Tell): Noah Kalina/PDT
Kettle of Fish: Joseph A. Rosen/Kettle of Fish
Bar at The Campbell Apartment: The Campbell Apartment
Rink Bar: Rink Bar

Metropolitan Opera Lobby: Marty Sohl/Metropolitan Opera
The Glass House: Eirik Johnson/Philip Johnson Glass House
Baked: courtesy of Baked

The Temple of Denur in The Sackler Wing at The Metropolitan Museum of Art. Photograph Courtesy The Metropolitan Museum of Art©Brookes Walker 2008

The Great Hall at the Metropolitan Museum of Art Photograph Courtesy The Metropolitan Museum of Art. ©Brookes Walker 2008

Maps Created by Mapping Specialists